D1612662

ENGLISH PLACE-NAME SOCIETY.   VOLUME LXI

FOR 1983-84

GENERAL EDITOR
KENNETH CAMERON

THE PLACE-NAMES OF
NORFOLK

PART I

ENGLISH PLACE-NAME SOCIETY

The English Place-Name Society was founded in 1923 to carry out the survey of English place-names and to issue annual volumes to members who subscribe to the work of the Society. The Society has issued the following volumes:

All communications concerning the Society and membership should be addressed to:

THE HON. DIRECTOR, English Place-Name Society, The University, Nottingham, NG7 2RD.

ENGLISH PLACE-NAME SOCIETY.   VOLUME LXI

THE PLACE-NAMES
OF NORFOLK

By

KARL INGE SANDRED and BENGT LINDSTRÖM

PART I

THE PLACE-NAMES OF
THE CITY OF NORWICH

ENGLISH PLACE-NAME SOCIETY
1989

Published by the English Place-Name Society

© English Place-Name Society 1989

ISBN: 0 904 88915 7

Printed in Great Britain
by Woolnough Bookbinding, Irthlingborough.

*The collection from unpublished documents
of material for the Norfolk volumes has
been greatly assisted by grants received from
the British Academy*

*The Camera-ready Copy of this volume
has been produced on equipment provided
by
Messrs Allied Breweries plc
and by
Messrs Advent Desktop Publishing Limited*

CONTENTS
(Norwich intra muros)

PREFACE

This is the first volume to come out of a project to edit the place-names of Norfolk. When the material collected over a period of about forty years by the late Dr O.K. Schram was transferred from the University of Nottingham, where it had been deposited since Schram's death in 1968, to the University of Uppsala in the summer of 1974, it formed the basis for the establishment of a Norfolk Archive in the English Department of the University. This was made possible with the help of a grant from the then Swedish *Humanistiska forskningsrådet*, which enabled me to purchase the necessary filing cabinets and to devote the time required (about one term altogether) to the task of arrangement. In order to provide effective access to the collection a complete gazetteer based on the Ordinance Survey six-inch maps for Norfolk was compiled by Dr Bengt Lindström, who a couple of years later joined me to work part-time on the project. The ultimate aim of the archive is to have the material processed, analysed and arranged for publication.

It was clear from the outset that, in spite of the size of the corpus, a great deal of collecting remained to be done. The files often contain plenty of material for major names, whereas they are very uneven as regards minor names and field-names. At Uppsala such material has been added, partly gathered by Dr Lindström and myself on visits to the Norfolk Record Office in our summer vacations, partly as a result of cooperation with voluntary helpers in Norfolk who have searched the Tithe Awards systematically and also earlier local documents. The collection of field-names is continuing without interruption, and this task would in fact be impossible without these voluntary helpers, many of whom are members of the Norfolk Research Committee. The present writer is especially indebted to the Committee's Chairman, Mr J.C. Barringer, M.A., and its Editor, Mrs Barbara Cornford, B.A., for implementing this cooperation. By electing me President for the academic session 1986-1987, the Norfolk Research Committee also gave me the opportunity of meeting several of its members personally.

The decision to produce a separate volume for the City of Norwich was taken when it was discovered what a large amount of

Middle English material there is for the Norwich street-names. Since Schram had never planned a separate volume on Norwich, most of this material had to be collected from the vast number of local documents in the keeping of the Norfolk Record Office. Urban archaeology had developed as a new discipline, Winchester and King's Lynn being two noteworthy sites where the new excavation and recording techniques had been used. Research into the topographical history of Norwich had been begun by the Norwich Survey, a division of the Centre of East Anglian Studies at the University of East Anglia. Contact was established between the Uppsala and Norwich projects through Professor K. Cameron at Nottingham, and on the 20th of July 1977, a meeting was arranged at Earlham Hall, where I had the opportunity of meeting and talking with Alan Carter, Director of the Norwich Survey, and Helen Sutermeister, Research Associate of the Survey. After an exchange of information about our separate plans, we decided upon cooperation, the archaeological and historical evidence to be studied at Norwich, the onomastic analysis to be carried out at Uppsala. Although the documentary evidence for the Norwich street-names is unusually good in the Middle English period, the pre-Conquest sources are extremely scanty. We have thus had to rely mainly on the findings of the archaeologists for the Anglo-Saxon period.

Our cooperation had hardly more than started when it was interrupted by the untimely death of Helen Sutermeister in 1979. Dr Lindström and I made a few visits to the Norfolk Record Office in the following summers, when most of the material found in this volume was collected. Files prepared by Helen Sutermeister, which were made available to us on these occasions, were a great help in leading us to the original documents. We also had the privilege of discussing various points of Norwich history with Alan Carter at the Centre of East Anglian Studies, which was then housed in Earlham Hall. It is sad to think that our thanks can no longer reach him either. He died in 1988. We dedicate this volume in grateful remembrance to these two scholars, who inspired us by their bravery and enthusiasm.

There have naturally been many other helpers, in ways great and small, over the years during which we have been preparing this volume. Personally, I feel specially indebted to Professor K. Cameron, Hon. Director of the English Place-Name Society. I had the honour of working with him at Nottingham University when I spent one year, i.e. the academic session 1971-1972, there as a Leverhulme European Visiting Research Fellow. During this stay I accepted the invitation to arrange the Schram collection for publication by the English Place-Name Society. Since I had a full-time teaching post at Uppsala University and a long time would elapse before any volumes could be published, it was decided to organise the Norfolk material into an archive in order to make it immediately useful and available for research. Thanks are also due to Dr Margaret Gelling, President of the Society, for the interest she has taken in this project.

Even though we have collected most of the street-name material for the present volume ourselves, the late Dr O.K. Schram should of course be given due credit, for without his tireless collecting of material for the whole county, there would be no project for the study of the place-names of Norfolk.

Miss Jean Kennedy, County Archivist for Norfolk, and her staff provided facilities for our work in the searchroom of the Norfolk Record Office. She also answered many queries and gave advice regarding Norwich documents, and so did Mr Paul Rutledge, Deputy Archivist.

In the Centre of East Anglian Studies we were given a separate room, typing- and copying-facilities and library-service, for which we are deeply grateful to Professors K.M. Clayton and A. Hassell Smith, Directors of the Centre at the times of our visits. While working there, we received help with documents from Mrs Elizabeth Rutledge, Mrs Margot Tillyard and Miss Serena Kelly.

Miss Barbara Green, Keeper of Archaeology, made me welcome in the Castle Museum and gave invaluable and energetic assistance when I was looking for information about the development of the Castle area. Mr P.D.T. Cattermole advised me on literature and generously lent me books about the history of the Norwich School and the Cathedral Close.

During the preparation of this volume Dr Mark Bateson, Research Assistant to the English Place-Name Society, provided forms from documents in the British Library and the Public Record Office. It is a pleasant task to express our gratitude to him and to Mr John Field, the Society's Editorial Assistant, who checked that our manuscript conformed to the Society's practice for its publications. We are also indebted to Mrs M.D. Pattison who prepared the whole manuscript for camera-ready publication.

Although we have spent several months altogether in Norwich over the years, most of our work on this volume has been carried out in Uppsala. We are grateful for having had the opportunity of consulting

Dr Rune Forsberg, our former teacher of Old English at Uppsala University, on points of Old English philology. Finally, I would personally like to record my indebtedness also to my former teacher and friend, the late Professor Erik Tengstrand, who took a lively interest in the Norfolk project and gave advice, particularly at the initial stage.

A grant from the Swedish *Humanistisk-samhällsvetenskapliga forskningsrådet* enabled me to have reductions in my normal load of teaching so that I could work half-time for short periods on this project. For our stays in Norwich in the summers, we are deeply indebted to Professor Peter Trudgill, a resident of Norwich, who made at least three of them possible by generously offering two Swedish scholars hospitality in his house for the length of time necessary for their research in the Norfolk Record Office and the Centre of East Anglian Studies.

Uppsala University   KARL INGE SANDRED
December 1988

ABBREVIATIONS AND BIBLIOGRAPHY

Abbrev	*Placitorum Abbreviatio* (RC), London 1811.
AD	*A Descriptive Catalogue of Ancient Deeds*, London 1890 and in progress.
AD	Unpublished Ancient Deeds in the PRO.
AddCh	Additional Charters in the BL.
AddR	Additional Rolls in the BL.
Angl	Anglian.
ANLett	*Anglo-Norman Letters and Petitions from All Souls MS 182*, ed. M.D. Legge (Anglo Norman Texts 3), Oxford 1941.
AOMB	Augmentation Office Miscellaneous Books in the PRO.
ASC	*Two of the Saxon Chronicles Parallel*, ed. J. Earle and C. Plummer, 2 vols, Oxford 1892-9.
Ass	Assize Rolls. *Rolls of the Justices in Eyre... 1218-19*, ed. Doris M. Stenton (Selden Society Publ. 53), 1934; *Pleas before the King or his Justices 1198-1202*, 2 vols (Selden Society Publ. 67-8), 1948-52.
Ass	Unpublished Assize Rolls in the PRO.
ASWills	*Anglo-Saxon Wills*, ed. Dorothy Whitelock, Cambridge 1930.
B, Blomefield	Francis Blomefield, *An Essay towards a Topographical History of the County of Norfolk*, vols III and IV, containing the history of Norwich, London 1806 (1741, 1745).
B 1746	*Plan of the City of Norwich...by...*Francis Blomefield, Rector of Fersfield in Norfolk. Published Sept. 29, 1746.
Banger	J. Banger, *Norwich at War*, Norwich 1982 (1974).
Baxter & Johnson	J.H. Baxter and C. Johnson, *Medieval Latin Word-List from British and Irish Sources*, Oxford and London 1934.
BCS	*Cartularium Saxonicum*, ed. W. de Gray Birch, 3 vols, London 1885-93.
Beecheno	F.R. Beecheno, *Notes on the Ditches of Norwich Castle* (MS copy in the Norwich Castle Museum), 1908.
Binh, Binham	The Cartulary of Binham Priory (BL MS Cott. Claud. D.XIII).
Björkman	Erik Björkman, *Scandinavian Loan-Words in Middle English* (StEPh 7, 11), Halle 1900-2.
BL	British Library.
BLR	Extracts from a Book of Langoll Rents, 1626, in K, pp. 111-13.
BM	*Index to the Charters and Rolls in the British Museum*, ed. H.J. Ellis and F.B. Bickley, 2 vols, London 1900-12.
BMC	*A Catalogue of English Coins in the British Museum.* Anglo-Saxon Series. I, ed. C.F. Keary and R.S. Poole. II, ed. H.A. Grueber and C.F. Keary. London 1887-93.
BMF	*Facsimiles of Ancient Charters in the British Museum*, ed. E.A. Bond with collaboration of E.M. Thompson, 4 vols, London 1873-8.
Bodl	*Calendar of Charters and Rolls in the Bodleian Library*, ed. W.H. Turner and H.O. Coxe, Oxford 1878.
Bond	F. Bond, *Dedications and Patron Saints of English Churches*, Oxford 1914.
Browne	Sir Thomas Browne, *Repertorium or Some Account of the Tombs and Monuments in the Cathedrall Church of Norwich*,

	1680. in vol. III of *The Works of Sir Thomas Browne*, ed. Geoffrey Keynes, London 1964 (1928).
BS	*Sir Christopher Hatton's Book of Seals*, ed. L.C. Loyd and Doris M. Stenton, Oxford 1950.
Buxton	The Buxton MSS in the CUL.
Camden	W. Camden, *Britannia*, London 1586.
Campbell	J. Campbell, *Norwich* (Historic Towns), London 1975.
Campbell OEG	A. Campbell, *Old English Grammar*, Oxford 1959.
Carter	Alan Carter, "The Anglo-Saxon Origins of Norwich" , *Anglo-Saxon England 7* (1978), 175-204.
Carthew	G.A. Carthew, *The Hundred of Launditch*, 3 vols, Norwich 1877-9.
CG	Church Goods in the PRO.
Ch	*Calendar of the Charter Rolls*, 6 vols, London 1903-27.
Ch	Charters relating to Norwich Cathedral in the NfRO.
ChancWarr	*Calendar of the Chancery Warrants*, London 1927 and in progress.
Chichele	*The Register of Henry Chichele, Archbishop of Canterbury, 1414-1443*, ed. E.F. Jacob, 4 vols, Oxford 1937-47.
ChNCP	*The Charters of Norwich Cathedral Priory*, ed. Barbara Dodwell (PRS New Series 40, 46), London 1974, 1985.
Cl	*Calendar of the Close Rolls*, London 1892 and in progress.
Cleer	*A New Mapp of the Ancient & Famous City of Norwich* by Thomas Cleer, 1696.
ClR	*Rotuli Litterarum Clausarum* (RC), 2 vols, London 1833-44.
CoinA	C.E. Blunt, "The Coinage of Athelstan, 924-939: A Survey", *The British Numismatic Journal* 42 (1974), 35-160.
Colvin	H.M. Colvin *et al.*, *The History of the King's Works*, 2 vols, London 1963.
CottCh	Cotton Charters in the BL.
Cottle	B. Cottle, *The Penguin Dictionary of Surnames*, London 1978 (1967).
CottR	Cotton Rolls in the BL.
Coxf	The Coxford Priory Cartulary, transcribed by W. Hudson (NPL MS 160).
CUL	Cambridge University Library.
Cuningham	William Cuningham's Map of Norwich of 1558. Key printed in K 118.
Cur	*Curia Regis Rolls*, London 1922 and in progress.
Dauzat	A. Dauzat, *Dictionnaire étymologique des noms de famille et prénoms de France*, 3rd edn, Paris 1960.
DB	*Domesday Book, seu Liber censualis Willelmi primi regis Angliae* ed. A. Farley and H. Ellis, 4 vols, London 1783-1816.
D&C	Deeds related to the property of the Priory of Holy Trinity, later the Dean and Chapter of Norwich Cathedral, in the NfRO.
DEPN	E. Ekwall, *The Concise Oxford Dictionary of English Place-Names*, 4th edn, Oxford 1960.
DGP	*Danmarks gamle Personnavne*, utg. af G. Knudsen, M. Kristensen og R. Hornby. 1. Fornavne, Copenhagen 1936-48. 2. Tilnavne, Copenhagen 1949-64.
Dietz	K. Dietz, "AE. *bēocere* 'Imker', ME. *bîke* 'Bienennest' und die Ortsnamen auf *Bick-*", *Anglia* 103 (1985), 1-25.
Douglas	D.C. Douglas, *The Social Structure of Medieval East Anglia* (Oxford Studies in Social and Legal History 9), 1927.

Drayton	M. Drayton, *Polyolbion*, London 1612 and 1622.
Dunn & Sutermeister	I. Dunn and Helen Sutermeister, *The Norwich Guildhall. A History and Guide.* Norwich 1978.
ECC	J. l'Estrange, *Eastern Counties Collectanea*, Norwich 1872-3.
EDD	J. Wright, *The English Dialect Dictionary*, 6 vols, Oxford 1896-1905.
E&S	Essays and Studies by Members of the English Association.
EETS	Early English Text Society. ES = Extra Series, OS = Original Series.
EG	*English Gilds*, ed. T. and L.T. Smith (EETS OS 40), London 1870.
EGS	*English and Germanic Studies*, University of Birmingham (publ. by W. Heffer & Sons Ltd, Cambridge), in progress.
EHN	O.S. Arngart (Anderson), *The English Hundred-Names*, 3 vols, Lund 1934-9.
ELPN	E. Ekwall, *Early London Personal Names*, Lund 1947.
EMC	C.E. Blunt, "St Edmund Memorial Coinage", *Proceedings of the Suffolk Institute of Archaeology* 31 (1970), 234-55.
ENS	*Early English and Norse Studies presented to Hugh Smith*, ed. A. Brown and P. Foote, London 1963.
EPNE	A.H. Smith, *English Place-Name Elements*, 2 vols (EPNS 25, 26), Cambridge 1956.
EPNS	Publications of the English Place-Name Society.
ERN	E. Ekwall, *English River-Names*, Oxford 1928.
ESts	*English Studies*, in progress.
Evans	J.T. Evans, *Seventeenth-Century Norwich*, Oxford 1979.
FA	*Inquisitions and Assessments relating to Feudal Aids*, 6 vols, London 1899-1920.
Falk-Torp	H.S. Falk and A. Torp, *Norwegisch-dänisches etymologisches Wörterbuch*, 2 vols, Heidelberg 1910-11.
Farmer	D.H. Farmer, *The Oxford Dictionary of Saints*, Oxford 1978.
Fees	*The Book of Fees*, 3 vols, London 1920-31.
Feilitzen	O. von Feilitzen, *The Pre-Conquest Personal Names of Domesday Book* (Nomina Germanica 3), Uppsala 1937.
FF	*A Short Calendar of the Feet of Fines for Norfolk*, ed. W. Rye, 2 vols, Norwich 1885-6.
Field	J. Field, *English Field-Names*, Newton Abbot 1972.
FieldGL	J. Field, *Place-Names of Greater London*, London 1980.
Fine	*Calendar of Fine Rolls*, London 1911 and in progress.
FineR	*Excerpta e rotulis finium 1216-72* (RC), 2 vols, London 1835-6.
Fisher	E.A. Fisher, *Anglo-Saxon Towers*, Newton Abbot 1969.
FK	Extracts from the papers of John Kirkpatrick, contributed by Robert Fitch, in *Views of the Gates of Norwich*, made by John Ninham, Norwich 1861.
Forsberg	R. Forsberg, *A Contribution to a Dictionary of Old English Place-Names* (Nomina Germanica 9), Uppsala 1950.
Forssner	T. Forssner, *Continental-Germanic Personal Names in England in Old and Middle English Times*, Uppsala 1916.
Fransson	G. Fransson, *Middle English Surnames of Occupation 1100-1350* (Lund Studies in English 3), Lund 1935.
Frere & St Joseph	S.S. Frere and J.K.S. St Joseph, *Roman Britain from the Air*, Cambridge 1983.
Gerv	Gervase of Canterbury, *Chronicle of the Reigns of Stephen, Henry II and Richard I*, ed. W. Stubbs (Rolls Ser.), 2 vols, London 1867-9.

Godefroy	F. Godefroy, *Dictionnaire de l'ancienne langue francaise et de tous ses dialectes du IXe au XVe siècles*, Paris 1881-1902
Green & Young	Barbara Green and Rachel M.R. Young, *Norwich, the Growth of a City*, Norfolk Museums Service 1981 (1963).
H	A. Hochstetter, *Plan of the City of Norwich*, London 1789.
Hald	K. Hald, "*A*-Mutation in Scandinavian Words in England", *The Vikings*, ed. T. Andersson and K.I. Sandred, Stockholm: Almqvist & Wiksell (1978), 99-106.
HarlCh	Harley Charters in the BL.
Harrod	H. Harrod, *Gleanings among the Castles and Convents of Norfolk* Norwich 1857.
HaRS	Publications of the Hampshire Record Society, in progress.
Hildebrand	B.E. Hildebrand, *Anglosachsiska mynt i svenska kongliga myntkabinettet, funna i Sveriges jord. Ny tillökt upplaga.* Stockholm 1881.
Hitzer	H. Hitzer, *Die Strasse vom Trampelpfad zur Autobahn*, Munich 1971.
HMC	Historical Manuscripts Commission.
HMC Var	*Report on Manuscripts in Various Collections* (HMC), 8 vols, 1901-23.
Holinshed	R. Holinshed, *The Firste Volume of the Chronicles of England, Scotlande, and Irelande*, 1577.
Holme	*St. Benet of Holme 1020-1210*, ed. J.R. West (NfRS 2, 3), 1932.
Holme	The Register of the Abbey of St Benet of Holme, BL Cott. Galba E.II (for spellings after 1210).
Hoyle	J. Hoyle, *A New Mapp of the City of Norwich*, 1728.
IA	*Itinerarium Antonini Augusti*, ed. G. Parthey and M. Pinder, Berlin 1848. A.L.F. Rivet, "The British Section of the Antonine Itinerary", with an appendix by K. Jackson, *Britannia* 1, 34-82 (1970).
Inq aqd	*Calendarium inquisitionum ad quod damnum* (RC), London 1803. *List of inquisitions ad quod damnum* (PRO, Lists and Indexes 17, 22), London 1904, 1906.
Ipm	*Calendar of Inquisitions post mortem*, London 1898-1921.
Jordan	R. Jordan, *Handbuch der mittelenglischen Grammatik*, 1. Teil: *Lautlehre*. Zweite Auflage bearb. von H.C. Matthes, Heidelberg 1934.
Journal	*EPNS Journal*, in progress.
Julian	*A Book of Showings to the Anchoress Julian of Norwich*, ed. E. Colledge and J. Walsh, 2 vols, Pontifical Institute of Medieval Studies, Toronto 1978.
K	J. Kirkpatrick, *The Streets and Lanes of the City of Norwich* (written c. 1720), ed. W. Hudson, Norwich 1889.
K^2	J. Kirkpatrick, *History of the Religious Orders and Communities, and of the Hospital and Castle, of Norwich* (written c. 1725), ed. D. Turner, London 1845.
KCD	*Codex diplomaticus aevi Saxonici*, ed. J.M. Kemble, 6 vols, London 1839-48.
Kelly	Serena Kelly, "The Economic Topography and Structure of Norwich c. 1300", *Men of Property*, ed. Ursula Priestley, Norwich 1983.
Ketton-Cremer	R.W. Ketton-Cremer, *Forty Norfolk Essays*, Norwich 1961.
King	Samuel King, *A New Plan of the City of Norwich*, Norwich

	1766.
Knights	M. Knights, *The Highways and Byeways of Old Norwich*, Norwich 1887.
Langley	The Register of Langley Abbey (BL Add. MS 5948).
LansdCh	Lansdowne Charters in the BL.
Latham	R.E. Latham, *Revised Medieval Latin Word-List*, London 1965.
LathamD	R.E. Latham, *Dictionary of Medieval Latin from British Sources*, London 1975 and in progress.
Leland	*The Itinerary of John Leland*, ed. L.T. Smith, 5 vols, London 1906-10.
Lib	*Calendar of the Liberate Rolls*, London 1916 and in progress.
LibEl	*Liber Eliensis*, ed. D.J. Stewart (Anglia Christiana Soc.), London 1848.
Lind	E.H. Lind, *Norsk-isländska dopnamn ock fingerade namn från medeltiden*, Uppsala 1905-15. Supplement, Oslo 1931.
LindB	E.H. Lind, *Norsk-is ländska personbinamn från medeltiden*, Uppsala 1920-21.
LindkvistY	H. Lindkvist, "A Study on Early Medieval York", *Anglia* 50 (1919), 345-94.
Lipman	V.D. Lipman, *The Jews of Medieval Norwich*, London 1967.
Löfvenberg	M.T. Löfvenberg, *Studies on Middle English Local Surnames* (Lund Studies in English 11), Lund 1942.
LöfvenbergC	M .T. Löfvenberg, *Contributions to Middle English Lexicography and Etymology* (Lunds Universitets Årsbok, NF, 41:8), Lund 1946.
Loyn	H. Loyn, "Towns in late Anglo-Saxon England: the Evidence and some Possible Lines of Enquiry", *England before the Conquest*, ed. P. Clemoes and Kathleen Hughes, Cambridge 1971, 115-28.
Luick	K. Luick, *Historische Grammatik der englischen Sprache*, Leipzig 1914-40.
ME	Middle English.
M&M	W.P. Millard and Josh. Manning, *Plan of the City of Norwich*, 1830.
MED	*Middle English Dictionary*, ed. H. Kurath and S.M. Kuhn, Ann Arbor 1954 and in progress.
Middendorff	H. Middendorff, *Altenglisches Flurnamenbuch*, Halle 1902.
MinAcct	Ministers' Accounts in the PRO.
Misc	*Calendar of Inquisitions Miscellaneous*, 4 vols, London 1916-57.
MLat	Medieval Latin.
MLN	*Modern Language Notes*, in progress.
Mousehold	*A trewe discription of Mushold heath ... And allso the trewe circumference of the Towne of Thorpe*. A 16th-c. map deposited in the Norwich Castle Museum in 1903 by C. Blackwell Foster.
MP	*Four Maps of Great Britain*, designed by Matthew Paris ab. AD 1250, ed. J.P. Gilson, British Museum 1928.
NAM	*The Norfolk Antiquarian Miscellany*, ed. W. Rye, 1877.
NAR	Accounts of the Bailiffs and Treasurers of the City of Norwich in the NfRO.
Nashe	Thomas Nashe, *Lenten Stuffe*, 1599.
NCReg, NCR	The Norwich Cathedral Register in the NfRO.
NF	Norman French.

Nf	Norfolk.
NfA	*Norfolk Archaeology*, publ. by the Norfolk and Norwich Arch. Soc., Norwich 1847 and in progress.
NfD	*Ancient Deeds belonging to the Duke of Norfolk* (HMC Var VII), 1914.
NfRO	The Norfolk Record Office.
NfRS	Publications of the Norfolk Record Society, in progress.
Niermeyer	J.F.Niermeyer, *Mediae Latinitatis Lexicon Minus*, Leiden 1954-76.
NLCh	*Newington Longueville Charters*, ed. H.E. Salter (Oxfordshire Record Soc.) 1921.
Nobbs	George Nobbs, *Norwich, City of Centuries*, Norwich 1978 (1971).
NoD	*A Short Calendar of the Deeds relating to Norwich 1285-1306*, ed. W. Rye, Norwich 1903. *A Calendar of Norwich Deeds 1307-1341*, ed. W. Rye, Norwich 1915.
NoLeet	*The Leet Jurisdiction of Norwich*, ed. W. Hudson (Selden Soc. 5), London 1892.
NoRec	*The Records of the City of Norwich*, ed. W. Hudson and J.C. Tingey, 2 vols, Norwich 1906-10.
Norvic	Registers of Norwich Priory in the NfRO: I. Registrum Primum (c. 1300), II. Registrum Secundum (Pt. i 13th c., Pt. ii 14th c.).
NoVis	*Visitations in the Diocese of Norwich*, A.D. 1492-1523, ed. A. Jessop (Camden Soc., NS 43), 1943.
NPD	Private Deeds relating to Norwich in the NfRO.
NPL	Norwich Public Library.
NSFL	*Nordiska studier i filologi och lingvistik*. Festskrift tillägnad G. Holm, Lund 1976.
ODEE	C.T. Onions, *The Oxford Dictionary of English Etymology*, Oxford 1966.
ODan	Old Danish.
OE	Old English.
OED	*A New English Dictionary*, ed. J.A.H. Murray *et al.*, Oxford 1884-1928. Re-issued with a supplement in 1933 as *The Oxford English Dictionary*.
OE *wīc*	E. Ekwall, *Old English* wic *in Place-Names* (Nomina Germanica 13), Uppsala 1964.
OF	Old French.
OFB	The Old Free Book in the NfRO.
Ogilby	J. Ogilby, *Itinerarium Angliae*, 1675.
OR	*The Early Communar and Pitancer Rolls of Norwich Cathedral Priory*, ed. E.C. Fernie and A.B. Whittingham (NfRS 41), 1972.
OR	Unprinted Obedientiary Rolls in the NfRO.
OS 1885	*Norwich within the Walls*: a reprint of 24 sheets from the first 1:500 Ordnance Survey published 1884-5.
OS 6" Map 1920	The 1920 edition of the 6" Ordnance Survey.
OUA	Ortnamnssällskapets i Uppsala Årsskrift.
Oxenedes	*Chronica Johannis de Oxenedes*, ed. H. Ellis (Rolls Ser.), London 1859.
P	*The Great Roll of the Pipe* (PRS).
Past	*Paston Letters and Papers of the Fifteenth Century*, ed. N. Davis, 2 vols, Oxford 1971-6.

Pat   *Calendar of the Patent Rolls,* London 1891 and in progress.

Pevsner   N. Pevsner, *The Buildings of England: North East Norfolk and Norwich,* Harmondsworth 1979 (1962).

Phillipps   The Phillipps Collection of Deeds in the NfRO.

PN Bk   A. Mawer, F.M. Stenton, *The Place-Names of Buckinghamshire* (EPNS 2), Cambridge 1925.

PN Brk   Margaret Gelling, *The Place-Names of Berkshire,* Parts 1-3 (EPNS 49-51), Cambridge 1973-6.

PN C   P.H. Reaney, *The Place-Names of Cambridgeshire and the Isle of Ely* (EPNS 19), Cambridge 1943.

PN D   J.E.B. Gover, A. Mawer, F.M. Stenton, *The Place-Names of Devon,* Parts 1 and 2 (EPNS 8, 9), Cambridge 1931-2.

PN Ess   P.H. Reaney, *The Place-Names of Essex* (EPNS 12), Cambridge 1935.

PN L   K. Cameron, *The Place-Names of Lincolnshire,* Part 1 (EPNS 58), Cambridge 1985.

PN La   E. Ekwall, *The Place-Names of Lancashire,* Manchester 1922.

PN O   Margaret Gelling, *The Place-Names of Oxfordshire,* Parts 1 and 2 (EPNS 23, 24), Cambridge 1953-4.

PN Sr   J.E.B. Gover, A. Mawer, F.M. Stenton, A. Bonner, *The Place-Names of Surrey* (EPNS 11), Cambridge 1934.

PN W   J.E.B. Gover, A. Mawer, F.M. Stenton, *The Place-Names of Wiltshire* (EPNS 16), Cambridge 1939.

PN Wa   J.E.B. Gover, A. Mawer, F.M. Stenton, *The Place-Names of Warwickshire* (EPNS 13), Cambridge 1936.

PN YE   A.H. Smith, *The Place-Names of the East Riding of Yorkshire* (EPNS 14), Cambridge 1937.

PN YW   A.H. Smith, *The Place-Names of the West Riding of Yorkshire,* Parts 1-8 (EPNS 30-7), Cambridge 1961-3.

PQ   *Philological Quarterly,* in progress, Iowa City.

PRO   Public Record Office.

PromptParv   *Promptorium Parvulorum,* ed. A.L. Mayhew (EETS ES 102), London 1908.

PRS   Publications of the Pipe Roll Society.

Ptolemy   *Claudii Ptolemaei Geographia,* ed. G. Parthy and M. Pinder, Berlin 1860, ed. C. Müller, Paris 1883.

QW   *Placita de quo Warranto* (RC), 1818.

R   Rolls of the Bailiffs' Court in the NfRO.

RAN   Registrum de Ornamentis Ecclesiarum Archidiaconatus Norwyci, in *Inventory of Church Goods temp. Edward III,* transcribed by D.A. Watkins (NfRS 19:I), 1947.

RC   Record Commission.

RCh   Royal charters relating to Norwich Cathedral in the NfRO.

Reaney   P.H. Reaney, *A Dictionary of British Surnames* (revised by R.M. Wilson), London 1976 (1961).

ReaneyFR   P.N. Reaney, "Some Extinct Fenland Rivers", *A Philological Miscellany presented to Eilert Ekwall,* Uppsala 1942.

ReaneyO   P.H. Reaney, *The Origin of English Surnames,* London 1969 (1967).

Reg I   The oldest cartulary of Norwich Cathedral, in the NfRO.

Reg(esta)   *Regesta Willelmi Conquestoris et Willelmi Rufi 1066-1100,* ed. H.W.C. Davis, Oxford 1913; *Regesta Henrici Primi 1100-1135,* ed. C. Johnson and H.C. Cronne, Oxford 1956.

RH   *Rotuli Hundredorum* (RC), 2 vols, 1812-18.

Rivet & Smith A.L.T. Rivet and C. Smith, *The Place-Names of Roman*

	Britain, London 1979.
Riddington Young	J. Riddington Young, *The Inns and Taverns of Old Norwich*, Norwich 1975.
Salzman	L.F. Salzman, *Building in England down to 1540*, Oxford 1952.
Sandred	K..I. Sandred, *English Place-Names in -stead* (Studia Anglistica Upsaliensia 2), Uppsala 1963.
Saunders	H.W. Saunders, *A History of Norwich Grammar School*, Norwich 1932.
SaundersI	H.W. Saunders, *An Introduction to the Obedientiary and Manor Rolls of Norwich Cathedral Priory*, Norwich 1930.
Savile	*Rerum Anglicarvm scriptores post Bedam praecipvi*, ed. H. Savile, London 1596.
Sawyer	P. Sawyer, *From Roman Britain to Norman England*, London 1978.
Saxton	Saxton, *Map of Norfolk*, 1574.
Schram	O.K. Schram, "Place-Names" , *Norwich and its Region*, ed. F. Briers, Norwich 1961, 141-9.
Seltén	B. Seltén, *The Anglo-Saxon Heritage in Middle English Personal Names* I (Lund Studies in English 43) and II (Acta Regiae Societatis Humaniorum Litterarum Lundensis 73), Lund 1972 and 1979.
SelténN	B. Seltén, *Early East-Anglian Nicknames. 'Shakespeare' Names* (Scripta Minora Reg. Societatis Humaniorum Litterarum Lundensis 1968-9), Lund 1969.
Sf	Suffolk.
SN	E. Ekwall, *Streeet-Names of the City of London*, Oxford 1954.
SNPh	*Studia Neophilologica*, in progress.
Solomons	Gerald Solomons, *Stories behind the Plaques of Norwich*, Norwich 1981.
SR	Unpublished Lay Subsidy Rolls in the PRO.
SrRS	Publications of the Surrey Record Society, in progress.
Stacy	*A Topographical and Historical Account of the City and County of Norwich*, printed by and for John Stacy, Norwich 1819.
StEPh	Studien zur englischen Philologie, ed. L. Morsbach.
Studies[1]	E. Ekwall, *Studies on English Place- and Personal Names* (Kungl. Humanistiska Vetenskapssamfundets i Lund årsberå ttelse 1930-1), Lund 1931.
Studies[2]	E. Ekwall, *Studies on English Place-Names* (Kungl. Vitterhets-, historie- och antikvitetsakademiens handlingar 42:1), Stockholm 1936.
Studies[3]	E.Ekwall, *Etymological Notes on English Place-Names* (Lund Studies in English 27), Lund 1959.
St Will	*The Life and Miracles of St William of Norwich by Thos. of Monmouth*, ed. A. Jessop and M.R. James, Cambridge 1896.
Tanner	A transcript of the Norfolk portion of the manuscript collections relating to the Diocese of Norfolk compiled by the Rev. Thos. Tanner, made by T.R. Tallack (NfA 1891).
Tengvik	G. Tengvik, *Old English Bynames* (Nomina Germanica 4), Uppsala 1938.
Tillyard	Margot Tillyard, "The Acquisition by the Norwich Blackfriars of the Site for their Church *c.* 1310-1325", *Men of Property*, ed. Ursula Priestley, Norwich 1983.
TophCh	Topham Charters in the BL.
Trevisa	Higden's *Polychronicon*, transl. by J. Trevisa, ed. C. Babington

	and J.R. Lumby (Rolls Ser.), 9 vols, London 1865-86.
Unwin	G. Unwin, *The Guilds and Companies of London*, London 1966 (1908).
Val	*The Valuation of Norwich*, ed. W.E. Lunt, Oxford 1926.
VE	*Valor Ecclesiasticus* (RC), 6 vols, 1810-34.
De Vries	J. De Vries, *Altnordisches etymologisches Wörterbuch*, Leiden 1957-61.
Wals	Cartulary of Walsingham Priory (BL MS Cott. Nero E.VII).
White	W. White, *History, Gazetteer, and Directory of Norfolk*, Sheffield 1845 (repr. 1969).
Wicks	W. Wicks, *Inns and Taverns of Old Norwich*, Norwich 1925.
Wilhelmsen	Leif J. Wilhelmsen, *English Textile Nomenclature* (Skrifter fra Norges Handelshøyskole i rekken språklige avhandlinger 1), Bergen 1943.
Will	The Will of Bishop Sampson, in the NfRO.
WillD	The Will of William of Dunwich, in the NfRO.
Winton	*The Register of John Pontissara* (SrRS), 1913-24. *The Register of John de Sandal and Rigaud de Asseris* (HaRD), 1897. *Wykeham's Register* (HaRS), 1896-99.
Worcestre	W. Worcestre, *Itineraries*, ed. J.H. Harvey (Oxford Mediaeval Texts), Oxford 1969.
WSax	West Saxon.
Zachrisson	E. Zachrisson, *A Contribution to the Study of Anglo-Norman Influence on English Place Names* (Lunds Universitets Årsskrift 4:3), Lund 1909.

NOTES ON ARRANGEMENT

(1) Because of the large amount of material for the street-names of Norwich, only the names within the old city walls have been included in this volume. The arrangement is very simple. The street-names have been arranged alphabetically in one big section. The headwords are always the modern names of the streets or, in the case of streets which no longer exist (marked as 'lost'), the names under which the streets were last recorded. In many cases a street has changed its name (and this may have happened several times in its history), or a part of a street was known by another name earlier. Then the names which are no longer current are listed chronologically under the modern street-name (or the name last recorded). The Index, which is complete, makes possible quick reference to a name, whether current or not.

(2) As can be seen from the Contents, the street-name section is preceded by a number of other sections, Medieval Leets, Watercourses, Staithes and Quays, Bridges, etc. Here, as well as in the street-name section, the early spellings are presented in the order 'spelling, date, source'. Religious houses, hospitals, schools and other buildings have a separate section. It may be noted that names of pubs and courts, which are not much evidenced in the early sources, have only been included if they have given names to streets.

(3) In explaining the names summary reference is made, by printing the elements in bold type, to the two volumes of *English Place-Name Elements* (EPNS 25, 26) and to *Addenda and Corrigenda* to these volumes in *English Place-Name Society Journal* 1.

(4) Unprinted sources of the early spellings of names are indicated by printing the abbreviation for the source in italics. The abbreviation for a published source is printed in roman type. The exact page, folio or membrane is only given where the precise identification of an entry is of some importance.

(5) Where two dates are given for a source (applies mainly to Old English sources), the first is the date at which the document purports to have been composed, and the second (within brackets) is the date of the manuscript copy which has come down to us. Sources which cannot be fixed to a particular year are dated by century, e.g. 11, 12, 13, etc. (or more specifically e13 or l13, etc., early or late 13th century respectively), by regnal date, e.g. Hy1, Hy3, Eliz, etc., or by a range of years, e.g. 1272-80.

(6) The sign (p) after the source or date indicates that the particular spelling given appears in that source as a person's surname, not primarily as a reference to the place.

(7) When a letter or letters in an early name form are enclosed in brackets, it means that spellings with and without the enclosed letter(s) occur.

(8) Putative forms of personal names and place-name elements appear asterisked in the analyses.

(9) In order to save space in presenting the early spellings, the preposition 'to' has been used to indicate that at least four but not more than nine identical spellings have been found between the dates (inclusive) in the source quoted, e.g. *Colegate* c. 1300 to 1501 *NPD*. '*Et freq* to' indicates that the number of identical spellings in the source is ten or more, e.g. *Berstrete* 1248 *et freq* to 1540 *NPD*.

THE CITY OF NORWICH

NORWICH

NORDVICO c. 900 EMC (?), *NORDWIC, NORWIC, NORW*
924- 939 CoinA, *NORDWIC, NORW, NORIDWC, NORWIC*
924-939 BMC, *NORD* 959-975 Hildebrand
Norðwic 1004 (E) ASC, 1035-40 (e11th c.; BMF IV 21, Sawyer
1489) ASWills 26, 1038 BM, *Northwic* l10th-e11th c. (l13th c.;
Sawyer 1525) ASWills 38
Norwic, Noruic 1086 DB
Nortwic Hy1 *CottCh,* 1250 MP, *Norhtwic* 1122 (E) ASC, *Nordwico*
1184 P, *Northwich* c. *1200 Gerv, Northwich'* 1223 Cur, *Nortwyc*
1237 Pat, 1239 Cl, *de Northewyco* 1284 Winton, *Norþwhiche* 1387
Trevisa, *Northwiche, Nortwyche* 1389 EG
Norwic 1130, 1201 P, 1250 MP, *Noruuic* 1137 (E) ASC, *Norwic'*
1156 *et freq* to 1202 P, 1199 *R,* 1201 FF, 1274 RH, 1292 *AddR,*
1401 *MinAcct, in (de) Norwico* 1176 *et freq* to 1187 P, 1212 Fees,
1262 *et freq* to 1615 *AddCh,* 1280 *LansdCh,* 1301 *CottR,* 1366
MinAcct, 1664 *AddCh, apud (iuxta) Norwicum* 1178 P, 1250 MP,
1327, 1383, 1407 *AddCh,* 1396 to 1545 *MinAcct, Norwice* 12 LibEl,
Norwiz 1194 *et freq* to 1211 P, 1226 Cur, 1361 Pat, *ciuitas Norwici,
ciuitatis Norwic, in (de) ciuitate Norwic'* 1366 *et freq* to 1545
MinAcct, 1613, 1662 AddCh
Norwich' 1173 to 1183 P, 1221 Cur, *Norwich(e)* 1482 *AddR,* 1550
et freq to 1556 *CG,* 1567, 1661 *AddCh, Norwych(e)* 1401 *MinAcct,*
1544 *et freq* to 1547 *AOMB,* 1550 *CG, Norwitch* 1599 Nash
Norewico 1188 P, *Norewic'* 1189 to 1202 P, 1202 FF, 1212 Fees,
Norewich 1195 P, *Norewiz* 1214-21 BM
Norwyc 1230 P, 1251 FF, 1265 Cl, *in (de) Norwyco* 1270, 1296
TopCh, 1296 to 1435 *HarlCh,* 1301 *CottR,* 1306 to 1379 *AddCh,*
1427-33 *MinAcct, Norwyz* 1230 P, 1253 Cl, *Norwy3* 1253 NoRec,
Norwicz 1351 Pat, *Norwych* 1375 Cl
Norweche 1443 Past, *Norwece* 1459 *ib*

v. **norð, wīc.** The present city centre is about five kilometres to the
north of the site of the Roman provincial capital of the *Iceni,* which is
recorded c. 150 AD in Ptolemy as *Venta,* the *polis* of the *Iceni,* and in
the 4th cent. in the IA as *Venta Icinorum* (cf. Rivet & Smith 492).

Today the parish church of Caistor St Edmund is found there and the place has not been built over (*v. Antiquity* 3, 1929, 182-7; Frere & StJoseph 157 f.). Caistor, from OE (Angl) **cæster**, is a common term for 'a (Roman) town' or 'an ancient fortification'. Whether *Venta* was abandoned at the end of the Roman period or continued to be used by the invading Angles into the seventh cent. is uncertain (Campbell 2).

The present city of Norwich seems to be the result of a merger of at least four separate settlements on the river Wensum. The names of these may be preserved in the names of quarters of the medieval city, such as Conesford, Westwick and Coslany, as suggested by Campbell (3). *v.* Map 1 and King Street, Westwick Street and Coslany Street *infra.* Instead of Conesford, Carter suggests that the name of one of the separate settlements was Needham (*v.* St Stephen's Street). To these we have to add a fourth, Norwich, which, because of its greater importance, gave its name to the whole. Coslany was situated north-west of Westwick and separated from it by the river Wensum *(ultra aquam).* Carter (197) places the original Norwich east and north of Westwick where there was a crossing of an east-west and a north-south road (both probably Roman). This route centre became the site of a lively market, especially because the river was navigable as far as this point (cf. Green & Young 9).

According to Ekwall (OE *wīc* 20), Norwich was so called because it is 'north of Ipswich and Dunwich'. This is possible, but since one of the other nuclear settlements out of which the city developed had the name Westwick, it seems even more plausible that Norwich, being itself one of these small separate settlements, was named in relation to the others. Ekwall's study of OE *wīc* is the most thorough of this place-name element to date (*Nomina Germanica* 13).

MEDIEVAL LEETS

Conesford

Leta de Cunisford 1288 NoLeet, *Cunesford* 1290 (2x), 1300 *ib*
(*ad Letam de/ Leta de/ amerciamenta Lete de*) *Conesford* 1289 to 1391
NoLeet, 1386, 1387 *NAR, ye Warde of Conesford* 1415 NoRec, *The Ward of* (*berstrete*) *Conford* (*and trowse*) 1551 NoLeet, *pro Warda de Conisford* (*Beerstreet & Trowse*) 1682, 1693 *ib, the Great Ward [of*

Conisford] 1802 *ib*

v. King Street. In the 13th-century rolls the references are to the Great Leet of Conesford; later the two combined subleets of North and South Conesford are usually referred to (*v.* Fig. 1:1-2). *Trowse* was a suburb which had not belonged to the subleet of South Conesford.

THE SUBLEET OF BERSTREET (*v.* Fig. 1:3)
Berstrette 1288, 1313 NoLeet, (*Leta de/ Presentationes Lete de/Veredicta Lete de*) *Berstrete* 1291, 1296, 1307, 1391 *ib, Berstret(e)* 1364, 1391 *ib, The Ward of berstrete (Conford and trowse), Berstret* 1551 *ib, pro Warda de (Conisford) Beerstreet (& Trowse)* 1693 *ib, Leta de Beerstreete* 1693, 1698 *ib*

v. Ber Street and All Saints Timberhill.

Mancroft

Manecroft 1288, 1291 NoLeet, (*Leta/ad Letam/ Presentationes Lete*) *de Nedham et Manecroft* 1289 to 1313 *ib, Presentationes de Nedham et Manecroft* 1296
Leta de Mancroft 1386, 1387 *NAR, Mancroft Warde* 1415 NoRec, *pro Warda de Mancroft* 1682, 1693 NoLeet

v. Market Place. *Nedham* is the original name of the district forming the parish and subleet of St Stephen. *v.* St Stephen's Street and Plain.

SUBLEETS (*v.* Fig. 1:4-5)
(*Leta/de Leta/ Veredicta Lete*) *Sancti Stephani* 1364 to 1698 NoLeet
de Leta Sancti Petri 1364 NoLeet, *Veredicta Lete Sancti Petri de Manecroft* 1391 *ib, Leta Sancti Petri* 1682, 1693, 1698 *ib*

For *Sancti Stephani* and *Sancti Petri de Manecroft, v.* Norwich Churches.

Wymer

(*ad Letam de/Leta de*) *Wymer et Westwyk* 1289, 1300, 1313
  NoLeet, *Presentationes de Wymer et Westwyk* 1393 *ib, Wimer et
  Westwyk* 1296 *ib*
Leta de Wymer 1291 NoLeet, 1386, 1387 *NAR, in Wymer Warde*
  1415 NoRec, *in Wymere Lete* 1416 *NAR, pro Warda de Wymer*
  1682, 1693 *ib*
Wymer and Mydyll Wymer & also Est Wymer Warde 1551 NoLeet,
  the Warde of Wymer 1552 *CG*

v. St Andrew's Street and Westwick Street.

SUBLEETS (*v.* Fig. 1:6-9)
(*de Leta/Veredicta Lete*) *Sancti Egidii* 1364, 1391 NoLeet
(*de Leta/Veredicta Lete*) *Sancti Gregorii* 1364, 1391 NoLeet, *Leta
  Sancti Gregorii infra Wardam de Wymer* 1551 *ib, Leta Sancti
  Gregorii* 1682, 1693, 1698 *ib*
(*de Leta/Veredicta Lete*) *Sancti Andree* 1364, 1391 NoLeet, *Leta
  Sancti Andree* 1682, 1693, 1698 *ib*
(*Leta/de Leta/Veredicta Lete*) *Sancti Georgii* 1364, 1391 NoLeet,
  1682, 1698 *ib*

For the names of the subleets, *St Giles, St Gregory, St Andrew* and *St
George* (*Tombland*), *v.* Norwich Churches.

Ultra Aquam

(*Leta/ad Letam/ de Presentationibus Lete/ Veredicta Lete*) *Ultra
  Aquam* 1288 to 1313 NoLeet, *Vltra Aquam* 1386, 1387 *NAR, ye
  Warde over ye Water* 1415 NoRec, *pro Warda Ultra Aquam* 1682,
  1693 NoLeet

SUBLEETS (*v.* Fig. 1:10-11)
(*de Leta/Veredicta Lete*) *Sancti Michaelis (ultra aquam)* 1364, 1391
  NoLeet, *Leta de Coslany* 1682, 1698 *ib*
(*de Leta/Veredicta Lete*) *Sancti Clementis* 1364, 1391 NoLeet, *Leta
  de Fibridge* 1682, 1693, 2698 *ib*

For *Leta de Coslany, v.* Coslany Street--Oak Street, and for *Leta de Fibridge, v.* Fye Bridge. For *Sancti Michaelis* and *Sancti Clementis, v.* Norwich Churches.

Fee of the Castle

(*Veredicta*) *Lete novi feodi Castri* 1391 NoLeet, *Leta Castri Feodi* 1698 *ib*

WATERCOURSES

COKEY (lost), (*super communem venellam que vocat'*) *kokeye* 1323 *NPD, kokeye* 1339 *ib, Cokeye, -am* 1339 to 1353 *ib.*

These documents concern property in St Vedast. The *cokey* referred to may be one which fell into the Wensum below *Fresflete* (*v.* Campbell Map 6). MLat *venella* 'lane'. For *cokey, v. Great Cockey.*

DALLINGFLEET (lost)
Kinges Flete 13 *D&C, Kinges-cokeye* Ed3 K
Dallingflette 1296 NoLeet
the Grey Fryers Creek c. 1720 K, *The Creke* 1746 B

v. OE **flēot**, ME **flēte** 'estuary, inlet', but also 'water course, ditch' (MED). For *creek, v.* Spiteldike. This was a brook that rose at the Grey Friary, crossed St Faith's Lane under a stone bridge (*Stone Bridge* 1766 King) and fell into the Wensum south of Lovell's Staithe (*v.* K 4). It is described as *aquam currentem sub Netherecunesford* 1255 *NPD* and *cursus aque currens usque ad magnam ripam* (1288 *R,* cf. K 100 f.). It was filled up in the early 19th cent. but the bridge still stood c. 1890 (K 4 note 8).

The *D&C* document was for some reason not available to Hudson (K 2 note 5), who expresses some doubt as to its authenticity. The document, assigned to 'the former part of K. Hen. 3' by Kirkpatrick, concerns a piece of land abutting north on 'the street which leads to Luuelestahte' and south on 'Kinges Flete'. There were several people in Norwich surnamed *(de) Dalling* from the late 13th cent. on. Field Dalling and Wood Dalling are Nf villages.

DALYMOND DYKE (lost)

Dalimund 1271 K, *communis watergate que dicitur Dalymund* 1345
   ib
Dalymond 1318, 1386 *ib, Dalimond* 1336 *ib*
Dalimont Diche 1383 K, *Dalymotdyche* 1488 *ib*
Dalymondes Dyke 1394 K, *Dalymondesdyke* 1394 *ib, Dalymondyk*
   1395 *ib*

This was a stream of some importance which entered the City
between St Augustine's Gates and Magdalen Gates, continued its
course in a south-easterly direction and fell into the Wensum
somewhere near St Edmund's Church (K 102). *Dalymond* 1318, 1386
and *Dalimond* 1336 would seem to have referred to a field or croft
north-east of St Augustine's Street--Botolph Street (K 80). All the
early forms end in -d, which points to ME **mund** 'protection' (MED s.v.
mound 1), by Smith connected with OE *mund* 'hand, security' (EPNE
s.v.) and ModE *mound* 'hedge, fence' (OED sb. 3), possibly also earlier
used in some topographical sense. Cf. Munstead Sr (Sandred 247).
For the first el., cf. John and Andrew *Daly* 1282 K. The second
component is ON **dík, díki** or OE **díc,** influenced by the Scand word.

FRESFLETE (lost), *communis fleta vocata Fresflet* 1290 K, was a
stream that fell into the Wensum a little to the south of Foundry
Bridge. OF *freis, fresche* 'fresh', OE **flēot,** ME *flēte* 'water course,
ditch'.

GREAT COCKEY (lost)
super foueam q. voc. Kokeye 13 D&C, *dyke called Kokeye* c. 1277 K
   Cokeye 1285, 1330, 1357 K, 1288, 1296 NoLeet, 1304 to 1320
   D&C, super Cokeyam 1288 R, *Cokeya* 1288 NoLeet, 1293 (2x)
   NoRec, 1304 to 1465 *D&C,* 1306 K, *cursus aque de Cokeye* 1386
   ib, commune Cokey 1391 NoLeet, *le comon Cokeye* 1419 K, *le
   Cokey* 1483 *ib*
regia fossa q. voc. Cokye 1286 K

The Great Cockey rose at JACK'S PIT (*Jakkes Pytt* 1496 K, *Jackes
Pitt* 1572 NoRec, *Jacks Pit* c. 1720 K) in Magna Neugate (now Surrey
Street) and flowed north through several parishes and entered the
Wensum west of Blackfriars Bridge. *v.* also Back of the Inns.
   In Norwich, and East Anglia generally, *cockey* was used as a

generic term. There were several Norwich *cockeys*. As they were used by the townspeople to carry off sewage, they were in due course vaulted over and the word *cockey* assumed the meaning 'sewer'. In the *Promptorium Parvulorum* (1440) it is glossed *priuy, cloaca* (cf. MED s.v. *cokei*). EDD defines it as 'a drain, sewer; a grate over a common sewer' (recorded from East Anglia). The second element of *cockey* is probably ME *ē* 'stream' (from OE *ēa*, suggested by MED s.v. *cokei*). The first element is more problematic. It cannot very well be OE **cwicu**, as suggested by Hudson (K 79), for the form *c(w)ucu*, the result of combinative back mutation, is found in WSax and Kentish writings only; in the Anglian dialect *i* remained unchanged before velar consonants (Luick § 221, Campbell OEG § 218). *Cock* is found with other names for a water-course, e.g. Cock Beck YW, Cofleet D (*Cokflute* 1298 FF) and the lost *Cocbroc* Brk (931 BCS 675). For Cock Beck Smith suggests (PN YW VII 123) either a compound of OE **cocc** 'wood cock' or an early back-formation from *Cocksford*. Different names may well have different explanations, but as Ekwall points out (ERN 83), in the earliest records *Co(c)k*, etc., occurs on its own without an adjunct, and this points to *Cock* being a real river-name. The authenticity of a Celtic noun *kok* 'hollow, water channel', quoted by Hudson (K 99), is open to doubt. Middendorff (28) posits an OE noun *cocc* meaning 'deep narrow valley, gully', but Ekwall (ERN 83) maintains that no such word is evidenced anywhere. However, the word may be of Scandinavian origin. Cf. ON *kók* 'gullet', Norw *kok* 'throat', Faroese *koka* 'pelvis' (*v.* De Vries s.v. *kók*).

SPITELDIKE (lost)
communis Fredisch 1285 K
Fossatum de Cokeye 1293 K, *communis Guttera que voc' Cokeya*
    1315 *ib, fossata que vocat' Cokeye* 1324 *ib*
Le Spiteldike 1311 K, *Spetyl Dyk* Ed3 *ib, Normanspitel dyk* 1358 *ib,*
    Le Spitel Pol 1351 *ib*
Spelunca Hospitalis Sci Pauli 14 K, *Fossatum de Normanspitele* 1369
    ib, Fossatum Hospitalis de Normans 1483 *ib*
the Cricke in St Paules 1630 K, *the Cricke near the Children's*
    Hospital 1631 *ib, the Creek in the Normans* 1637 *ib, the Normans*
    Creek 1637 *ib, the Cricke at St Edmunds on the backside of the*
    Children's Hospital 1651 *ib*

This ditch ran from the area north of Norman's Hospital, from which it was named, to Dalymond Dyke (*q.v.*). *Fredisch*, OE **frēo** 'free (from charge)' and **dīc** 'ditch', presumably a ditch that could be used without restriction by anyone (for the deposition of refuse). MLat *fossatum, fossata* 'ditch', *guttera* 'channel, gutter', *spelunca* 'covered passage' (Latham s.vv.); ON **dík, díki** 'ditch'; OE **pōl** 'pool, pond'; ME **crike** 'cove, small stream', from ON **kriki** 'nook, bend' or OF *crique*; ME *crēke*, either from MDu *krēke* or from *crike* by lengthening.   Cf. ReaneyFR 103 f., MED s.v. *crike* 1, ODEE s.v. *creek*; *v.*   Norman's Hospital and Spitellond.

WENSUM

Wenson 1096, 1119, 15, 1418, 1443 *NCReg*, 1250 *Ass*, 1543 NoRec,
    1585 *Mousehold, Weneson* 15, 1418 *NCReg, Wensonne* 1462, 1556
    NoRec, *Wensun* 15 *NCReg*, 1535-43 Leland
Wensum 1250 *Ass*, 1443 NoRec, 1461-83 K, 1462 Ch, *Wensom(e)*
    1307-27 Tanner, 1343, 1556 NoRec, Hy6 K
Weysum 1325 Cl
Wantsume 1577 Holinshed, *Wentsum* 1586 Camden, 1622 Drayton
Winsder 1574 Saxton, 1675 Ogilby, *Wentsar* 1586 Camden

Ekwall (ERN 434), quoting Bradley (E&S I 34), gives OE ***wendsum** (earlier ***wændsum**) 'winding' as the etymon (cf. EPNE).

STAITHES AND QUAYS

BALTIC WHARF, is a landing place on the south side of Foundry Bridge. A lane connects it with Mountergate.

FRANKESTATHE (lost), *Frankestathe* 1290 K, was a quay approximately where Carrow Bridge now is, named after one Goscelin *Franke* 1290 K (cf. John *Franke* 1289 NoRec). Kirkpatrick mentions a walkway called *Frankestathe* (K 6).

NEW COMMON STAITHE (lost)
Calves Stathe c. 1397 NoRec, *Caluestathe* (2x) 1411 *NPD*,
    Calvestathe 1419 *NAR*
mesuagium vocat' the comen Stathe 1481 *NPD, the new common
    Stath* c. 1720 K, *the New Common Stathe* 1746 B, *New Com.*

Staithe 1766 King, *Newcom St* (sic) 1789 H, *New Common Staithe* 1830 M&M

This quay was situated in the parish of St Edward, practically opposite the church. Blomefield (IV 70) identifies *Calves Stathe* with the New Common Staithe. *Calf* is well attested as a Norwich surname: William *Calf* 1286 to 1301 NoD, 1288 NoRec, John *Calf* 1319 NoD, 1345 NoRec, Roger *Calf* 1339 (2x) NoD, 1365, 1369, 1375 NoRec. According to Blomefield (IV 70) one Richard *Blackamore* (cf. Richard *Blakehumoure* 1389, 1397 NoRec) had a crane set up here in Henry IV's time and, for a time, the quay also went by the name of *Blackamore's stathe* (*v.* Campbell Map 6).

OLD COMMON STAITHE (lost)
(*lez*) *Stath'* 1378 NoRec, *the Stathe* 1382 to 1397 *ib*
the Comon Stathe c. 1397 to 1414 NoRec, *the Common Staith* 1474
    ib, *the comon stathe in Norwich* 1527 *ib*
the old stathe 1437 NoRec
Old Common Stathe 1746 B, *Old Common Staith*(*e*) 1766 King,
    1789 H, 1830 M&M, *the old common stathe* 1819 Stacy
Town Stathe 1696 Cleer, *Town-stathe* 1745 B

The earliest evidence (1378) refers to all the common staithes in Norwich. The Old Common Staithe, in the parish of St Clement, was purchased by the City in 1379 from Hugh Holond and the Abbot of Wendling. The New Common Staithe, in the parish of St Edward further south, was acquired by the City in the same year (NoRec II xxxv f.), but it did not supersede the Old Staithe, which was rebuilt in 1432: 'John Marwe, citeseyn of Norwich, fremason,...xal make er don make the newe comon kaye of Norwich lying in the paros of Seint Clement of Conesford' (NoRec II 390, Salzman 502). This actually refers to the Old Staithe in St Clement's, not to the New Staithe in St Edward's as maintained by Campbell (15 note 15). The Old Staithe remained the principal place for loading and unloading ships and boats, witness the designation *Town Stathe* as late as the 18th century. In 1474 it was ordained that 'all aliens bringing any merchandise by water shall lodge it at the Common Staith and not elsewhere' (NoRec II 101).

QUAY SIDE

super Cayo de Fibrigghe 13 Holme, *cayum de fibrighe* 1259 *NPD,*
    Kayum de Fibrigge 1265 K, *kayum de Fibrigg'* 1271 *D&C,*
    Cayum de Fibrigg 1288, 1289, 1290 *R,* 1290 NoRec, *Cayum de*
    Fibriggat' 1290 *R, Cayum de Fibrig(ge)* 1301 NoD, 1323 K,
    Fybriggkay 1519 NfRS, *Fybriggekey* 1524 *ib*
magna ripa de Fibrigge 1282 *D&C*
le Stath' de Fibrigge 1285 Norvic, *Fybrigge Stathe* 1307, 1316 K,
    Fibrigge Stathe 1316 *ib, le Fibrigge Staye* 1316 *ib, Fybriggestathe*
    1523 NfRS, *Fibrig stathe* 1543 *ib*
Five Bridge Key or Stathe 1746 B, *Fye Bridge Key* 1766 King, *Fye*
    Bridge Quay 1789 H, 1830 M&M
Quay Side 1845 White, 1885 OS, 1920 OS 6" Map

    Quay Side runs from Fye Bridge to Bedding Lane, which is close to
St Martin at Palace Plain, the site of the medieval *Bichil,* a gravel
terrace where waterborne goods were landed in the very early period
from the incoming merchant ships. *v.* further St Martin at Palace
Plain.

RUSHWORTH STAITHE (lost)

Luuelestathe 13 *D&C, Louelestath in Norwico* 1291 Abbrev, *ad kayum*
    quod vocatur loulestathe 1292 *AddR, Nouelstathe* (sic) 1350
    D&C, Lovellstathe 14 Binham, *Lovellestath* R2 NoRec, *Lovelstathe*
    1566 K, *Lovel Stath* 1609 *ib*
une place quest apellee Roscelinestath 1343 NoRec, *Russhlyng Stathe*
    1451 *ib, Rushlyng Stath* 1475 K
Rushworth(e) Stath 1526 K, c. 1720 *ib*

    This was a landing stage a little to the south of Pull's Ferry. The
first elements preserve two family names, those of Roger *Lovell* who
lived in the time of Henry III (K 6 note 5; cf. *ad terram que fuit Rogeri*
Luuel 1257 NoRec) and Sir Peter *Roscelin,* recorded in 16 Edward I,
i.e. 1288 (K 6 note 4). *Rushworth* is considered to be a corruption of
the name *Roscelin.*

ST ANN'S STAITHE

St Ann's Stath(e) 1546, 1614, 1678 K, 1746 B, *St Anns Staith(e)* c. 1720
    K, 1766 King, *Saint Annes Staith(e)* 1789 H, 1830 M&M, *St Anne's*
    staith 1845 White, *St Ann's Staithe* 1885 OS

The staithe and the lane leading to it (St Ann Lane) acquired their names from St Ann's Chapel nearby, demolished c. 1270 (Blomefield IV 78). The name *Saint Annes Staith(e)* is actually printed along the lane leading to it on two of the maps (1789 H, 1830 M&M). The same applies to *St Anns Staithe* 1766 King. In 1614 it was decided 'that St. Ann's stath should from thenceforth be used for a Common washing stath and not for the loading and unloading of Goods as heretofore' (K 8). Today's *St Ann's Wharf* is slightly to the north of the original staithe.

ST EDMUND'S QUAY (lost)
caium Sci Edmundi 1313, 1338 K
St Edmunds stath, St Edmunds Watering c. 1720 K, *Fishers Gate Staithe* 1766 King

In Kirkpatrick's time (c. 1720) a street from Fishergate to the river, along the west end of St Edmund's churchyard, led to *St Edmunds stath* or *St Edmunds Watering*, which served as a watering place for horses (K 86). This is opposite the present Quay Side.

ST JAMES'S STAITHE (lost), *ad Kayum Sci Jacobi* 1313 K, *St James stath* c. 1720 K.
On the south side of Barrack Street a common lane led to this staithe on the river. St James's Church is situated nearby.

ST JULIAN'S WHARF
Tepeystathe 1275 *R*, 1290 NoLeet, *Teppeystathe* 1290 *R, Teppaystathe* 1296 *ib, Tepaystathe* 1303 *NPD*, 1304 *R*
Tepperestath(e) 1357 to 1379 *NPD*
Mendham Stathe 1519 (2x) K
Briggs Staith(e) 1766 King, 1789 H, 1830 M&M
St Julian's Wharf 1885 OS

This staithe was situated below St Julian's Church. The old spellings all seem to preserve personal names. *Tepeystathe* has been derived 'from a certain Alexander *Teppay*' 1289 (K 7 note 6). *Tepperestathe* may derive from Nicholaus *Tepede* (assuming this is a scribal error; cf. Ulfuine *Teperesune* c. 1095 Bury Sf in Reaney 316) who in 1290 narrowed the lane by 'eight feet and more' by building a house and a raised footway down to the river (NoLeet 36). *Mendham Stathe* is from someone surnamed (*de*) *Mendham*, such as Robertus de *Mendham*

1288 NoLeet, Robert de *Mendham* 1305 NoD, Ralph de *Mendham*
1308, 1314 NoD, Godefr. de *Mendham* 1311 NoRec, etc. (Mendham is
in Suffolk).   *Briggs Staithe* contains the family name *Briggs*, also found
in Briggs Street (formerly Lane) from Augustine *Briggs* the Elder (died
1684) and the Younger (died 1704), both aldermen and mayors (K 17,
Blomefield IV 217 ff.). The name *Briggs Staith(e)* is actually printed
along the lane leading to the river on the three maps dated 1766, 1789
and 1830.

ST MARGARET'S STAITHE (lost)
St Margaret's Stathe in St George at Muspol 1546 K, *St Margarets Stathe*
    1746 B
St George's Stathe c. 1720 K

On Blomefield's map (1746 B), *St Margarets Stathe* is printed along
Water Lane, which runs from St George's Church in Colegate to the
river, where the site of this staithe would thus seem to have been. This
is where St Margaret Newbridge Church once stood. It was converted
to a hermitage chapel in 1349 (when this parish was depopulated by the
plague) and later pulled down.   The parish was united to St George
Colegate (Blomefield IV 474 f.).
     Campbell (on Map 2) gives another St Margaret's Staithe on the
south bank of the river, below St Margaret Westwick Church. This
seems to derive from King 1766.

ST OLAVE'S STAITHE (lost)
Cayum Sci Olavi n.d. K, *St Olave's Quay in Conesford* 1346 NoRec
St Olaves Stath c. 1720 K

This quay was situated just north of present-day Carrow Bridge. It
was named from the Chapel of St Olave, which was pulled down before
1345.

BRIDGES

BISHOP BRIDGE
ad pontem episcopi c.1250 *NPD*, 1272-89 ChNCP, *sub ponte Episcopi*
    1371 NoLeet
Busshoppys Brygge 1331 NoRec, *Bisshopesbrege* 1332 AD, *Bishops
    Bridge* c. 1720 K, 1746 B, 1766 King, 1789 H, *Bishop's Bridge* 1845

White
le pount le Euesqe 1343 NoRec
Bishops Gate Bri. 1728 Hoyle, *Bishopgate Bridge* 1830 M&M

It was so called because it originally belonged to the episcopal see.
At the end of the fourteenth century it passed into the citizens' hands
(*v.* Blomefield IV 402). The present bridge is supposed to date back to
c. 1340 and is the only medieval bridge in Norwich (Pevsner 266).

BLACKFRIARS BRIDGE
de novo ponte 1257 *NPD, Neubrigg* (p) 1265 *ib, Neubrigge* 1265, 1273
    (p, 2x) *ib, Newebrigg*(*e*) 1284, 1294 (p) *ib,* 1289 to 1313 (p) *R*
Black Friers Bridge 1696 Cleer, c. 1720 K, 1746 K, 1766 King, *Blackfriars
    Bridge* 1789 H, *Black Friars Bridge* 1830 M&M, 1845 White
St George's Bridge 1885 OS

This bridge, still usually called Blackfriars Bridge after the
Dominican Friary which stood nearby, was called *Newebrigge* in
relation to earlier bridges (*v.* **nīwe**). The present bridge was built in
1783 (Pevsner 266). An earlier bridge, built in the reign of Henry V,
was of timber. It was rebuilt in Edward IV's time, and in 1586 it was
made of stone. *v.* Blomefield IV 353.

CARROW BRIDGE
Opened in 1923, it is the most recent of the Norwich river crossings.
It is just inside the Walls. Its predecessor, built in 1810, was further
down the river, outside the Walls.

CARROW is one of the eight villages which, in the course of the
centuries, were incorporated into Norwich. The others are Bracondale,
Earlham, Eaton, Heigham, Hellesdon and Pockthorpe.
Charho 1158 *et freq* to 1193 P, *Carho* 1159 *et freq* to 1230 *ib, Charrou*
    1194, 1195 *ib, Carrho* 1196 *ib, Carrou* 1197 *et freq* to 1211 *ib, Karhoge*
    1198 FF, *Karro* c.1200 Gerv, *Carhow* 1212 Fees, 1492 NoVis, *Karhowe*
    eHy3 HMC, 1234 FF, 1250 *Ass,* 1275 RH, *Carhou* 1223 Cur, 1229-51
    Ch, 1269 *Ass,* 1307 Pat, *Karhou* 1225 (2x) Cur, *Carroue* 1229 BM,
    Carhowe 1229-51, 1302 Ch, c.1250 BS, 1254 Val, 1286 *Ass,* 1289, 1307
    R, 1307, 1333 Ipm, 1316, 1428 FA, 1336 Pat, 1406 BM, 1429 *AddCh,*
    Karho 1234 Pat, 1250 *Ass, Carhoue* 1272 Ch, *Karowye* 1274 RH,
    Carowe 1282 BM, 1535 VE, 1537 *MinAcct, Carrowe* 1285 to 1313 *R,*
    1286 *Ass,* 1384 Pat, 1389 EG, 1530, 1544 *AOMB,* 1535 VE, *Carehowe*

1288 NoLeet, 1292 (p), 1312, 1313 *R*, 1314 Ipm, 1445 BM

The second element of the name is OE **hōh,** one of whose meanings was 'a low projecting piece of land in the bend of a river'. Carrow lies in a fork of low-lying land near the junction of the rivers Yare and Wensum. The first el. cannot very well be ON **kjarr,** ME *kerr* 'bog, marsh', seeing that there is not a single ME form with *Kerr-*. Ekwall (DEPN) suggests that the first el. is OE **carr** 'rock'.

A convent of Benedictine nuns, CARROW PRIORY, was built here in King Stephen's time (Blomefield IV 525). Some of the ruins still remain. *v.* also Carrow Hill--Carrow Road.

DUKE'S PALACE BRIDGE, *Dukes Palace New Bridge* 1830 M&M, *Duke's Palace Bridge* 1845 White, 1885 OS, is of 1822. It was at first a toll-bridge. The toll was removed in 1855 (NoRec II cxxxv, Wicks 98 f.). Cf. Duke Street.

FOUNDRY BRIDGE, *the Foundery Bridge* 1819 Stacy,   *Foundry Bridge* 1830 M&M, 1845 White, 1885 OS, is a river-crossing at the eastern end of Prince of Wales Road.   The present bridge is the third on the site. The first was opened in 1811, the second in 1844, the third in the eighteen-eighties.   The first was a toll-bridge, but the second was thrown open to the public (*v.* Stacy 123, White 81, Pevsner 266). The Iron Foundry (1830 M&M) was on the west bank of the river.

FYE BRIDGE

Fifbrig' 1130-33 ChNCP, *Fibrigg*(*e*) 1140-53 Holme, 1205-11, 1274
   ChNCP, 1286 (p) to 1290 *R*, 1539 NfRS, *Fifbrege* 1141-9 Holme,
   Fifbrigge 1176 K, *Fybrige* 13 *D&C,* 1250 (p) *Ass,* *Fyfbrig*(*g*)*e* 1257,
   1269 *ib, Fyfbrig* 1269 *ib, Fybrigg*(*e*) 1283 to 1683 *NPD* , 1317 Inq
   aqd, 1368 Ipm, 1535 VE, *Fybrygge* 1535 *ib, Fibridge* 1547 Pat,
   Febrige 1547 *ib, Febridge* 1547 *ib, Fybridge* 1548 *ib,* c. 1720 K,
   Fibrige 1567 *AddCh, Fybriddge* 1627 *NPD, Fy Bridge* 1696 Cleer,
   Five Bridge 1746 B, *Fye Bridge* 1766 King, 1819 Stacy, 1830 M&M,
   1845 White, 1885 OS

Although Whitefriars Bridge (*q.v.*) is the earliest recorded bridge in Norwich, Fye Bridge is considered to be at least equally old. The first element is in all probability the numeral *five* (OE **fīf**). Cf. *Fye Foot*

Lane in the City of London (SN 100) and *Omannebrugge* 1398 'one-man bridge' in Aylesbury (PN Bk 257). The name appears to be elliptical. Schram (148) suggests the meaning 'the bridge that is five times the width of an ordinary footbridge'. To our knowledge, no information is available as to the width of the early Fye Bridge, but as it was the principal river-crossing, it ought to have been the widest of the Norwich bridges. The original Fye Bridge is believed to have been contemporary with Whitefriars Bridge, evidenced in 1106. The present bridge is of 1829 (Pevsner 266).

ST MILES BRIDGE
Coslaniebrigge 1186-1210 Holme, (*in parochia S. Laurencii... inter*)
   duos pontes de Koselanye ? 1287 NoRec, (*in parochia Sci Laurentii
   prope / apud*) *pontem de Coselanye* 1289, 1295 *R*, (*ad emen-
   dacionem / sustentacionem*) *pontis de Coslanye* 1296 *NAR*, 1341,
   1349 *NPD*
Coslanybrigge 1419 *NAR, Cos(e)lany Bridge* 1696 Cleer, 1746 B, 1766
   King, 1789 H, 1819 Stacy
St Miles Bridge 1830 M&M, 1885 OS, *St Miles' bridge* 1845 White

The second quotation is puzzling, since it refers to two bridges. The present bridge was built in 1804 (Pevsner 266). St Michael's Church (*q.v.*) is in Coslany Street, just north of the junction with Colegate. For *Miles* as a popular variant of *Michael's, v.* Reaney, s.n. *Michael.*

WHITEFRIARS BRIDGE
a ponte Sci Martini usque ad terram Sci Michaelis 1106, 1136 Regesta,
   1157 ChNCP, *pons Sci Martini* 1290 *R, a ponte Sancti Martini* 1292
   AddR
White Friers Brigge 1552 *CG, the bridge called the Whyghtfriers Bridge*
   1579 NoRec, *White Friers Bridge* 1696 Cleer, c. 1720 K, 1746 B, 1766
   King, *the White Friars Bridge* 1830 M&M, *Whitefriars' Bridge* 1845
   White, 1885 OS

This is the earliest recorded bridge in Norwich. As is obvious from the first quotation, there was a bridge at this place long before the foundation of the Monastery of the Carmelites (or White Friars) on the north bank of the river in 1256. St Martin at Palace Church is some distance to the south of the bridge. The present bridge dates from 1925.

GATES AND TOWERS

BER STREET GATE
(*prope/iuxta*) *portas de Berstrete* 1297 *R*, 1521 *NPD*, (*apud*) *portas de
    Berstrette* 1298 *ib*, (*a*) *portis de Berstrete* 1322 *D&C, la porte de Berstret*
    1343 NoRec, *portas Berstreteyatis* 1428 FA, *Berstrett gats* 1508 FK,
    Bear-Street Gate 1696 Cleer, *Berstreet Gates* 1746 B, *Bear Street Gate*
    1766 King, *Ber Street Gate* 1789 H

This was the most important entrance to Norwich, Ber Street
leading to the Castle. The gate was taken down in 1726 and rebuilt
with red brick. It was finally demolished in 1808 (FK 5 ff.).

BISHOP GATE
la porte sur le pount le Evesqe 1343 NoRec, (*apud*) *Byshopgates* 1419
    NAR, le Bishopesyates 1422 NoRec, (*the*) *Busshopp(e)s gates* 1451
    Past, 1530 Harrod, *Bisshoppes Gates* 1481 NoRec, 1581 *D&C,
    Busshoppesʒates* 1529 *NPD, Bishoppes Gate* 1558 Cuningham,
    Busshopps gate 1585 *Mousehold, Bishops Gate* 1696 Cleer, 1746 B,
    1766 King, *Bishop Gates* c. 1720 K, *Bishop's Gate* 1789 H

So called because it led to the Bishop's Palace. The taking down was
accomplished by 1791 (FK 33 ff.)

BLACK TOWER
the Blak Toure 1451 NoRec, *the Black Tower* 1591 FK
the Governo(u)r's or Black Tower 1746 B, 1819 Stacy
Earl of Buckinghamshire's Tower 1766 King
Snuff Mill 1789 H

The remains of a tower in the City Wall on the top of Carrow Hill.
This tower 'was made a prison for unruly, infected persons, in 1625
and 1636' (FK 3). It may have been called the Black Tower because it
was faced with black flint (Stacy 62).

BRAZEN DOORS
(*ad*) *portam de Swynemarket* 1290 *R*, (*apud*) *portas de Swynmarket*
    1298 *ib*, (*iuxta*) *portas ferreas* 1385 *NAR, Irendore* 1443 FK, *the
    Irendore* 1451 NoRec, *Brazen Dore* 1513 FK, *Brazen Tower* 1541,
    1543 *ib, Brasendore* 1558 Cuningham, *Brason Doors olim Porte de*

Swinemarket & le Irondore 1696 Cleer, *New Gate* 1726 FK, *Brasen Doors* 1746 B, 1766 King, *Brazen Doors* 1789 H

This was a postern not large enough for the passage of carriages. In 1726 it was widened and after this also called *New Gate*. It was situated at the entrance of the present All Saints Green, formerly Upper Surrey Street (*q.v.*). It was finally removed in 1792 (FK 9 f.).

CONESFORD GATE -- SOUTHGATE

(*extra/ad*) *portas de Cunesford* 1295 R. 1386 *NAR, la porte de Conesford* 1343 NoRec, *portas Cones fordyatis* 1428 FA, *a porta de Consford* 1480 Worcestre, *South Gate, Conesford Gates* 1696 Cleer, *South* or *Conisford Gate* 1746 B, *Conisford Gate* 1766 King, 1789 H

This was the gate at the south entrance of King Street. The late name Southgate also appears in Southgate Lane (*v.* Butter Hills). Contractors for its demolition were invited in 1794 (FK 1 ff.).

COW TOWER

castrum voc. Cowholme 14 *Binham*
Le Dongon 1395 NoRec, *the dongeon by the Hospitall medewes* 1451
   ib, the Tower in the Hospital medowe 1541 K, *the Dungeon Tower in*
   St Giles' Hospital meadow 1845 White
the Cowes Tower 1696 Cleer, *Cows Tower* 1711 ECC, 1766 King, 1789
   H, 1830 M&M, *Cows Tower or Hassets Tower* 1746 B, *Cow's tower*
   1819 Stacy, *Cow Tower* 1885 OS, 1920 6" Map

A ruinous tower north of Bishop Bridge, in a sharp bend of the Wensum. Bills of 1378 for the purchase of bricks are extant (Pevsner 259). Cf. NoRec II 50: 'To Richard Blakehumoure for six lighters to the tower with bricks, 3 *s.*' (1389) and *ib* II 52: 'The Dungeon. Paid Robert Perkyns for 1,000 bricks, 5 *s.* 6 *d.*' (1399). Built as a fortress and river tollhouse, it later became a prison for the jurisdiction of the Cathedral.

   Cowholme (*Couholm* 1253 K) was the name of an area to the south of Holmstrete (now Bishopgate, *q.v.*). From the earliest quotation, however, it would seem that *Cowholme* was once the name of the grassland on both sides of Holmstrete. *Cow Tower* might be elliptical, reduced from *Cowholme Tower*. ME *dongeon, dongoun* (OF *donjon*) meant 'fortress, underground prison cell' (MED). The name *Hassets*

Tower was due to *Hassets House* (1746 B) or *Hasset's Hall* (1845
White) on the other side of the river, called after William *Blenarhasset,*
a sixteenth-century owner (Knights 111).   This was the old manor
house of Pockthorpe, which originally belonged to the Cathedral
Priory, and at that time it went by the name of the *grangia monachorum*
'the Monks' Grange' 1318, 1384 *OR*. Cf. (*versus*) *Grang'* 1285 OR,
(*pro*) *grangea* 1327 *ib*, (*ad*) *grangeam* 1327 *ib*. Another name was *The
Lathes* 1585 *Mousehold,* from ON **hlaða** 'barn'. *v.* SaundersI 36.

HEIGHAM GATE
Blake Gate 1221 FK
la porte de Hegham 1343 NoRec, *Heygham Gates* 1676 NoRec, *Hayham
     Gate* 1696 Cleer, *Heigham* als *Hell gates* c. 1720 K, *Heyham Gate*
     1766 King, *Heigham Gate* 1789 H
port' Inferni 1393 FK, *Helle Yate* 1397 *ib*, *Helgate* 1541 K, *Hellgates*
     1558 *ib*, *Helle Gate* or *Heyham Gate* 1746 B

This was a postern, only wide enough for small carts to pass. It was
situated at the entrance of the present Westwick Street (*q.v.*). It was
removed some years before 1792 (FK 21 f.). Smith (EPNE) suggests
that OE **hell** may occur as a term of contempt in some later pl.ns.
There is also a tradition that the nearby St Benedict's (or Over
Westwick) Gate was known as Heaven Gate because the way to the
shrine of the Queen of Heaven at Walsingham led through it (Knights
62, Nobbs 36).
     HEIGHAM is one of the eight villages which, in the course of the
centuries, were incorporated into Norwich.
Echam, Hecham 1086 DB, 1108 *et freq* to 1210 Holme, 1253 *Holme,*
     1256 (p) Lib, *Heham* 1127-34 Holme, *Hegham* 12 Douglas, 1214-5
     Fees, 1243, 1255, 1281 FF, 1257 (p) Lib, 1257, 1286 *Ass*, 1303 (2x) *R*,
     1316 FA, 1325, 1329 NoD, 1325 NfD, *Heyham* 1269 *Ass*, 1389, 1548
     Pat, 1402 FA, *Hekame* 1269 *Ass*, *Heghham* 1317, 1319 FF, *Heigham*
     1356 *ib*, 1384 Cl, *Heygham* 1383 Cl, 1548 Pat, *Heyham* 1389 *ib*,
     1401-2 FA, *Heiham* 1432 AD, *Higham* 1467-72 ECP, 1525 VE,
     Hygham 1534 AD, *Hayham* 1675 Ogilby

The early forms seem to point to OE **hæcc,** or rather its side-form
hecc (*v.* DEPN s.n. Heigham). It had a variety of meanings, including
'floodgate' and 'grate to catch fish at a weir'; Heigham is in a loop of
the Wensum.   The second element may be OE **hamm** 'water meadow'

as well as OE **hām** 'homestead'.

MAGDALEN GATE

portam de Fibrigge 1286 K, *Fibriggeyate* 1332 AD, *la porte de
Fibriggate* 1343 NoRec, *portas vocat' Fibriggegates* 1366 *MinAcct,
Fibrig Gates* 1391 FK, *Fibriggeyatis* 1428 FA, *Fybrigge ʒate* c. 1500
NPD, ye Gates of Magdalen 1556 FK, *Maudelyn Gates* 1591 *NPD,
Magdalen Gate* 1664 to 1783 FK, *Magdalen Gate olim Porte de
Fybriggegate* 1696 Cleer, *Fibridge* or *Magdalen Gate* 1746 B,
Magdalen Gate 1766 King, 1789 H

Like Magdalen Street, whose entrance it formed, this gate took its
name from the Chapel and Hospital of St Mary Magdalen, situated
about half a mile beyond the gate (cf. *de domo sancte Marie Magdalene*
1257-66 ChNCP, *hospitali beate Marie Magdalene* 1272 *WillD, hospital'
Sancte Marie Magdalene* 1288, 1289 *R*, 1364 *OR*, 1461 K, *magist' hosp'
Marie Magdalen'* 1416 *NAR, Magdalen Chappell* 1585 *Mousehold*). This
was the last gate to be destroyed, in 1808 (FK 27 f.). *v.* also Fye
Bridge and Fye Bridge Street.

POCKTHORPE GATE

(*le*) *Barregates* 1269 *Ass*, 1323, 1338, 1346 K, 1323 to 1519 FK, R2, 1461
NoRec, *Barregatys* 1331 *ib, Barrygatys* 14 *Binham;* (*le*) *Barregate* c.
1270, 1280, 1328 *D&C,* 1237 FK, 1286 K, 1330 (p) *SR,* c. 1500 *NPD,
porta que dicitur Barregate* 1280-9 ChNCP, *Barrechate* 1338 K, 1340
FK

portam de Barreyats 1286 K, *le Barreyate* 1332 AD, *la porte de Barreyates*
1343 NoRec, (*apud*) *Barreyates* 1386 *NAR*, 1386 NoRec, (*portas
vocatas*) *Barreyatis* 1428 FA, *berre ʒate, barre ʒate* c. 1500 *NPD
Pokethorp(e) Gate* 1542, 1757 FK, 1696 Cleer, 1789 H, *Pokethorp(e)
Gates* 1547 Pat, 1558 Cuningham, 1591 *NPD, Pockthorp* or *Barr Gate*
1746 B, *Pockthorp(e) Gate* 1757 FK, 1766 King

The present Barrack Street runs where this gate was situated. The
bar (OF *barre*, MLat *barra*) was perhaps originally an obstruction
outside the gate (*v.* MED s.v. *barre* 1a), or the meaning may simply
have been 'the gate that bars entry into town', as suggested by Reaney
(s.n. *Bargate*). The gate seems to have been renamed *Pockthorp(e)
Gate(s)* relatively early. It was removed in 1792 (FK 29 ff.). *v.*
Barrack Street.

POCKTHORPE is one of the eight villages which, in the course of time, were incorporated into Norwich.

Poketorp 1203 FF, 1268 Abbrev, *Pokethorp(e)* 1250 NoRec, 1257, 1269, 1286 *Ass*, 1330 *SR*, 1345, 1394, 1488 Pat, 1370 FF, 1428 FA, 1524 NAM, 1535 VE, 1547 Pat, 1576 AD, *Pokethorp(e)* 1305 NoD, 1306 *R*, 1535 VE, 1558 K, 1585 *Mousehold, Pokethorpp* 1461 K

'*Poka's* village'; OScand **þorp**. Cf. PN YE 95.

ST AUGUSTINE'S GATE

(*extra*) *portas Sancti Augustini* (*de Norwico*) 1268 to 1293 *NPD, portas ciuitatis Sancti Augustini* 1290 *ib, la porte de Saint Austyn* 1343 NoRec , *Seynt Austynesyatis* 1428 FA, *portas Sancti Augustini* (*Norwici*) 1483 *AddCh, Saynt Austyns gates* 1544 *NPD, St Augustines gates* 1601, 1626, 1667 *ib, St Austins Gate* 1696 Cleer, 1746 B, 1766 King, *St Augustine's Gate* 1789 H

This gate stood at the entrance of St Augustine's Street which passed St Augustine's Church. It was taken down in 1794 (FK 25 f.).

ST BENEDICT'S GATE

(*extra*) *portas de Westwyk* 1298 *R, la porte de Westwyk* 1343 NoRec, (*ad*) *portas de Westwyk* 1386 *NAR, Westwyk yates* 1427 Past
St Benedict's Gate 1558, 1746 FK, *St Benedicts Gate olim Porte de Westwyk* 1696 Cleer, *St Bennets Gate* 1746 B, *St Benedicts Gate* 1766 King, *St Benedict's Gate* 1789 H

Situated at the entrance of the present St Benedict's Street, formerly Upper Westwick Street (*q.v.*), it was taken down in 1793 (FK 17 ff.). As regards the once popular name Heaven Gate, *v.* Heigham Gate.

ST GILES'S GATE

Port' S. Egidii 1288, 1289 FK, *la porte de Saint Gile* 1343 NoRec, *la porte de Seint Gyle* 1343 *NPD, St Giles Gate* 1696 Cleer, 1766 King, *St Giles's Gate* 1746 B, 1789 H

This gate, at the entrance of the present St Giles Street, was demolished in 1792 (FK 15 f.).

ST MARTIN'S GATE

Porte de Coslayn 1275 FK, *la porte de Coselanye* 1343 NoRec, (*apud*)
   Coslanyates 1421 *NAR, Coslanyeyatis* 1428 FA, *Coslany Gates* 1461
   FK, *Coslany Gates* 1553 *ib*
St Martins Gate olim Porte de Coslanye 1696 Cleer, *Coselany* or *St*
   Martin at the Oak Gate 1746 B, *St Martin's at Oak Gate* 1757 *ib*, *St*
   Martins Gate 1766 King, 1789 H

It stood at the entrance of the present Oak Street, called from the
church of St Martin at the Oak or Coslany (*q.v.*).   It was demolished in
1808 (FK 23 f.).

ST STEPHEN'S GATE

(*a*) *porta de Nedham* 1290 *R*, (*in emendatione*) *portarum de Nedham*
   1296 *NAR, Nedham Gates* 1299 *NPD, la porte de Nedham* 1343
   NoRec, *Nedeham yates* 1427 Past, *Nedeham gates* 1537 *MinAcct*,
   Nedehamgates 1547 Pat
St Stephen's Gates 1556 AD, *St Stephens Gate* 1696 Cleer, *St Stephen's*
   Gate 1746 B, 1754, 1757, 1761 FK, 1789 H, *St Stephens Gate* 1766
   King

This gate stood at the entrance of the present St Stephen's Street,
formerly Needham Street (*q.v.*).   It was taken down in 1793 (FK 11
ff.).

NORWICH CASTLE

CASTLE

(*XVII mansure uacue que sunt in occupatione*) *castelli...* (*LXXXI in*
   occupatione) *castelli* 1086 DB
apud Norwicense (*Norwycum*) *castrum* W2 *NCReg* 1, *ad castrum*
   Norwyc' 1247 ChNCP, *de feodo dicti castri* 1345 Blomefield, *Castro*
   Norwic' 1535 VE
Castellum de Norwico 1108-21 Holme, *ante portam castelli* 1157, 1162
   ChNCP, (*in emendatione*) *castellorum de Norwic'* 1191 P, *in castello*
   de Norewic 1193 *ib*, *Turris quadratus castelli Norwici* 1479 Worcestre

The building of the castle was ordered by William I shortly after the

Conquest. According to DB (*v. supra*), 98 properties were laid waste
in order to make room for the motte-and-bailey earthwork. The great
stone keep is considered to have been built by Henry I. *v.* Harrod
(1857) and Colvin *et al.* (1963).

BAILEY

This was the semicircular enclosure which formed the first line of
defence of a feudal castle, and Norwich Castle had more than one. In
the records the term *bailey* usually occurs with reference to the church
St Martin Bailey (*q.v.*). The Latinized forms *de Ball'ia* 1254-75, etc.,
and *de Balliua* 1554, 1555 represent MLat *ba(i)llium, ba(i)llia* 'bailey,
courtyard of a castle' and *ba(i)lliva* 'bailiwick; area of such jurisdiction'.
MLat *ba(i)llia* is also recorded in the latter sense (LathamD).
Beecheno (19) notes a great number of different spellings: *St Martin
in le Baille* 1315, *in le Bailli* 1322, *in le Balye* 1328, *in le Baillie* 1340, *en
la Baillie* 1382, *at Bailyff* 1508, *apud le Bale* 1556, 1570, *de Bale* 1578, *de
le Bale* 1582.

These spellings indicate either ME **baille, bail(l)i** (from OF *baille,*
MLat *ba(i)llium, ba(i)llia* 'wall surrounding a castle') or ME **bailli(e),
bali(e)** (from OF **baillie** 'authority of an official, district under such
authority'). There was considerable confusion of spellings for these
words in Middle English (*v.* OED and MED).   *at Bailyff* 1508 reflects
the officer in question. Beecheno suggests that the church had its
name because it was situated within the bailiwick rather than in the
bailey. Campbell, however, places the church inside a smaller, outer
bailey (Map 2).

CASTLE DITCH

in fossato Castri 1257 *Ass,* (*de ruina*) *fossati castri* 1305 *Beecheno,*
  (*circa*) *fossata castri* 1345 Blomefield, *Fossat' Castri* (*Norwici*) 1401,
  1404, 1557 *R,* 1421 *NPD,* 1439 *Beecheno, foueam* (*castri*) 1435 to
  1556 *ib*
Castyll dyche 1543 *Beecheno, le castell dyke* 1568 *NPD, le Castledyk*
  1569 *Beecheno, le Castle Dykes* 1571 *ib, le Casteldickes* 1577 *ib, Castle
  Dikes* 1630 to 1705 *ib*

It is generally assumed that the earthworks surrounding the castle
were made immediately after the Conquest. Their exact extent has
long been controversial. For a recent discussion and reconstruction, *v.*
Campbell 8 note 89 and accompanying maps. *v.* also York Alley.

CASTLE HILL
Castellond 1390, 1392 *Beecheno*
Schirhousyerd Ed3 K^2, *Curia vocata Shirhousyerd* 1401 *ib*,
   Shirehouse Yard 1533 Harrod, *Sherehouseyard* 1534 *Beecheno,*
   Sherehouseyerde 1545, 1546 *ib*
le Shirehouse Green 1495 Harrod
Garter Hill c.1720 K, *Garter-hill* c.1725 K^2

These name forms refer roughly to the area where the medieval *Curia Comitatus* was situated (*v.* Shire House *infra*). Castle Hill is at the top of the old Cattle Market, on the north-west side of Bell Avenue. The medieval *Curia Comitatus* could be approached by way of a lane that approximately followed the line of the present Orford Street (*v.* Streets and Campbell Map 6). Kirkpatrick's statement that Garter Hill was 'so called from its being used formerly for the warping of garters there' (K^2 312) does not carry conviction. *Garter Hill* could be a modification of **Galtre Hill*, from OE *galgtrēow* 'gallowstree', due to interchange of the liquids *l* and *r* (Zachrisson 121). Cf. *(apud) Galchtrehil* 13 *D&C*, (*in campo qui vocatur*) *Galghetrewong'* c. 1280 *ib*, *Galtre*, or *Gallows-hill by Norwich* 1745 B, all referring to a piece of high ground outside Magdalen Gates, on the Sprowston road. Castle Hill is known to have been the scene of public hangings.

CASTLE MEADOW, now AGRICULTURAL HALL PLAIN
Castelmedwe 1349 *Beecheno*, *Castel Medew* 1375 K^2, *pratum vocat' le Castell medewe* 1429 *NPD*, *Castell Medowe* 1564 Harrod, *Castle Meadow* 1766 King, 1789 H, 1830 M&M
Pelloures Medwe 1395 *Beecheno*
pratum Castri 1421 to 1438 *NPD*

The original Castle Meadow, not to be confused with the modern street of this name, was east of the Castle, where the Anglia TV studios are now. These are partly housed in the old Agricultural Hall, which dates back to 1882 (Pevsner 261). For *Pelloures, v.* Pellour Lane *infra*.

SHIRE HOUSE (lost)
Curia Domini Regis 1285 to 1305 *R, Curia Comitatus* 1287, 1294, 1305 K^2, 1295, 1306, 1311 *Beecheno,* (*versus*) *Comitatum* 1306 *ib*
(*in domo nostra que vocatur*) *Shirehous* 1326 NoRec, (*in domo vocata*)

le Shirehous 1345 Blomefield, 1434 Harrod, 1435, 1458, 1534
Beecheno, the shirehous, the schirehows 1461 Past, *the shirehows* 1464
ib, the shire hous 1465 *ib, the sherhous* 1472 *ib, le Shire howse* 1546,
1609 *Beecheno, le Shyre house* 1558 *ib, le Sherehous* 1568 *NPD, le
Sherehows(e)* 1568, 1581 *Beecheno, le Sherehowsse* 1580 *ib, le
sheirehowse* 1600 *ib, le oldesherehowse, oldeshirehowse* 1612 *ib, the old
Sherehowse* 1631 *NPD, the old Sheirhouse* 1699 *Beecheno, the Old
Shirehouse* 1705 *ib*

This was the medieval County Court on Castle Hill (*v.   supra*). It
was replaced by an Elizabethan Shire House near the Castle Keep
(Harrod 153). Kirkpatrick relates that old inhabitants had told him
about walls of a stone house, with iron bars in the windows, still
standing when they were young, which would seem to have been the
last remains of the old (medieval) Shire House (K^2 312).

SHIRE HOUSE GAP (lost)
Le Shire hous gap 1375 K, *Le Shirhous Gap* 1379 *ib, Shire hous Gappe*
    1533 *ib, Sherehous gappe* 1533 to 1592 *Beecheno, Sherrod's Gap*
    1712 *ib, Sherwood's Gap* 1833 *ib*
le Shirehouslane 1495 *Beecheno*
Pig Lane 1861 *Beecheno*

Kirkpatrick (12) identifies the ancient Shire Hous Gap with Golden
Ball Lane (*v.* Golden Ball Street). According to Beecheno (Map) and
Campbell (Map 6), Shire House Gap was further to the east,
connecting Beaumont's Hill (*v.* Cattle Market Street) with Garter Hill
(*v.* Castle Hill).

NORWICH CATHEDRAL

CATHEDRAL CHURCH OF THE HOLY TRINITY
(*in*) *Ecclesia Sce Trinitatis apud Norwycum* Hy1 *Reg I, ecclesia sancte
    Trinitatis* 1101 *ib,* (*monachis suis in*) *Ecclesia Sce Trinitatis de*   ˙
    Norwyco Hy1 *ib,* (*concessisse*) *Sce Trinitati & monachis de Norwyco*
    Hy1 *ib,* (*pratis que pertinent*) *ecclesie Sce Trinitatis* (*de*) *Norwyco)* Hy1
    ib, (*ecclesia/ conuentus*) *sancte Trinitatis* 1117, 1155-6 Holme, 1136-45
    CottCh, Ecclesia Sancte Trinitatis Norwici (*Norwyc'*) 1274 to 1306
    RCh, (*ante portas*) *Ecclesie Sce Trinitatis* 1285, 1288 *R,* 1314 to 1360

NPD, (ante portam) Sce Trinitatis 1287, 1288 (2x), *(Priori) Ecclesie sce Trinitatis* 1287 *D&C, (in portam) Sce Trinitatis* 1288 *R, ecclesia Sce Trinitatis de Norwico* 1289, 1290 *R, (prope portas) Sce Trinitatis Norwyci* 1309 *NPD, (ex aposito) Ecclesie Sce Trinitatis* 1333, 1334 *ib, (ad portas) ecclesie sancte Trinitatis* 1378 *NPD, ecclesia Sce Trinitatis Norwici* 1399 *NAR, (ecclesia) Sce Trinitatis Norwici* 1483 *AddCh,* 1535 VE, *the Cathedrall Church of the holly Trynytye of Norwich* 1538 *AddCh*

(Episcopi) ecclesie Cathedralis 1420 *NAR, (in fine orientali) ecclesie cathedralis Sancte Trinitatis Norwici* 1444 Past, *þe Chathedrall chirch of Norwich* 1452 *ib, (ecclesia cum choro) cathedralis Norwici* 1479 Worcestre, *ecclesia cathedralis Sce Trinitatis Norwici* 1535 VE, *(Sacrist') ecclesie cath' Norwici* 1535 *ib, the Cathedrall Chyrche (Church) of the holy Trinite* 1540, 1597 *D&C, (Decanus) Ecclesie Cathedralis Sce Trinitatis* 1559 *NPD, the cathedrall churche of the holy Indivisible Triniti of Norwich* 1581 *D&C, the cathedrall church of the holy and indevided trinity* 1598 *ib, the Cathedral Church of the only and vndivided Trinity* 1620 to 1673 *ib*

Crystechyrche 1425 Past, *Cryst's Church in Norwich* 1515 Harrod, *Cryst's Chyrch* 1521 *ib, (to) ye Mother Church, that is to Cristis Church in Norwich* 1525 *ib, Cryste Chyrch* 1551 *ib, Christes Churche* 1558 Cuningham, *Christchurch* 1680 Browne

Conuentus (Sce Trinitatis) de Norwic' (Norwyco) 1248 to 1314 *RCh, Conuent' Ecclesie sce Trinitatis Norwyc' (Norwici)* 1283, 1435 *D&C, (mesuagium Prioris et) conuentus ecclesie Sce Trinitatis* 1330 *ib*

(prope portam) prioratus sce trinitatis 1303 (2x) *NPD, (ad portas) Prioratus sce Trinitatis* 1303 *ib, Priori et conuentui ecclesie sce Trinitatis* 1339 *D&C, þe priorie of þe Trinite´ chirche of Norwiche* 1427 Past, *Prioratu Norwici* 1479 Worcestre

(infra septa) Monasterii Sce Trinitatis Norwyci 1331 *D&C*

(John Reppys, Priour of) the Abbey of Norwiche 1437 Past, *the Abbey* 1451 *ib, the abbay* 1456 *ib, the abbey of Norwyche* 1466 (2x) *ib, the Abbeys* 1470 *ib*

The greater part of the Cathedral took some fifty years to build (1094-1145) under the supervision of Bishops Herbert and Eborard. Uncommonly much of the original Norman work has survived; thus the great nave and the transept remain much as they were built (*v.* Pevsner 210 ff.).

Bishop Herbert Losinga had the Cathedral built on a part of Cowholme (*v.* Bishopgate and Cow Tower). Pevsner (211 n.) says that Herbert built 'on a virgin site', but Harrod (235 f.) maintains that he erected his church on the site of a yet more ancient one, also dedicated to the Holy Trinity and also monastic, and quotes in support of his thesis a will of the late 10th or 11th century -- 'And ic [Siflæd] an into Northwich to Cristes kirke .iiii. retheren ...' ASWills 38 (BCS 1014, KCD 947; Birch and Kemble mistakenly print *recheren* for *retheren* 'oxen') -- and a statement of Ingulphus, the abbot and chronicler of Croyland, who on his arrival at Croyland in 1076 found more than a hundred monks of external origin there (besides the sixty-two regular ones), fourteen of whom came from Christ Church, Norwich ('Fuerunt enim tunc nostri comprofessi ... ecclesiæ Christi Norwici 14', Savile fol. 515a). This church also occurs in Domesday Book (1086) as *Ecclesia Sancte Trinitatis.* The designation of the old church was transferred to the Cathedral, which was called Christ Church into the 19th century by the common people.

The Benedictine Priory at the Cathedral was founded by Bishop Herbert. While it was being built, the monks lived at St Leonard's Priory on Mousehold Heath (cf. *apud sanctum Leonardum* m13 ChNCP), opposite Bishop Bridge. In 1101 the Cathedral was so far completed that they could move in. Over the centuries the number of monks dropped from an original sixty to about thirty at the time of the Dissolution.

The monastery was ruled by the Prior and twelve departmental executives, the Obedientiaries. Their accounts have come down to us in 1,500 rolls of varying length, only a fraction of which have been printed.

ALMERY (lost), (*in*) *domo Elemosinarii* 1275 *OR,* (*super*) *terram Elemosinar' ecclesie Cathedralis* 1443 *D&C.* The Almery was in the south-west angle of the Outer Court (or Almery Green), along the east side of St Cuthbert's churchyard. MLat *eleemosynarius* 'almoner'. *Almery* is OF *almarie*, MLat *almarium* 'place for storing, storehouse', in mistake for *almonry*, OF *au(l)mosnerie* 'place where alms are distributed' (*v.* OED s.v. *ambry*).

ALMERY SCHOOL (lost)
scolas Norwycensis (*ecclesie/episcopatus*), *Scolas Norwycenses* 1155 to 1274 ChNCP, (*in*) *Scolis* 1298 *OR,* (*iuxta*) *scole chat'* 1327 OR, (*in*)

Scol' 1330 *ib*, (*in scola grammatical' vocat'*) *Le Almery Scole* 1535
VE

The third quotation actually reads *Item in petra de Kam empta pro portis et hostiis iuxta scolethat' 13s. 0d.* (OR 106). The editors of OR hesitatingly gloss *scolethat'* as 'school thatch' (127), but this does not make sense. The meaning would seem to be: 'Likewise for stone from Caen bought for the gates and doors next to the Cathedral School - 13*s.* 0*d.*', *that'* being an error for *chat'*, i.e. *cathedralis*. It is true that *iuxta* normally governs the accusative but, in the words of the editors, 'usage [in OR] is very inconsistent, particularly in case and number', and the entry is corrupt anyway. The gates referred to cannot very well be any other than St Ethelbert's Gate, immediately north of the Almery. This gate was finished by 1317, but 'the vaulting of the gateway was inserted later, being ... of about 1330' (OR 33). The Scola Grammaticalis, which probably prepared boys for the monastic life, had only thirteen pupils (SaundersI 124).

BAKEHOUSE (lost) (*in stipend' coopertor'*) *Pistrini* 1285 *OR*, (*de*) *pistrino* 1304 *ib*, *Pistrinum* 1285 to 1349 *ib*, (*in*) *pistrino* 1379 *ib*, (*in*) *pistrina* 1384 *ib*. The Bakehouse and the other houses devoted to household work and storage were to the south-east of the Cathedral and Priory, round Brewer's Green, the present Lower Close. MLat *pistrinum* 'bakehouse'.

BARGEHOUSE (lost), (*Emendacio*) *Galy'* 1291 OR, (*Expense*) *galye* 1298 *ib*, (*Expensis circa*) *domus galye* 1299 *ib*. Only the last quotation actually refers to the bargehouse itself; the other two refer to repairs of a galley or barge, MLat *galia* 'galley'. The Bargehouse stood at the west end of the canal originally built to transport Caen stone for the construction of the Cathedral. This canal, apparently still used in the days of the Priory, no longer exists. A later rebuilding of this house is said partly to survive in No. 29, The Close (OR 31).

BAUCHUN CHAPEL
(*de argento*) *Bauchun* 1324 OR, (*pro roba*) *Bauchun* 1330 *ib*, (*propter superexpensas*) *capello Bauchun* 1330 *ib*
Beauchampes chappell 1680 Browne, *Chapel called our Lady the Less, or Beauchamp's Chapel* 1745 B, *the chapel of St Mary the less, called also Beauchamp's chapel* 1819 Stacy, *Beauchamp Chapel* 1885 OS

On the south side of the Cathedral presbytery. Finished by 1330, but remodelled in the 15th or early 16th century (Pevsner 215 f.). The founder was one William Bauchun. His name was inscribed on the outside of the south wall, but the inscription had become all but defaced by 1680: hence the corruption to *Beauchamp* (*v.* Browne 138). At the east end there is a canopied niche, where there was formerly an image of St Mary the Less, to whom the chapel was dedicated.

BELFRY or GREAT TOWER (lost), (*Compot' Exp'*) *turris magis* 1298 *OR*, (*in cord' ad*) *campan'* 1298, 1305 *OR*, (*le*) *Ber(e)fry* 1301 to 1308 *OR*. The building of a detached belfry south of the Erpingham Gate was a costly and long-drawn-out operation. The first Belfry account is to be found in the 1297-8 Sacrist Roll, which states, however, that the work was actually started as early as 1291-2. The 1312 Sacrist Roll contains no Belfry account, so the tower should have been completed by then (*v.* SandersI 109 f.). Fernie and Whittingham (OR 28) say that the tower was erected between 1298 and 1307. MLat *campanile* 'belfry' (Latham); ME *berfrey*, OF *berfrei*, later *belfrei* through dissimilation (Zachrisson 120). *v.* ODEE s.v.

BISHOP'S PALACE
Palacii Episcopi Norwicen' 1292 *RCh, Curia episcopi* 1315 *OR*, (*ad capellam in*) *curia episcopi* e14 Harrod
the Bishops palace 1680 Browne, *Bishops Pallace* 1696 Cleer, *the Palace* 1746 B, *Bishops Palace* 1766 King, 1830 M&M, *(the) Bishop's Palace* 1789 H, 1819 Stacy, 1885 OS

The Palace is to the north of the Cathedral. It consists of a north-south range and a west-east range. Both ranges contain some traces of the original Norman palace. The present palace dates from the middle of the 19th century (*v.* Pevsner 229).

BISHOP'S PALACE CHAPELS
(*capelle/capellam*) *sancte Marie* (*in curia episcopi*) 1136 to 1274 ChNCP, (*emendac' organ' in*) *capell' sce Mar'* 1346 *OR*, ad *capellam in curia episcopi* e14 Harrod
the old Bishops chappell now demolished 1680 Browne, *chapel dediated to the Virgin Mary* 1745 B

Browne (134) and Blomefield (IV 48) give Bishop Salmon as the founder of the old chapel, the Chapel of St Mary, which stood south of its successor, Bishop Reynolds's Chapel: *the Bishops chappell* 1680 Browne, *Bishops Chappel* 1696 Cleer, *Bps. Chapel* 1746 B, (*the*) *Bishop's Chapel* 1845 White, 1885 OS. This chapel was built in 1661-76 by Bishop Edward Reynolds, who was buried there (Browne 134 and Blomefield IV 49 f.).

BREWERY (lost)
(*in stipend' coopertor'*) *Bracini* 1285 OR, (*de*) *bracino* 1304 to 1308 *ib,*
   (*in*) *bracino* 1308 (3x) *ib,* (*pro dealbacione*) *Bracini* 1309 *ib*
(*in*) *granario brasei* 1309 OR

The Brewery was next to the Bakehouse, along the east side of Brewer's Green (the Lower Close). MLat *bracinum* 'brewhouse', *braseum, bracium* 'malt'; the *granarium brasei* was 'the malt store'. Cf. Latham s.vv.

CAMERA PRIORIS (lost), (*iuxta*) *cameram Prioris* 1303 OR, (*in*) *camera prioris* 1307 to 1410 OR, (*in*) *Camera domini Prioris* 1385 *ib.* The Prior's House, of which the Prior's Chamber was a part, was an extension of the east range along the cloister walk.

CARNARY COLLEGE, now NORWICH SCHOOL
(*in*) *carnario ... subtus ... Capellam Sci Johannis* 1316 Ch, *del Charnel*
  (p) 1345 OR, (*de*) *Capell' Sci Johannis ad portas ecclesie* 1364 *ib,*
  (*capellani*) *carnarii* 1373 Saunders, (*capellani*) *Sci Johannis*
  Ewangeliste de Carnarii 1379 *ib,* (*juxta porticum*) *capelle Carnarii*
  1422 Harrod, (*juxta portam*) *Carnarie* 1494 Saunders, *Carnar' in*
  Norwico 1535 VE, *the Charnell* 1551 *et freq* to 1583 Saunders,
  the Charnell House 1554 *ib, the Charnell howse* 1555 *ib,* ye
  Charnell c. 1720 K, *the Charnell-house, now the Free-School*
  1745 B
the skolehowse 1564 Saunders, *the Scho*(*o*)*lehows, -hous* 1571 *et freq* to
  1602 *ib, the Skoolehowse* 1637 *ib, the chappell of St John the*
  Evangelist ... now the Free-schoole 1680 Browne, *the School* 1696
  Cleer, *Grammar School* 1789 H, *the Free-School* 1819 Stacy, *Free*
  Grammar School 1830 M&M, *the Free Grammar School* 1845
  White, *King Edward VI Grammar School* 1885 OS

Near the west entrance of the Cathedral, just within the Erpingham

Gate. The oldest part of the building, the Chapel, was erected in 1316 at the command of Bishop Salmon. The basement was to serve as an *ossuarium* or charnel for the City. The foundation letter is still extant (*v.* the first quotation). After the Reformation the Chapel was converted into a school by the government of Edward VI in 1547 (Pat 1547-8), the present Norwich School (Blomefield IV 55 ff., Saunders 3 ff., Pevsner 231 f.). MLat *carnarium* 'carnary, charnel-house' (LathamD).

CHAPTER HOUSE (lost), (*ad fenestram*, etc.) *capituli* 1288 to 1327 *OR*. Half way down the east walk of the Cloisters is the Chapter House entrance. The Chapter House itself is gone. It was founded before 1288 by Richard Uphall of Tasburgh and was finished by 1303 (*v.* OR 29).

CLOISTERS
(*in albacione*, etc.) *claustri* 1294 to 1327 OR, *Claustrum* 1304 *OR,* (*ad*) *claustrum* 1308, 1324 (2x) OR, 1309 *OR,* (*pro*) *claustro* 1327 OR, (*longitudo*) *claustri ecclesie cathedralis* 1479 Worcestre

The work on the present Cloisters was begun in 1297 in front of the Chapter House (the east walk; *v.* Worcestre 396-7). They were not completed until c. 1450 and thus display several styles of stonework. For a detailed account, *v.* OR 31 ff. At the south end of the east walk is the Dark Entry, which leads into a vaulted cell. Worcestre (396) calls it the Infirmary Door (*hostium quo transitur ad infirmariam*). MLat *claustrum* 'cloister in a monastery' (LathamD). Prior to these Cloisters there existed a Norman cloister, of which nothing remains (*v.* Pevsner 226). This explains the date of the first quotation above. Presumably the first cloisters were damaged in the 1272 riots.

DORMITORY (lost), (*Emendacio*, etc.) *dormitorii* 1289 to 1294 *OR,* (*Emandacione lectorum*) *dormitorie* 1299 *ib.* MLat *dormitorium* 'dormitory in a monastery' (Latham). This building was situated south of the Chapter House. Cf. also the DORMITORY CHAPEL, (*in*) *Capella dormitorii* 1376, 1377, 1383 *OR.*

EAST GATE
the owtward Est gate of the late Priorie or Monasterie towards the hospital of Saynt Giles 1539 NoRec, *the Hospital-gate* 1745 B

This is the Bishopgate entrance to the Cathedral Precinct. St Giles Hospital is now the Great Hospital.

ERPINGHAM GATE

(*ad*) *portam Trinitatis* 1254-75 Val, (*ad*) *portas Ecclesie* 1337 OR, (*ante*) *portas Ecclesie Cathedralis Sancti Trinitatis* 1428 FA
Erpingham's, or *the Lower-gate* 1745 B, *Erpingham Gate-house* 1819 Stacy, *Erpingham Gate* 1845 White, 1885 OS

This is the main entrance to the Cathedral Precinct, facing the west end of the Cathedral. The present gate was built in 1450 by Sir Thomas Erpingham, reputedly as 'a penance for Lollardy' (Blomefield IV 54).

GREAT GRANARY (lost), (*in emendacione*) *Granar'* 1337 *OR*, (*pro*) *granar'* 1340 *ib*, (*ad/pro*) *granar' domini Prioris* 1346 (2x) *ib*, (*pro emend' hostiorum*) *granarie* 1384 *ib*. The Great Granary was along the north side of Brewery Green (the Lower Close).

GREEN YARD

(*in cimiterio ecclesiae Christi Norwycensis Monasterii, qui* (sic) *vulgariter dicitur*) *Grene Yard* 1448-50 Harrod, *the Green yard* 1680 Browne, *the Green Yard now the Palace Yard* 1746 B, *Green Yard* 1885 OS

The cemetery or Green Yard was on the north and west sides of the Cathedral. It was known as *the preechyng yard* and contained a pulpit as early as 1437. In 1644 'this pulpitt was taken downe and placed in Newhall green' (Browne 141). *v.* St Andrew's Hall.

GUEST HALL (lost)

Hospicium 1289 *OR*, (*Ferramentis utriusque hostiorum*) *hospitii* 1303 OR, (*ad hostium*) *aule* 1299 *OR*, (*ad murum*) *aule* 1327 OR, (*in*) *aula* 1347 to 1435 *OR*, (*in emendacione fenestrarum*) *aule* 1425 *ib*, (*in*) *magna aula* 1437 *ib*, (*cum ... hostio*) *Aulae hospitum* c. 1480 Worcestre
(*pro/in*) *camera hospitum* 1347 (2x) *OR*
(*in*) *communi hostilaria* 1421 *OR*, (*in*) *hostilar'* 1421 *ib*

The Guest Hall (*aula*) was in the west range (along the west walk of the Cloisters).   Over the Hall there was a chamber (*camera*) where visitors slept.   MLat *hospitium* 'guest house', *hostilaria* (= *hospitalaria*) 'guest house of a monastery' (Latham).

INFIRMARY (lost)
(*ad nouam Cameram*) *Infirmar'* 1309 (5x) *OR*, (*circa nouam Cameram*)
   Infirmatorii 1309 *ib*, (*super murum*) *Infirmarie* 1325 OR, (*pro*)
   Infirmaria 1327 *ib*, (*in fenestra vitrea*) *Infirmarie* 1330 *ib*, (*in/versus*)
   infirmar' 1346, 1348 *OR*, (*solut'*) *Infirmaria* 1349 *ib*

The Infirmary stood to the south of the Cloisters and the Refectory. Apparently a new chamber was added to the others c. 1309 (*v.* the first two quotations).   Mlat *infirmaria, infirmatorium* 'infirmary of a monastery' (Latham).   The *Chapel of St Nicholas* was situated in the east part of the Infirmary (OR 31):   (*Emendacio*) *capelle Sancti Nicholai* 1289 OR, (*in reparacione goter*) *capell' Infirmar'* 1345 *OR*, (*clerico*) *capell' infirmar'* 1346, 1348 *ib;* (*altar'*) *Sci Nicholai* 1297 *OR*, (*clericis*) *sancti Nicholai* 1435 *ib.*

KITCHEN (lost), (*ad fenestram versus*) *coquinam* 1349 *OR.* The Kitchen ran south off the west end of the Refectory.   MLat *coquina* 'kitchen' (Latham).

LIFE'S GREEN, *Lifes Green* 1745 B, 1766 King, 1789 H, 1830 M&M, *Life's Green* 1845 White, 1885 OS, lies to the east of the south transept, also known as the *Sextry Yard.*   It was formerly a cemetery.

LOWER CLOSE, *Lower Green* 1696 Cleer, *Lower Close* 1746 B, 1766 King, 1789 H, 1819 Stacy, 1830 M&M, 1845 White, 1885 OS, south-east of the Cathedral and Cloisters, is the old *Brewer's Green; v.* Brewery.

PALACE GATE
ad portas (*portam*) *Episcopi* 1254-75 Val, c. 1368 RAN, (*St Martin at*)
   Bishop's Gates 1346 NoRec, *the Bishop's Great-gate* 1745 B
ante portas Palacii Norwicensis Episcopi 1428 FA, *the Pallis Gate* 1558
   Cuningham, *St Martin's Palace Gate* 1819 Stacy

This is the north entrance to the Cathedral Precinct. Work on the present gate was begun by Bishop Alnwik (c. 1430).

PULL'S FERRY
Sandlings Ferry 1696 Cleer, 1728 Hoyle, 1746 B, 1766 King, 1789 H,
    1830 M&M, *Sandlin's Ferry* 1711 ECC
Pull's Ferry 1885 OS

This is a fifteenth-century watergate between the Foundry and
Bishop bridges. A canal for the transportation of the stone with which
the Cathedral was built ran from here into the Close (*v.* also
Bargehouse). *Sandling* kept a ferry here in the seventeenth century.
He was probably identical with the John *Sandlin* who informed Sir
Thomas Browne about the inscriptions and monuments that had been
destroyed in the Cathedral during the Civil War (Browne 123). John
Poole, ferryman and inn-keeper, kept the ferry to his death in 1841.

REFECTORY (lost), (*in emendacione fenestre*, etc.) *Refectorii* 1312,
1349 (2x) *OR, (in) Refector'* 1314 to 1410 *ib*, (*pro*) *refector'* 1349 *ib*.
MLat *refectorium* 'refectory' (Latham). The south range (parallel to
the south cloister-walk) contained the Refectory. Some remains,
notably the north wall, still stand (*v.* Pevsner 228).

ST ETHELBERT'S GATE
the Ambry Grene gate 1572 K, *Upper Gate* 1746 B, *St Ethelbert's or the
    Monastery Gate* 1819 Stacy, *St Ethelbert's Gate* 1845 White, 1885 OS

The first gate on this site was destroyed in the 1272 riot together
with St Ethelbert's Church, which stood to the east of the gate. The
present gate was built by the citizens as an act of reparation and is
believed to have been completed by 1316 (*v.* Green & Young 17 and
Pevsner 232). *Almery Green* or *Outer Court* (now *Upper Close*) was
just inside the gate.

UPPER CLOSE
(*usque*) *magnam curiam* 1289 (2x) OR, (*in*) *curia* 1304, 1327 *ib*
Vpper Green 1696 Cleer, *Upper Close* 1746 B, 1766 King, 1789 H, 1819
    Stacy, 1830 M&M, 1845 White, 1885 OS

The Upper Close was formerly the *Almery Green* inside St
Ethelbert's Gate (*q.v.*). At the present day Almery Green only applies
to a grass plot south of the gate.

NORWICH CHURCHES AND PARISHES

ALL SAINTS FYEBRIDGE

(*ad ecclesiam*) *Omnium Sanctorum* 1086 DB

(*Ecclesia*) *Omnium Sanctorum* 1205-11 to 1281 ChNCP, 1254-75 Val,
   c.   1368 RAN, 1379 *OR*, (*in parochia*) *Omnium Sanctorum de
   Fibrygge* 1421 *NPD*, 1428 FA, (*rectoria*) *Omnium Sanctorum in
   Fybrygge* 1535 VE

(*the late parish of*) *All Saints* 1581 *D&C*, (*the parish(e) of*) *All Saints in
   Fibriggate* (*streete*) 1627 to 1673 *D&C*, 1713 *NPD*

In 1550 this church was deconsecrated and the parish was united to
St Paul's. The church itself was demolished. Blomefield IV 438 f.
The number of church dedications to All Saints (All Hallows) in
England was over 1,200, surpassed only by those to the Blessed Virgin
Mary (Bond 191, Farmer 12).

ALL SAINTS TIMBERHILL

(*Ecclesia*) *Omnium Sanctorum in Swinemarkette vetere* 1254-75 Val,
   Omnium Sanctorum de Berestrete c. 1368 RAN, *Omnium
   Sanctorum in Oldswynmarket* 1428 FA, (*rectoria*) *Omnium
   Sanctorum in Berestrete* 1535 VE

(*in parochia*) *Omnium Sanctorum in* (*de*) *Swinemarket* 1255 *NPD*, 1288,
   1289 *R, de Swynemarket* 1290 to 1296 *ib, de Swynemarkette* 1294,
   1295, 1297 *ib*, (*in parochia*) *Omnium Sanctorum apud Suynmarket
   hil* 1364 *NPD, Omnium Sanctorum de Timbermarket* 1364 *ib*, (*apud
   Tymmermarket*) 1372 *ib*, (*apud Oldswynmarkethill*) 1437, 1449, 1454
   ib, Omnium Sanctorum 1527, 1532 *ib*

(*in the parysshe of*) *All Sayntes in Berstrete* 1540 *D&C, all saynt' of
   Berestrete* 1547 *AOMB, All Sayntes in Berestrete warde, All Saints in
   Berstrete ward* 1636 *ib, in Berestreet ward* 1672 *ib, in Berstreet ward*
   1846 *ib*

v. All Saints Green. The additions *in Berestrete, Berstrete*, etc., refer
to the subleet or ward. Blomefield IV 130.

ST ANDREW

(*Ecclesia*) *Sancti Andree* 1254-75 Val, 1337 *OR*, c. 1368 RAN, 1428
   FA, (*rectoria*) *Sancti Andree* 1535 VE

(*in parochia*) *Sancti Andree* 1257 *et freq* to 1491 *NPD*, 1285 to 1296 *R*,

1366 to 1545 *MinAcct*, 1467 to 1512 *AddCh, in Seint Andrues parissh*
1454 Past, *(the parishe of) Sainte Andrewe* 1556 *CG, Saint Andrew(s)*
1754, 1762 *NPD*, 1830 *D&C*

According to Blomefield (IV 300 ff.) there was a pre-Conquest
church on this site. *St Andrew* had 637 medieval dedications in
England (Bond 40, Farmer 16).

ST AUGUSTINE

(Ecclesia) Sancti Augustini 1254-75 Val, c. 1368 RAN, 1394 *NPD*, 1428
    FA, *(rectoria) Sancti Augustini* 1535 VE
(in parochia) Sancti Augustini c. 1260 to 1596 *NPD*, 1257 to 1297 *R*,
    1537, 1541 *MinAcct, (in the parisshe of) Seynt Austyn* 1511 *NPD*,
    Saynt Austyn 1547 *AOMB*, 1556 *CG, (parish of) St Austen* 1620
    NPD, Saint Augustine 1710 *ib*

Blomefield IV 475 ff. *v.* St Augustine's Street.

ST BARTHOLOMEW

(Ecclesia) Sancti Bartholomei 1254-75 Val, c. 1368 RAN, 1428 FA,
    (rectoria) Sancti Bartholomei 1535 VE
(in parochia) Sancti Bartholomei de Bergstrete 1258, 1265, 1269 *NPD*,
    Sancti Bartholomei (de Berstrete) 1288 to 1295 *R*, 1317 *D&C*, 1407 to
    1532 *NPD*, 1429, 1430 *AddCh*, 1537 *MinAcct, Saynt Bartilmue in
    Berstrete* 1540 *NPD, (ye parishe of) sancte bartilmwe* 1547 *AOMB*

This church was deconsecrated in 1549 and fell into ruin. The
parish was united to St John Sepulchre's. Blomefield IV 136 f.

ST BENEDICT

(Ecclesia) Sancti Benedicti 1155, 1176, 1274 ChNCP, 1254-75 Val, 1285
    R, c. 1368 *RAN*, 1428 FA, *St Bennett within the Cite of Norwich* 1556
    CG
(in parochia) Sancti Benedicti 1268 *D&C*, 1285 *et freq* to 1298 *R*, 1312 to
    1549 *NPD, (the parish of) Saint Benet* 1547 *AOMB, Saint Benedict*
    1834 *D&C*

The church was destroyed by enemy action in 1942. Only a round
tower remains (Banger 47). The dedication is to the founder of the
Benedictine Order. Blomefield IV 248 ff.

ST BOTOLPH

(*Ecclesia*) *Sancti Botulphi* 1254-75 Val, 1298 *R*, 1337 *OR*, c. 1368 RAN,
    1428 FA, (*rectoria*) *Sancti Bothulphi* 1535 VE, *S. Butholdes* 1558
    Cuningham
(*in parochia*) *Sancti Bothulphi* 1256, 1274 *D&C*, 1290 to 1297 *R*, 1446 to
    1538 *NPD*, (*the parishe of*) *saynt Botolffe* 1547 *AOMB*, *The Pageant
    Howse, in late St Buttolph's* 1626 BLR, (*the late dissolved parish
    of*) *St Buttolph* 1649 *NPD*

By 1548 the church had been deconsecrated and demolished, and
the parish was united to St Saviour's. Blomefield IV 442 f. St Botolph
was founder of a monastery at Icanho in 654 (ASC) on land given by
the king of East Anglia.

ST CATHERINE

(*Ecclesia*) *Sancte Katerine que quondam fuit Sancti Winewalocy* 1254-75
    Val, *Sancti Wynowal* c. 1368 RAN
(*Ecclesia*) *Sancte Katerine* 1428 FA, (*Capella*) *Sancte Katerine* 1535
    VE
(*in parochia*) *Sancte Katarine* 1527 *NPD*, *Sancte Katerine* 1532 *ib*, 1537
    MinAcct

This parish never recovered after being depopulated by the plague
in 1349. The church was then converted into a chapel and the parish
was united to that of St Stephen. The church was first dedicated to St
Winwaloe, a saint regarded as evidence of early Flemish or Picard
influence (*v.* J. Campbell in *Studia Hibernica* 15, 1975, 177 ff.). It was
early rededicated to St Catherine. *v.* All Saints Green. Cf. St
Winwaloe's Priory in Wereham (*St Winewalloe* 1241 Lib, *St Winewal*
1296 Ipm, etc.). Blomefield IV 143 ff.

ST CHRISTOPHER

(*Ecclesia*) *Sancti Cristofori* 1190-1200 Holme, 1254-75 Val, (*in
    parochia*) *Sancti Christoferi* 1287, 1289 *R*, (*in parochia que fuit*)
    Sancti Christoferi 1296 *R*

This was a church on the east side of St Andrew's Hill which was
burnt down in the reign of Henry III. The greater part of the parish
was united to St Andrew's and a smaller part to St. Michael's at Plea.
The parish had disappeared by 1286. Blomefield IV 319, Tillyard 7.

ST CLEMENT CUNESFORD

(*Ecclesia*) *Sancti Clementis* 1254-75 Val, *de Conesford* c. 1368 RAN,
   1428 FA, (*rectorie*) *Sanctorum Edwardi, Juliani et Clementis* 1535 VE,
   St Clement at the Well 1745 B

(*in parochia*) *Sancti Clementis in* (*de*) *Conesford* 1266 *et freq* to 1480
   NPD, 1287 to 1295 *R*, (*cimiterium ecclesie*) *Sancti Clementis* 1303,
   1353, 1357 *NPD*, (*in parochia*) *Sancti Clementis in Cunesford* 1309
   AddCh

According to Blomefield, this church was of pre-Conquest origin.
The advowson belonged to the Abbey of Wendling (founded by
William de Wendling in 1267). For *at the Well, v.* Abbey Lane. The
parish was joined to St Julian's in 1482. The church was deconsecrated
in 1550 but it was still standing, although it was a ruin, in 1744.
Blomefield IV 77 ff. St Clement, pope and martyr (d. c. 100), is represented on painted screens in East Anglia (Farmer 83 f.).

ST CLEMENT FYEBRIDGE or COLEGATE

(*in parochia*) *Sancti Clementis de Fibrig*(*g*)*ate* (*Fybriggate*) 1252 *et freq*
   to 1567 *NPD*, 1285 to 1294 *R*, (*ad pontem*) 1379 *R*, (*in cimiterio*
   parochiae) *Diui Clementis iuxta Fibrige* 1567 *AddCh*

(*Ecclesia*) *Sancti Clementis ad Pontem* 1254-75 Val, c. 1368 RAN, 1428
   FA, (*rectoria*) 1535 VE, (*ecclesia*) *Sancti Clementis apud Pontem de*
   Fybridges 1554 *AddCh, Saynte Clement at Fybrygge gate* 1547 *AOMB*,
   (*parrishe Churche of*) *saincte Clementis by Fybridge* 1567 *AddCh*

According to Blomefield (IV 453 ff.), this church is 'one of the most
ancient in the city'. It belonged originally to the manor of *Tokethorp*
(*Toketop* 1086 DB, *Thoketorp* 1203 Cur), later *Tolthorp* (*v.* Peacock
Street).

ST CROUCHE

(*Ecclesia*) *Sancte Crucis* 1157 to 1281 ChNCP, 1257-75 Val, 1293 *R*, c.
   1368 RAN, 1428 FA, 1535 VE, (*the cherch of*) *Saynt Crouche* 1543
   NPD

(*in parochia*) *Sancte Crucis* 1287 to 1298 *R*, 1293, 1308, 1529 *NPD*, (*the*
   parysshe of) *the Crosse* 1547 *AOMB*

The church was deconsecrated in 1551 and the parish was divided
between St Andrew and St John Maddermarket. In Blomefield's time

(1745) it was totally demolished and a pub called the *Hole in the Wall* stood on the site. Blomefield IV 299, Tillyard 7. *v.* School Lane. The Holy Cross was venerated with numerous dedications in Britain (Farmer 93 f.). OE **crūc**³ 'cross', evidenced in early ME as *cruche, crouche* (*v.* OED, MED and Löfvenberg 48).

ST CUTHBERT
(*Ecclesia*) *Sancti Cuthberti* 1157, 1273 ChNCP, 1254-75 Val, 1337 *OR,*
   c. 1368 RAN, 1428 FA, (*super cimiterium ecclesie*) *Sancti Cuthberti*
   1303, 1309, 1346 *NPD,* (*rectoria*) *Sancti Cuthberti* 1535 VE
(*in parochia*) *Sancti Cuthberti* 1285 to 1298 *R,* 1290 *et freq* to 1368 *D&C,*
   1352 *et freq* to 1535 *NPD* (*in the late dissolued parishes of St Mary*
   Little and) *St Cuthbert* 1634 *NPD*

This parish was joined to that of St Mary the Less in 1492 and the church was demolished in 1530-35. Blomefield IV 116. St Cuthbert, Bishop of Lindisfarne 685-7, has numerous church dedications both in Scotland and England (Farmer 94 ff.).

ST EDMUND
(*Ecclesia*) *Sancti Eadmundi in Fisscheresgate* 1254-75 Val, *Sancti*
   Edmundi c. 1368 RAN, 1428 FA, (*rectoria*) 1535 VE, *Se*(*y*)*nt*
   Edmundes 1452, 1479 Past, *Seint Edmondes* 1481 *ib*
(*in parochia*) *Sancti Edmundi in Fibriggate* 1285 *R, in Fyscheregate* 1288
   ib, in Fisscheregate 1291 *ib, de Fischeregate* 1293, 1295 *ib, de*
   (*in*) *Fisshergate* 1342, 1383 *AddCh, de Fyschergate* 1400 *NPD, the*
   parish of seint Edmunde 1547 *AOMB, the parisshe of St Edmund*
   1556 *CG*

According to Blomefield (IV 403), the church was founded in the time of William the Conqueror. The dedication is to St Edmund, King of East Anglia and martyr (870). Because several relics of the King were preserved here, the church was once a place of pilgrimage. It is now disused.

ST EDWARD
(*Ecclesia*) *Sancti Edwardi* 1254-75 Val, 1267 *NPD,* 1295 *R,* 1337 *OR,*
   Sancti Eadwardi c. 1300 *NPD,* (*Ecclesie*) *Sanctorum Edwardi et*
   Juliani c. 1368 RAN, 1428 FA, (*rectorie*) *Sanctorum Edwardi,*
   Juliani et Clementis 1535 VE

(*in parochia*) *Sancti Edwardi* 1270 *et freq* to 1481 *NPD,* 1290 *D&C,*
    Sancti Eadwardi 1277 *NPD,* 1288 to 1294 *R*

In the late 13th century this parish was united to St Julian's. The
church served as the church of Hildebrond's Hospital until the
dissolution of the monasteries, when it fell into ruin. Blomefield IV 69
f.

ST ETHELDRED
(*Ecclesia*) *Sancte Etheldrede* 1254-75 Val, 1270, 1281 ChNCP, c. 1368
    RAN, 1428 FA, *(Firma)* 1535 VE
Sca Ethelreda (p) Hy3 *AddCh,* (*in parochia*) *Sancte Etheldrede 1285,*
    1322 D&C, 1286 *et freq* to 1295 *R,* 1367 *Phillipps,* 1391 *NPD*

This is said to be the oldest church in the city (White 109). The
dedication is to St Etheldred (OE *Æþelþryþ* 630-79), Queen of
Northumbria, founder and Abbess of a convent at Ely. Blomefield IV
72 ff. Before the demolition of St Peter Southgate, the living of the
latter was united with that of St Etheldred.

ST GEORGE COLGATE
(*Ecclesia*) 1157 to 1274 ChNCP, *Sancti Georgii de Coslane* 1254-75 Val,
    Sancti Georgii de Colgate c. 1365 RAN, *in Mospool* 1394 *OR, de*
    Collegate 1428 FA, *(rectoria) Sancti Georgii de (in) Colgate* 1535 VE
(*in parochia*) *Sancti Georgii de (in) Col(e)gate* c. 1250 *et freq to 1580*
    NPD, 1268 *D&C,* 1287 *et freq* to 1298 *R, de Muspol* 1296 *ib, iuxta*
    Mosepol 1351 *NPD, apud Muspol* 1251 *ib, de Mospole* 1397 *ib, Saynte*
    George of Colgate 1547 *AOMB, the parishe of Sainte Georges of*
    Colgate 1556 *CG*

Mos(e)pol was a spring or pool near the church, from which it was
sometimes called. Blomefield IV 466 ff. *v.* Muspole Street, St
George's Alley and Street.

ST GEORGE TOMBLAND
(*Ecclesia*) *Sancti Georgii ad portam Trinitatis* 1254-75 Val, *ad portas*
    Ecclesie 1337 *OR,* c. 1368 RAN, *ante portas Ecclesie Cathedralis*
    Sancti Trinitatis 1428 FA, (*Churche Wardens of*) *St Georges of*
    Tumlounde 1556 *CG*
(*in parochia*) *Sancti Georgii ante portas (portam) Ecclesie Sancte*

Trinitatis 1285 *et freq* to 1298 *R*, 1253 *et freq* to 1482 *D&C*, 1314 to 1378 *NPD, Sancti Georgii de Tomlond* 1539 *NPD, (the parish of) Saynte George at Tomplonde* 1547 *AOMB, St George of Tombland* 1692 *NPD,* 1834 *D&C*

The *portam Trinitatis* and *portas (portam) Ecclesie* in the 13th and 14th-century quotations above would seem to refer to some predecessor of the present Erpingham Gate to the Cathedral Precinct. Blomefield IV 361 ff. *v.* Tombland.

ST GILES
(*Ecclesia*) *Sancti Egidii* 1136-45 *CottCh,* 1155 *et freq* to 1281 ChNCP, 1254-75 Val, 1281 *CottR,* c. 1368 RAN, 1428 FA, 1479 Worcestre, (*rectoria*) 1535 VE, *apud sanctum Egidium in Norwyco* 1163-8 Holme, *apud Norwicum ad monasterium sancti Egidij* 1175-86 *ib* (*in parochia*) *Sancti Egidii* 1280 to 1343 *NPD,* 1274, 1317 *D&C,* 1285 *et freq* to 1298 *R,* (*in superiori Neweport/Neuport*) 1287, 1291, 1292 *ib,* (*the parisse of*) *Saynt Giles* 1547 *AOMB, Saynte Gyles* 1556 *CG, St Gyles* 1597 *AddCh*

The church was founded in the reign of William the Conqueror by Elwyn, the priest, on his own estate, according to Reg. I (quoted in Blomefield IV 238). For *Superior Neweport, v.* Bethel Street. *St Aegidius* or *Giles,* a hermit in Provence (c. 700), was popular as the patron saint of cripples and beggars. *v.* Great Hospital.

ST GREGORY
(*Ecclesia*) *Sancti Gregorii* 1254-75 Val, 1276 to 1289 ChNCP, c. 1368 RAN, 1337 *OR,* 1428 FA, (*rectoria*) 1535 VE
(*in parochia*) *Sancti Gregorii* 1255 *et freq* to 1561 *NPD,* 1284 *et freq* to 1342 *D&C,* 1285 *et freq* to 1298 *R, in vico de Tonsoria* 1287, 1288, 1295 *ib, in vico de Stongate* 1290, 1298 *ib, in vico de Inferiori Neuport* 1297 *ib, Sent Gregorys parysh* 1452 Past, *Seynt Gregorys paryche* 1463 *ib,* (*the parissche of*) *Seynt Gregory* 1552 *CG,* (*the parisshe of*) *Sainte Gregories* 1556 *CG*

For *Stongate, v.* Goat Lane; for *Tonsoria, v.* Charing Cross; for *Inferior Neuport, v.* St Giles Street. Blomefield IV 272 ff.

ST HELEN
(*Ecclesia*) *Sancte Helene* 1273 ChNCP, c. 1368 RAN, *Sancte Elene in Norwico* 1535 VE
(*in parochia*) *Sante Elene* (2x) *NPD, Sancti Helene* 13 *ib*

This church originally stood to the south of Holmstrete/Bishopgate, in the Cathedral Precinct. It was demolished and the parish was united to the hospital church of St Giles, which was re-dedicated to St Helen. Blomefield IV 376 f. *v.* Great Hospital. *St Helen* (*c.* 250-330), mother of the Emperor Constantine, had numerous church dedications in England because of her reputed British origin, most frequent in the north-east (Farmer 188).

ST JAMES
(*Ecclesia*) *Sancti Jacobi* 1157 to 1281 ChNCP, 1254-75 Val, 1337 *OR*, c. 1368 RAN, 1428 FA, c. 1500 *NPD*, (*rectoria*) 1535 VE, (*ecclesia parochial'*) *Sci Jacobi* 1615 *AddCh*
(*in parochia*) *Sancti Jacobi* 1283, 1591 *NPD*, 1289 to 1298 *R*, 1302 to 1321 *D&C*, (*de parochia*) *Sancti Jacobi* 1479 Worcestre, *Saynt Jamys parische* 1547 *AOMB*, (*the parishe of*) *Saint(e) Jamys* (2x) 1556 *CG*

The church is said to have been founded in the time of William the Conqueror. Part of Mousehold Heath and the hamlet of Pockthorpe were included in the parish. Blomefield IV 423 ff.

ST JOHN THE EVANGELIST
(*placea ubi fuit aliquando Ecclesia*) *Sancti Johannis Ewangeliste ubi est taberna W. Seysun* 1254-75 Val, (*Ecclesia*) *Sancti Petri de Permontergate et Johannis Evangeliste* c. 1368 RAN

According to Blomefield (IV 102), this parish was united to that of St Peter Parmountergate about 1300, when the Grey Friars appropriated the site for their convent. The church was pulled down. Judging by the entry in Val *supra*, it would seem to have ceased to function as a church even earlier. Campbell 12.

ST JOHN MADDERMARKET
(*Ecclesia*) *Sancti Johannis de Madermarket* 1254-75 Val, 1337 *OR*, 1428 FA, *de Madyrmarket* c. 1368 RAN, (*rectoria*) *Sancti Johannis de Mathermarkett* 1535 VE

(*in parochia*) *Sancti Johannis de Madermarket* c. 1250, 1351 *NPD*, 1285
   et freq to 1297 *R*, 1286 *et freq* to 1490 *D&C, Sancti Johannis de*
   Madelmarket 1289 (2x) *R, de Madelmarket(t)e* 1292 to 1295 *ib, de*
   Mather Market 1557 *NPD, Seint John of Madermarket* 1529 *ib,* (*the*
   parishe of) *Saint Johns of Madermarkett* 1556 *CG*

The dedication was originally to the Holy Trinity and St John the
Baptist. According to Blomefield the church was founded before the
Conquest and probably built by twelve burgesses who then had the
patronage. *Maddermarket* refers to an old market at the northern end
of the churchyard. Today *St John Maddermarket* also refers to a street
along the east side of the churchyard. Blomefield IV 287 ff. *v.* St
John Maddermarket (Streets). The church is now leased to the Greek
Orthodox Congregation.

ST JOHN SEPULCHRE
(*Ecclesia*) *Sancti Sepulchri* 1136-9 *et freq* to 1281 ChNCP, 1254-75 Val,
   c. 1368 RAN, 1428 FA, (*rectoria*) *Sancti Johannis in Sepulcro*
   (*Cepulcro*) 1535 VE, *S. Johns at the gates* 1558 Cuningham
(*in parochia*) *Sancti Sepulcri* 1286 *et freq* to 1298 *R*, 1486 *D&C, Sancti*
   Johannis (*Sepulcri*) 1527, 1532 *NPD, St John sepulture* 1556 *CG*

The dedication is to St John the Baptist and the Holy Sepulchre.
According to Blomefield (IV 137), this church was founded in the
Confessor's reign. The appellation *at the gates* 1558 refers to Ber
Street Gate.

ST JOHN TIMBERHILL
(*Ecclesia*) *Sancti Johannis ante portam Castelli* Hy1 *Beecheno*, 1157,
   1162 ChNCP, *de* (*in*) *Ber*(*e*)*strete* 1254-75 Val, c. 1368 RAN, 1428
   FA, (*rectoria*) 1525 VE, *the parish church of St John of Berstrete* 1631
   NPD
(*in parochia*) *Sancti Johannis de Bergstrete* 1265, 1267, 1279 *NPD, de*
   (*in*) *Berstrete* 1287 *et freq* to 1401 *R, de Bergstrete* 1289 *et freq* to 1341
   NPD, 1294 to 1380 *D&C*, 1306 *AddCh, St Johns parisshe in Bearstrete*
   1552 *CG*
(*in parochia*) *Sancti Johannis de Berstrete iuxta le Tymbermarket* 1350
   D&C, (*in the parysshe of*) *Seynt John de* (*of*) *Tymberhyll* 1556, 1641
   NPD, S. Johns on the hill 1558 Cuningham

This church is said to have been built by Wodowin, the priest, who gave it to Norwich Priory soon after its foundation. Blomefield IV 126 ff. *v.* All Saints Green and Timberhill.

ST JULIAN

(*Ecclesia*) *Sancti Juliani de Cunegesford* 1254-75 Val, *Sancti Juliani* c.
    1368 RAN, (*rectorie*) *Sanctorum Edwardi, Juliani et Clementis* 1535
    VE
(*in parochia*) *Sancti Juliani* 1260 et freq to 1324 NPD, 1288 to 1293 *R,*
    in Conesford 1348 *Phillipps*

According to Blomefield, the church was founded before the Conquest. It was given to the nuns of Carrow by King Stephen. The rectory of St Edward was united to that of St Julian in 1269 and that of St Clement Cunesford was added in 1482. Blomefield IV 78 ff.

The dedication is to *Julian the Hospitaller,* almost certainly a mythical saint (Farmer 226 f.). The church was destroyed by enemy action in 1942 (Banger 65), but owing to its association with Julian of Norwich, anchoress and visionary, the church was rebuilt despite the fact that Norwich is a decidedly 'over-churched' city. Julian of Norwich was probably born in 1342 and lived into the fifteenth century. In the will of Thomas Emund, a chantry priest of Aylesham in Norfolk, proved in 1404, there is a bequest of one shilling to 'Juliane anchorite apud St Juliane in Norwice' (Julian I 33). The church was not named after the anchoress; she assumed the name of the church's patron saint.

ST LAWRENCE

(*Ecclesia*) *Sancti Laurentii* 1086 DB
(*Ecclesia*) *Sancti Laurentii* 1254-75 Val,*Sancti Laurencii* c. 1368 RAN,
    1428 FA, (*rectoria*) *Sancti Laurencij* 1535 VE
(*in parochia*) *Sancti Laurentii* 1254 *et freq* to 1649 *NPD,* 1285 *et freq* to
    1298 *R,* 1306 *D&C, Seynt Laveransis parysh* 1451 Past, *Sci Laurencij*
    1537 *MinAcct,* 1664 *AddCh,* (*the parrish of*) *saynct Laurence* 1547
    AOMB, Saint Larraunce 1556 *CG*

Founded in the reign of Edward the Confessor. The old church was pulled down about 1460 and the present one erected. Blomefield IV 260 ff.

ST MARGARET FYEBRIDGE

(*Ecclesia*) *Sancte Margarete ubi sepeliuntur suspensi* 1254-75 Val,
   Ecclesia Margarete c. 1368 RAN, *Sancte Margarete* 1428 FA,
   (*Gardian' capelle*) *Sancte Margarete ... in Fybrygge* 1535 VE
(*in parochia*) *Sancte Margarete* 1289 *R*, 1485 *NPD*, (*ground with an
   house therevpon standing & builded heretofore called*) *the Chapell of
   Sct Margarette* 1661, 1669, 1672 *D&C*

This church, sometimes called St Margaret *in Combusto* (cf. St
Mary Combusta) or by the Gates, stood on the west side of
Magdalen Street. The gallows was just outside Magdalen Gates,
and persons executed there had the right to be buried in this
churchyard. At the Dissolution the church was deconsecrated and
the parish was united to that of All Saints Fyebridge, which in its
turn was made part of St Paul's parish. Blomefield IV 439 f. More
than 200 English churches were dedicated to St Margaret, including
58 in Norfolk (Farmer 260 f.).

ST MARGARET NEWBRIDGE

(*Ecclesia*) *Sancte Margarete* 1157 to 1281 ChNCP, *Sancte Margarete
   super pontem de Newebrigg* 1254-75 Val, *Margarete de Neubryg'* c.
   1368 RAN
(*in parochia*) *Sancte Margarete de* (*apud*) *Newebrigg* 1289, 1295 *R*

When this parish was depopulated by the plague of 1349, the church
was converted into a hermitage chapel. The parish was united to St
George Colegate. The church was also called St Margaret Colegate.
Blomefield IV 474 f. *v.* Water Lane[1] and Blackfriars Bridge.

ST MARGARET WESTWICK

(*Ecclesia*) *Sancte Margarete in Westwick* 1254-75 Val, *de Westwyk* c.
   1368 RAN, 1428 FA, (*rectoria*) *Sancte Margarete de Westwik* 1535
   VE
(*in parochia*) *Sancte Margarete de Westwyk* 1284 to 1429 *NPD, de
   Westwyk* 1286 to 1298 *R*

The site of the church is between Lower and Upper Westwick
Street (St Benedict's Street). Blomefield IV 257 ff. The church is
now disused.

ST MARTIN BAILEY

(*Ecclesia*) *Sancti Martini de Ball'ia* 1254-75 Val, *Michaelis in Berestrete et Martini* c. 1368 RAN, (*rectoria*) *Sancti Martini de Berestrete* 1535 VE, (*in Berestret*) 1537 *MinAcct*

(*in parochia*) *Sancti Martini de Ball'ia* 1287 to 1294 *R*, 1387, 1421 *NPD*, *Sancti Martini de Balliua* 1554, 1555 *R*, (*in the parish of*) *St Martens of Balle* 1556 *CG*, *St Martyn at Bayle* 1631 *R*, *St Martins at Bale* 1691 *ib*

(*in parochia*) *Sancti Martini de Tymmerhill* 1537 *MinAcct*, *S. Martines on the hill* 1558 Cuningham

Ball'ia, Balliua, Bayle, etc., refer to the bailey or bailiwick of the Castle. The church was also called St Martin at the Castle Gate. Those who died in the Castle, or were executed there, were buried in this churchyard until 1562, when the church was deconsecrated and the parish united to that of St Michael at Thorn. The church was eventually demolished. *v.* also Bailey (Castle) *supra.* Blomefield IV 120 ff. *Martin* (c. 316-397), bishop of Tours, was a popular saint, with 173 ancient church dedications in Britain (Farmer 265 f.).

ST MARTIN COSLANY

(*Ecclesia*) *Sancti Martini de Coslane* 1254-75 Val, *Sancti Martini Coselan'* c. 1368 RAN, (*rectoria*) *Sancti Martini de Coslany* 1535 VE

(*in parochia*) *Sancti Martini in* (*de*) *Cos(e)lanie, -lanye* 1288 *et freq* to 1298 *R*, 1288 *et freq* to 1394 *NPD*, 1426 *D&C, de Coslany* 1519 *NPD*, 1634 *Phillipps*, (*the parissh of*) *saynct Martins in Coslany* 1547 *AOMB, St Martyns parisshe of Coslany* 1556 *CG*

S. Martines at th' Ooke 1558 Cuningham, *St Martines at Oake* (*the Oake*) 1661 *AddCh*

The name *St Martin at the Oak* is from a large hollow oak which formerly stood in the churchyard, with an image of St Mary in it (*v.* also Coslany Street - - Oak Street). Blomefield IV 479 ff.

ST MARTIN AT PALACE

(*Ecclesia*) *Sancti Martini* 1086 DB

(*Ecclesia*) *sancti Martini* 1236 to 1281 ChNCP, *Sancti Mantini ad portam Episcopi* 1254-75 Val, *ad portas Episcopi* c. 1368 RAN, *ante portas Palacii Norwidensis Episcopi* 1428 FA, (*rectoria*) *Sancti*

Martini ad Portas Palacij Episcopi 1535 VE, *St Martins at the*
   Pallis Gate 1558 Cuningham
(*in parochia*) *Sancti Martini ante portam (portas) Episcopi (palacii*
   Episcopi) 1259 *et freq* to 1481 *NPD*, 1282 *D&C*, 1287 to 1290 *R*, *seynt*
   Martyns at the palis Gate 1552 *CG*, *Saynte Martyns at the Pallis Gate*
   1556 *ib*, (*in the parish of*) *Saint Martin at Palace alias Saint Martin's*
   before the Gates of the Palace of the Bishop of Norwich 1731 *NPD*
(*in parochia*) *Sancti Martini del Hill* 1288 *R*, *Sancti Martini ad Montem*
   1290 (2x) *ib*, *Sancti Martini super Montem* 1627 *NPD*

The name derives from the situation opposite the entrance to the
Bishop's Palace. The church was founded before the Conquest.
Bishop Stigand held it TRE (DB). The addition *del Hill, ad Montem,*
etc., refers to the feature also called *Bichil*, etc. *v.* St Martin at Palace
Plain. Blomefield IV 367 ff.

ST MARY COMBUSTA
(*in parochia*) *Sancte Marie Arse* 1233 *Phillipps, Sancte Marie Combuste*
   c. 1250 to 1385 *NPD, Beate Marie Combuste* 1272, 1274 *ib, Sancte*
   Marie Combuste 1287 to 1291 *R*, (*in vico de Fybriggate*) 1296 *AddCh*
(*Ecclesia*) *Sancte Marie Combuste* c. 1250 *NPD*, (*in cimiterio*) *Beate*
   Marie uirginis combuste c. 1250 *Phillipps, Sancte Marie Combuste* 1252
   NPD, (*Ecclesia*) *Sancte Marie Combuste* c. 1250 *NPD*, 1254-75 Val,
   1337 *OR, Conbuste* c. 1368 *RAN, Sancte Marie Combuste* 1428 FA
(*rectoria*) *Beate Marie Incombuste* 1535 VE, (*Ecclesia*) *Sancte Marie*
   Vnburnte 1559 *NPD*
(*in parochia*) *Sancte Marie Vnburde* 1537 *MinAcct, Sancte Marie*
   incombuste 1541 *ib*, 1557 to 1580 *NPD*, (*cum cimiterio parochie*) *Beate*
   Marie Incombuste 1557 *ib*, (*in nuper parochia*) *Sancte Marie*
   Incombuste 1565 *Phillipps*

This church stood in the part of the city that was burnt in a great fire
in the Conqueror's time; hence *Sancte Marie Arse* or *Combuste*. *In*
combusto loco or *in combusta area* led to the appellation *Incombuste* or
Unburnt. The church was demolished after the Dissolution and the
parish united to St Saviour's. Blomefield IV 449 f. *v.* Golden Dog
Lane, formerly Brent Lane.

ST MARY COSLANY
(*cimiterium*) *sancte Marie in Coslania* 1175-86 Holme, (*Ecclesia*) *Sancte*

Marie de Coslane 1254-75 Val, *de Coselanye* c. 1368 RAN, *de Coslanye* 1428 FA, *de Coslanie* 1437 *OR*, (*rectoria*) *Beate Marie de Cosseney in Norwic* 1535 VE

(*in parochia*) *Sancte Marie de Cos(e)lanie, -lanye* c. 1250 to 1303 *NPD*, 1261 to 1412 *D&C*, 1287 *et freq* to 1298 *R, de Coslanye* 1294 *NPD,* (*in the paryssh of*) *Seint Marie of Coslany* 1525 *ib, Seynt Mary(e) of Coslanye* 1547 *AOMB,* 1552 *CG, Sainte Maries of Coslaine* 1556 *ib, St Mary of Coslany* 1619 *NPD*

This church has a round Anglo-Saxon tower (Pevsner 247, Fisher 173). Blomefield IV 286 ff. *v.* also St Mary's Alley and St Mary's Plain.

ST MARY THE LESS

(*Ecclesia*) *Sancte Marie* 1155, 1176, 1273 ChNCP, *Sancte Marie Parue* 1254-75 Val, 1269, 1283 *D&C*, c. 1368 RAN, (*rectoria*) *Sancte Marie Parve* 1535 VE, (*Ecclesia*) *Beate Marie vocata little Seynt Maries* 1544 *NPD*

(*in parochia*) *Beate Marie Parue* 1261, 1276, 1504 *NPD*, 1545 *MinAcct, Beate Marie de Tumlond* 1541 *ib, Sancte Marie Parue* 1276 *et freq* to 1535 *ib,* 1281, 1378 *D&C, Sancte Marie le Litle* 1280 *ib,* 1282 *NPD,* 1294 *R, Sancte Marie Minoris* 1416 to 1437 *NPD, Sct Mary called Sct Mary Little* 1632 *D&C, in the late dissolued Parishes of St Mary Little and St Cutbert* 1634 *NPD*

This parish was united to that of St George Tombland, together with St Cuthbert's (earlier dissolved), in 1542. The church was not demolished. In the 17th and 18th centuries it was the church of the Walloon and French congregations. It is now leased to the Catholic Apostolic Church. Blomefield IV 118 ff.

ST MARY IN THE MARSH

(*ecclesia*) *Sancte Marie in (de) Marisco* 1155 to 1274 ChNCP, 1254-75 Val, 1329, 1331 *D&C,* 1428 FA, *Sancte Marie del Merssh* 1378 *D&C,* (*cimiterium*) *Beate Marie de le Merssh* 1393 *ib,* (*Ecclesia*) *Beate Marie de Marisco* 1435 *NPD,* (*rectoria*) *Beate Marie in Marisco* 1535 VE

(*in parochia*) *Sancte Marie de (in) Marisco* 1272, 1286, 1380 *D&C,* 1346 *NPD, Beate Marie de Marisco* 1334 *D&C*

This church stood in the Cathedral Precinct. It was built by Bishop

Herbert and replaced an earlier chapel which belonged to Thorpe. In 1564 the parishes of St Mary in the Marsh and St Vedast (the church of which was demolished) were united to St Peter Parmountergate. The church of St Mary was deconsecrated and turned into a dwelling-house, and it remained as such in 1745. Blomefield IV 50 ff.

Near St Mary in the Marsh church there was an area of empty land called *Londenefyerd* 1377 *D&C*.

ST MATTHEW

(*Ecclesia*) *Sancti Mathei ad portam scolarium* 1254-75 Val, c. 1368 RAN

(*in parochia*) *Sancti Mathei ad portas Scolarum* (*contra Scolas gramaticales*) 1275 *et freq* to 1360 *NPD*

Situated near the old grammar school, to the east of St Martin at Palace church, to which the parish was joined after the great pestilence in 1349. The church fell into ruin. Blomefield IV 375. *v.* World's End Lane.

ST MICHAEL CONESFORD

(*Ecclesia*) *sancti Michaelis uidelicet in Cunesford/Cuningefordia/ Cunesfordia* 1147-9, 1183, 1186- 1210 Holme, *Sancti Michaelis* 1254-75 Val

(*in parochia*) *Sancti Michaelis de* (*in*) *Conesford* 1287 to 1289 *R, in Cunesford* 1290, 1292, 1298 *ib*, 1308 *D&C*

This church was sold about 1360 to the Augustinian friars, who demolished it and built their own establishment in its place. The parish was united to that of St Peter Parmountergate. Blomefield IV 84 ff. The cult of Michael, the Archangel, was strong in the British Isles. The medieval church dedications in England numbered 686 (Farmer 277 f.).

ST MICHAEL COSLANY

(*Ecclesia*) *Sancti Michaelis de Coslane* 1254-75 Val, *de Coslan'* 1337 OR, *de Coselan'* c. 1368 RAN, *de Coslanye* 1428 FA, *the parissh cherch of Seint Michael of Coslany in Norwich* 1482 Past, 1482 *AddR*, (*ecclesia/rectoria*) *Sancte Michaelis in Coslany* 1535 VE, *St Mychels of Coslanye* 1556 CG

(*in parochia*) *Sancti Michaelis de* (*in*) *Cos(e)lanye, -lanie* 1268 *D&C*,
   1286 *et freq* to 1298 *R*, 1296, 1302 *HarlCh*, *Sancti Michaelis in*
   Muskepole 1537 *MinAcct*

Commonly called *St Miles* (cf. St Miles Bridge and Colegate).
Blomefield IV 492 ff. The church is now disused.

ST MICHAEL AT PLEA
(*ecclesia*) *sancti Michaelis* (*de/in Norwico*) 1126-7 to 1190-1200
   Holme, *sancti Michaelis ad placita* 1147-9, 1183 *ib*, (*Ecclesia*) *Sancti*
   Michaelis ad Placita 1254-75 Val, c. 1368 RAN, 1428 FA, (*rectoria*)
   1535 VE, *Sainte Mychell(s) at the ple(a)* (2x) 1556 *CG*, *St Michael of*
   Musball c. 1720 K
(*in parochia*) *Sancti Michaelis de Placitis* 1283 to 1294 *D&C*, 1287 to
   1293 *R*, *ad Placita* 1285 to 1298 *ib*, 1333 to 1399 *D&C*, 1337 *OR*, 1394
   to 1506 *NPD*
(*in parochia*) *Sancti Michaelis de Motstowe* 1289, 1298 *R*, *de Motstouwe*
   1349 *D&C*, (*the parisshe of*) *Saincte Michaell at the plee otherwise*
   called Mustow 1547 *AOMB*

Blomefield says that *ad Placita*, *at Plea*, *de Motstowe* refer to the
court meetings of the Archdeacon of Norwich. Blomefield IV 319 ff.
v. Bank Plain for further discussion.

ST MICHAEL AT THORN
(*Ecclesia*) *Sancti Michaelis in* (*de*) *Ber(e)strete* 1254-75 Val, c. 1368
   RAN, 1428 FA
(*in parochia*) *Sancti Michaelis in* (*de*) *Berstrete* 13 *Phillipps*, 1284 *et freq*
   to 1532 *NPD*, 1289 *et freq* to 1297 *R*, *de Berestrete* 1563 *NPD*, 1596 to
   1638 *AddCh*, (*the parish of*) *St Mychaell of Berestrete* 1612 *ib*

The modern name *at Thorn* is said to refer to a large thorn which
grew in the churchyard. Blomefield IV 134 ff., White 115. This
church was destroyed by enemy action in 1942. *v.* also Thorn Lane.

ST MICHAEL ON TOMBLAND
(*Ecclesia*) *Sancti Michaelis*, (*terre*) *Sancti Michahelis de Norwic* 1086
   DB, (*Ecclesia*) *sancti Micha(h)elis* 1136-43, 1146-74 ChNCP
(*terram*) *Sancti Michaelis* W2 *Reg I*, 1107-16, 1136, 1157 ChNCP, (*terra*)
   Sancti Michaelis & nunc est ibi Tomblond c. 1306 *Reg I*

According to Blomefield, this church was founded by the earls of East Anglia and served as a chapel to their palace before the Cathedral was built. When he founded the Cathedral and Priory, Bishop Herbert procured of Roger Bigod the palace and the church of St Michael, both of which he caused to be demolished. A stone cross was placed on the spot where the chapel had stood. This marked the boundary between the liberties of the church and the city. In recompense for the demolished church, Bishop Herbert founded a chapel dedicated to St Michael on the summit of Thorpe Hill on the other side of the river. Blomefield IV 116. *v.* Tombland.

ST OLAVE
(*capella*) *sancte Ol(aue*) *in Norwico* 1186-1210 Holme, *de ecclesiis sanctorum Martini et Olavi* 1227-36 ChNCP, (*Ecclesia*) *Sancti Olaui* 1254-75 Val, *Sancti Olavi* c. 1368 RAN, 1428 FA
(*in parochia*) *Sancti Olaui* 1256 to 1410 *D&C*, 1287 *et freq* to 1557 *R*, 1294 to 1492 *NPD*, (*in the parisshe of*) *St Olau'* 1614 *ib*

This church stood on the north side of Cherry Lane (*St Tooley's-lane* 1745 B). It was demolished in 1546 and the parish was united to that of St George Colegate. The cult of Olaf, King of Norway (d. 1030), was strong in the Viking areas of Britain. *Tooley* developed by the addition of the final *t* in *Saint.* Blomefield IV 475. *v.* Cherry Lane and Cherry Tree Opening.

ST OLAVE'S CHAPEL
Capella Sancti Olaui in parochia Sancti Petri 1254-75 Val, (*Fuitque in eadem parochia antiquis temporibus*) *una capella de Sancto Olavo* 1368 RAN

This was a parochial chapel before the Conquest, situated on the east side of King Street near Conesford Gates. It was pulled down before 1345, but judging by the above evidence, the cure was joined to the parish church of St Peter Southgate a century earlier. Blomefield IV 65. *v.* St Olave's Staithe.

ST PAUL
(*Ecclesia*) *Sancti Pauli* 1139-45 to 1281 ChNCP, 1254-75 Val, 1301 *CottR*, c. 1368 RAN, 1428 FA, (*rectoria*) 1535 VE, (*ecclesia*) *de Sco*

Paulo 1301 *CottR*
(*in parochia*) *Sancti Pauli* c. 1270-1300 ChNCP, 1313 *et freq* to 1376
  D&C, (*the parysh, parisshe of*) *Seint powle* 1547 *AOMB*, *St Pawle* 1556
  CG, *St Paule* 1620 *AddCh*, (*in parochia*) *Sancti Pawli* 1623 *ib*, *Sancti*
  Pauli 1615, 1649, 1662 *ib*, (*the parisshe of*) *St Paule* 1620 *ib*, *Saint*
  Paul 1834 *D&C*

This church with the adjoining St Paul's Hospital was dedicated to
St Paul the Apostle and St Paul the first hermit. Blomefield IV 429 f.
The church was destroyed by enemy action in 1942.   *v.* Norman's
Hospital, Norman's Lane and St Paul's Square.

ST PETER HUNGATE
(*Ecclesia*) *Sancti Petri de Hundegate* 1254-75 Val, 1479 Past, *de*
  Hondegate c. 1368 *RAN*, *de Hundgate* 1428 FA, *Seynt Peters of*
  Hundgate 1479 Past, (*the cherch of*) *Seint Petre of Hungate* 1482 *ib*,
  (*rectoria*) *Sancti Petri de Hungate* 1535 VE, *Sainte Peters of*
  Houndgate 1556 *CG*
(*in parochia*) *Sancti Petri de Hundegate* 1248 *et freq* to 1435 *NPD*, 1277
  et freq to 1442 *D&C*, 1285 to 1294 *R*, *de Houndegate* 1322, 1413 *NPD*,
  1385, 1393 *D&C*, (*the parissh of*) *Seint Peter of Hungate* 1482 *AddR*,
  Saint Peter of Hungate 1620 *D&C*

The present church (now a museum) dates from 1460. It is the
successor to an older church which was demolished. In 1458 John
Paston and Margaret, his wife, received the advowson of the rectory.
Blomefield IV 329 ff. *v.* Princes Street.

ST PETER MANCROFT
(*Ecclesia*) *Sancti Petri de Manecroft* 1254-75 Val, (*cimiterium*) 1289 *R*,
  (*ecclesia*) *Sancti Petri de Manecroft* 1292 to 1298 *ib*, *Sancti Petri de*
  Mancroft(*e*) 1337 *OR*, c. 1368 (2x) RAN, 1428 FA, (*ecclesia*) *Sancti*
  Petri 1479 Worcestre, (*rectoria*) *Sancti Petri in Mancrofte* 1535 VE,
  1545 *MinAcct*
(*parochia*) *Sancti Petri de Mannecroft* 1280 *LansdCh*, 1282 *Phillipps*,
  1294 *AddCh*, *de Manecroft* 1285 *et freq* to 1298 *R*, 1370 *Phillipps*, *de*
  Mannescroft 1316 *HarlCh*, *de Mancroft* 1407 *AddCh*, 1531 *Phillipps*,
  1537 *MinAcct*, *de Mancrofte* 1568 *NPD*, (*the parish of*) *seint Peter of*
  Mancroft 1547 *AOMB*

The present church was begun in 1430 on the site of an older one and was finished in 1455.   Blomefield IV 184 ff.   *v.*   Market Place, Mancroft.

ST PETER PARMOUNTERGATE

(*Ecclesia*) *Sancti Petri in Parmenterestrete* 1254-75 Val, *de Permontergate* c. 1368 RAN, 1428 FA, (*rectoria*) *Sancti Petri de Montergate* 1535 VE, (*the churche of*) *seint pettr permontgate* 1547 *AOMB*

(*in parochia*) *Sancti Petri de Parmentergate* 1269 *Ass*, 1286 to 1660 *D&C*, 1287 *et freq* to 1312 *R*, 1302 to 1395 K, 1355 Bodl, *Parmenter*(*e*)*sgate* (2x) Hy3 K, *de Parmetergate* 1291 to 1361 *D&C*, *Sancti Petri de Parmontergate* 1377 K, 1516 to 1535 *D&C*, *Parmountergate* 1393 K, 1494, 1613 *NPD*, *Permontergate* 1428 FA, 1537 to 1660 *NPD*, (*in the parissh of*) *Seint Petir of Parmontergate* 1516 *D&C*, *Seint Petre of Parmontergate* 1522 *ib*, *seint* (*seynt*) *Petir Parmontergate* 1552, 1553 *CG*, *St Peter Parmontergate* 1556 *ib*

A rectory in the patronage of Roger Bigot, who gave it to the Priory of Norwich (Blomefield IV 91 ff.).   The monks rebuilt the church in 1486 (Pevsner 252).   *v.* Mountergate -- St Faith's Lane.

ST PETER SOUTHGATE

(*ecclesia*) *sancti Petri in Cuningesford/Cunggesforde/Cuningefordia* 1175-86 to 1190-1200 Holme, (*Ecclesia*) *Sancti Petri de Suthgate* 1254-75 Val, 1322 *D&C*, *de Southgate* c. 1368 RAN, 1428 FA, 1521 *NPD*, (*rectoria*) *Sancti Petri de Southgate* 1535 VE

(*in parochia*) *Sancti Petri de Suthgate* 1257 *Ass*, 1269 *NPD*, 1285 to 1292 *R*, *de Southgate* 1296 to 1429 *NPD*, 1350 Pat, 1428 FA, 1535 VE, *de Sudgate* 1269 *Ass*, *de Sugate* 1269 *ib*

This church at the south end of King Street (*prope portam ciuitatis Norwici* 1175-86 Holme) was demolished in 1887.   Only a small part of the tower remains.   Blomefield IV 65 ff.   *v.* Southgate Lane.

ST SAVIOUR

(*Ecclesia*) *sancti Salvatoris* 1186-1200 to 1281 ChNCP, *Sancti Saluatoris* 1254-75 Val, 1337, 1340 *OR*, *Salvatoris* c. 1368 RAN, 1428 FA,

(*rectoria*) *Sancti Salvat' in Fybrygge* (*Sylvat' in Fybrygge*) 1535 VE

(*in parochia*) *Sancti Saluatoris* 1287 to 1296 *R*, *Sancti Salvatoris* 1559

NPD, (the parisshe of) St Savyors 1556 *CG*

The dedication is to the Transfiguration of Christ. Blomefield IV 443 ff. *v.* St Saviour's Lane.

SS SIMON AND JUDE

(*Ecclesia*) *Sanctorum Simonis & Jude* 1086 DB
(*Ecclesia*) *Sanctorum Simonis et Jude* 1285 *et freq* to 1298 *R,* 1366
     MinAcct, 1404, 1541 *D&C, (in parochia) Simonis & Jude* 1537
     MinAcct, (the parish of) saynt Symond' & Jude 1547 *AOMB, St*
     Symon and Jude 1556 *CG, Saint Simon & Jude* 1591 *AddCh, Saint*
     Simon and Jude 1769 *Phillipps*

This was the Bishop's own church before the see was moved to Norwich. It is now used for secular purposes. Simon and Jude are two saints of the first century who are always commemorated together (Farmer 225, 357 f.). Blomefield IV 353 ff.

ST STEPHEN

apud Norwycum ad monasterium sancti Stephani 1114-6 Holme,
     (*Ecclesia*) *Sancti Stephani* 1155 *et freq* to 1325 ChNCP, 1254-75 Val,
     (*cimiterium*) 1289 *R (ecclesia)* 1317 *D&C,* 1337 *OR,* c. 1368 RAN,
     1428 FA, 1535 VE, *Seint Stephenes Chirche in Norwiche* 1437 Past
(*in parochia*) *Sancti Stephani (in Nedham)* 13 *Phillipps,* 1270 *et freq* to
     1470 *D&C,* 1285 *et freq* to 1296 *R,* 1537, 1545 *MinAcct*

The dedication is to St Stephen, the first Martyr. This church was founded before the Conquest but was rebuilt in the 16th century. Blomefield IV 145 ff. *v.* St Stephen's Street and Plain.

ST SWITHIN

(*Ecclesia*) *Sancti Swithuni* 1254-75 Val, 1428 FA, *Sancti Swythuni* c.
     1368 RAN, (*rectoria*) *Sancti Swithuni* 1535 VE
(*in parochia*) *Sancti Swythini* 1288 (5x) *R, Sancti Swythuni* 1292, 1294
     R, (the parysshe of) sent Swythune 1547 *AOMB, (the parisshe of) St*
     Swythons 1556 *CG*

This church is now used for secular purposes. It had its tower pulled down in 1870. St Swithin or Swithun (d. 862) was Bishop of Winchester (Farmer 365). Blomefield IV 251 ff. *v.* St Swithin's

Alley.

ST VEDAST

(*Ecclesia*) *sancti Vedasti* 1157 to 1281 ChNCP, *Sanctorum Vedasti et*
    Amandi 1254-75 Val, *Sancti Vedasti* 1337, 1340 *OR,* c. 1368 RAN,
    1428 FA, (*rectoria*) *Sancti Devasti* (sic) 1535 VE
(*parochia*) *Sancti Vedasti* 1285 *et freq* to 1298 *R,* 1285 to 1467 *D&C,* (*in*
    Norwyco) 113, 1435, 1484 *HarlCh,* (*in vico de Conesford inferiori in*
    Norwico) 1523 *AddCh*

The dedication is to two Flemish saints, St Vedast (Vaast) and St
Amand, which suggests Flemish connections or a Flemish colony. The
name was confused with that of St Faith the Virgin (*v.* Mountergate --
St Faith's Lane). The church was founded before the Conquest; a
pre-Conquest cross shaft was found in the 19th century built into a
house on the site of the church (NfA 10:140, 13:116). The church was
pulled down in 1540 and the parish was united to that of St Mary in the
Marsh until both were united to St Peter Parmountergate in 1564.
Blomefield IV 105 f.

RELIGIOUS HOUSES, HOSPITALS, SCHOOLS AND
OTHER BUILDINGS

ABRAHAM'S HALL (lost)

the messuage of Abraham the Jew 1248 NoRec, *Abrahameshalle* 1346 *ib,*
    Abrammeshalle (2x) c. 1397 *ib, Abrahammeshalle* 1397 *ib,*
    Abrahamall 1398 *ib, Habramhall in Norwich* 1401 Pat, *Abraham's*
    Hall c. 1720 K, 1746 B, *Abrahams Inn* 1766 King

This house fronted north on the Haymarket (now Hay Hill) and
south on the Horsemarket (now Rampant Horse Street), and the
parish boundary between St Peter Mancroft and St Stephen's ran
through it from east to west. It had its name from a Jew, *Abraham*
filius Deulecresse (i.e. *Dieu l'accroisse,* a translation of the Jewish name
Gedalaya; v. PN O xlvi), who was executed in 1279 on a charge of
coin-clipping and blasphemy (Blomefield IV 184, Lipman 171). In
the eighteenth century there was an inn on the site with Abraham
offering up his son as its sign (K 29).

ASSEMBLY HOUSE, *v.* College of St Mary in the Fields.

AUSTIN FRIARS (lost)
fratres Sancti Augustini 1290 NoLeet, *de ordine de S. Augustino* 1290
    NoRec, *fratribus Sancti Augustini* 1302 *NAR,* (*longitudo ecclesie*)
    fratrum Sancti Augustini Norwici,...fratrum Augustinensium 1479
    Worcestre, *fratres Augustinienses* 1480 *ib*

The Austin friars were established in the parish of St Michael
Conesford early in the reign of Edward I on a site given to them by
Roger Miniot.   In 1368 they acquired the church of St Michael
Conesford, which they demolished to make room for their own
establishment.   After the Dissolution this establishment became
private property in 1547.   It soon came into the hands of the Duke of
Norfolk; the monastic buildings were demolished, and the area was
turned into gardens by Lord Henry Howard (hence *my Lord's gardens*
c. 1720 K, *the Lord's Gardens* c. 1725 K^2, *My Lords Gardens* 1766
King).   *v.* St Anne Lane and Blomefield IV 85 ff.

BETHEL HOSPITAL
Bethel or *Bedlam* 1746 B, *Bethel* 1766 King, 1789 H, *Bethel Hospital*
    1830 M&M, 1845 White

The Bethel Hospital was built in 1712-3 by Mary Chapman, wife of
the Rev. Samuel Chapman, rector of Thorpe by Norwich, 'for the
convenient reception and habitation of Lunaticks, and not for
natural-born fools or ideots (sic)' (Blomefield IV 236). Alterations to
the original building were made in 1807 and later. *v.* Bethel Street.

BLACK FRIARS (lost)
fratribus predicatoribus 1248 NoRec, 1272 *Will,* (*iuxta portas*) *fratrum*
    predicatorum 1313 NoLeet, *de domo Fratrum Praedicatorum Norvici*
    1413 K^2, *in the chyrche of the Frer' Prechowrys* 1451 *ib,* (*longitudo*
    navis) *ecclesie fratrum predicatorum* 1480 Worcestre, *the chapell of*
    our Lady of the Fryer Precheours, the Black Freres 1502 K^2, *the*
    convent of the Blak Frers 1509 *ib*

The Black Friars were originally (1226) established north of the
river, in the vicinity of Colegate. In 1307 they acquired the site of the
Sack Friars (friars *de penitentia*), situated south of the river, when the

latter order was dissolved by the Pope, and here a Dominican Friary
was built. The abandoned site became known as Old Friars' Yard (*the
Oldefreres yerd ... iuxta vicum vocat' Colgate* 1380 *NPD, the late
Blackfriers Garden* c. 1720 K). *v.* further Tillyard 6 ff. On the later
history of the Dominican Friary, *v.* St Andrew's Hall.

BOYS' AND GIRLS' HOSPITAL SCHOOLS -- ST GEORGE'S CHAPEL

The house called the Children's Hospital(l) 1623 NoRec, (*The*) *Boys
    Hospital*(*l*) 1696 Cleer, 1746 B, 1766 King, 1830 M&M, *Boy's
    Hospital* 1789 H, *The Boys' and Girls' Hospital Schools* 1819 Stacy,
    1845 White

The Children's Hospital or Boys' Hospital, founded c. 1620 with
money bequeathed by Thomas Anguish, finally Mayor of the City (*v.*
Blomefield IV 407 ff.), stood on the north side of Fishergate. In 1802
it was united with the Girls' Hospital (*q.v.*). The building is now a
Roman Catholic church (St George's Chapel-of-Ease). Past the north
side of the Hospital there used to flow a water-course (*v.* Spiteldike).

BREWHOUSE (lost), (a house called) *le Brewhous* 1347 *NPD* (in the
lost parish of St Matthew, near St Martin at Palace Plain), *le Brewehus*
1349 *ib.*

CALK MILLS (lost)

Calk milnes 1186-1210 Holme, *Calkmilles* 1291 NoLeet, 1299 *R,* 1346
    NoRec, *Calkemills* 1341 K, *Calkemylles* 1391 (p) NoLeet, *Le
    Calkemyll* 1422 NoRec
(*water called*) *Calkmille-dam* 1329 *R*

These mills may have been situated at the end of a lost lane out of
Coslany Street -- Oak Street called Water Lane (K 73). It is possible,
however, that they were across the river, on the Heigham side.   *v.*
Water Lane[2].   OE (Angl) **calc** 'chalk', OE **myl(e)n** 'mill'.

CARDINAL'S HAT (lost), (*void ground once edified by Andrew Mase
    called the*) *Cardinals Hatt* 1627, 1670, 1673 *D&C.*

The whereabouts is not known, but it is worthy of note that there
was an alehouse called *The Cardinal's Hat* or *Cap* just west of the

junction of Ten Bell Lane with St Benedict's Street. There is a tradition that this sign commemorated Cardinal Wolsey's visits to Norwich in 1517 and in 1520 (Wicks 103, Riddington Young 32).

CITY GAOL (lost), *(the) City Goal* 1746 B, 1789 H, *Goal* 1766 King. To the north of the Market Place, between St Giles Street and London Street, stood the Gaol, which had earlier been a building owned by the Gild of St George, called the Lambe or the Lambe Inn: *(ad domum vocatum, hospicio vocato,* etc.) *Le Lambe* 1504 to 1515 NfRS 9, *the Lambe grounde* 1537 *ib.* This property was acquired by the Gild in 1504 (NfRS 9:22).   Another prison was built in 1827 outside St Giles's Gate in Unthank Road (on the site of the present RC Cathedral). This second City Gaol was replaced by the present one (on Mousehold Heath) in 1881.   The site of the Lambe Inn is now occupied by the one-time Norwich Subscription Library.   The street between the site of the old Gaol and the Guildhall is called GUILDHALL HILL, but the part that is south of the Guildhall is called GAOL HILL.

COLLEGE OF ST MARY IN THE FIELDS or CHAPEL FIELD HOUSE (lost)

Capella Beate Marie de Campis 1254-75 Val, 1287, 1288, 1289 R, *(ad terram) Capelle Beate Marie in Campis* (2x) 1268 *D&C, (ad emendationem)* 1272 *WillD, Capella Sce Marie Collegiat' in Campis* 1372 *NPD, (Decanus) Ecclesie (Collegiate) Beate Marie de (in) Campis* 1385 to 1429 *NPD,* 1416, 1420, 1430 *NAR, (Maistre del) Chapel in þe Felde* 1406 *ANLett, the Chapell of Feld* 1482 Past, *Collegium Beate Marie de Campis* 1520, 1553 *NPD, the College of oure blessed lady in Norwich called the chapell of the felde* 1530 *NPD, (Magistro) capelle in Campis in Norwico* 1535 VE, *Capell' in campis iuxta Norwicum* 1545 *MinAcct, the late college of our lady in the fyld* 1547 *AOMB*

Cruftum Capelle Beate Marie de Campis 1285 to 1306 *R, Cruftum Beate Marie in Campis* 1301, 1303 (2x), 1304 *ib, le Chapel Croft* 1332 K, *Chapelle of Field Croft* 1507 *ib, Chapell of Feld Crofft* 1541, 1565 *ib, le Chappell Felde Croftes* 1549 Pat, *Chapile fylde croftes* 1568 *NPD, Chappile filde croftes* 1569 *ib, Chappel a fyeld Crofte* 1583 *ib*

(in) campo de Capella beate Marie de Campis 1287 *R, (in) camp' capelle Beate Marie de Campo* 1313 *NPD, (in) camp' Capelle Collegiate Beate Marie de Camp'* 1485 *NPD, Chappel a feld feld* (sic) 1549 K, *Chapelfield* 1596 Buxton, *Chapply Feild* 1696 Cleer, *Chapel*

Fields 1746 B, *Chapel Field* 1746 B, 1766 King, 1789 H, 1830 M&M,
Chapelfield Gardens 1885 OS

The Chapel of St Mary was built before 1250 and soon became a
college, i.e. a resident community of priests (the first Dean was the
founder, John le Brun); *v.* Blomefield IV 170 ff. At the Dissolution the
College became private property (*v.* NfA 27, 1939-40, 351-84). On the
site of the College (in Theatre Street) now stands the ASSEMBLY
HOUSE, built in 1745; fragments of the College building are to be
found in the west wing of the present building (*v.* Pevsner 261).

According to hand-written information on Cleer's Map (1696), the
Croft and the Field were two separate open spaces. The Croft was
roughly coextensive with the area now bounded by Malthouse Road,
Chantry Road, Chapel Field East and Chapel Field Road (= CHAPEL
FIELD GROVE 1885 OS, 1920 OS 6" Map). The Field was
coterminous with the present CHAPEL FIELD GARDENS.
Differently in Stacy (53). Chapel Field Gardens became a public park
in 1852.

COMMON INN (lost), *at Geywood's* 1382 NoRec, *the Inne* 1394 *ib*, *the
Common Inn* 1440, 1445, 1474 *ib*. In 1384, when the Worsted Seld (*q.v.*)
was established, the municipality acquired from John de Welbourn
most of a block of buildings bounded by Pottergate on the north side,
Stongate Magna (Goat Lane) on the west, Hattere Rowe (Guildhall
Hill) on the south and Holdtor (Dove Lane) on the east. The
southern part of this block was the Common Inn. *Geywood* was the
sitting tenant at the time of the transfer (NoRec II xxxv.).

COOK'S HOSPITAL
Cook's Hospital 1746 B, *Cooks Hospital* 1766 King, 1830 M&M,
Cookes' Hospital 1819 Stacy, *Cooke's Hospital* 1845 White

Cook's Hospital, east of Quakers Lane, originally stood in Rose
Lane. It was built c. 1700 by the brothers Robert and Thomas *Cooke*,
both of whom were aldermen and mayors (Blomefield IV 102 f.). The
removal to the present site took place in 1892.

DOUGHTY'S HOSPITAL
Doughties Hospital 1696 Cleer, *Doughtys Hos.* 1728 Hoyle, *Doughty's
Hospital* 1746 B, 1789 H, 1845 White, *Doughtys Hospital* 1830 M&M

Douglass Hosp 1766 King

Doughty's Hospital, an old people's home, was founded by William Doughty, whose will is dated 15 April 1687 (Blomefield IV 448 f., Stacy 204 f., White 135 f., NoRec II cxv f.). The buildings are west of Calvert Street and north of Golden Dog Lane.

FISH HOUSE (lost)

(*le*) *Fishus* 1272 *NPD*, 1272, 1299 *R, fishouse* 1286 *ib, medietatem cuiusdam Fishhus* 1288 NoRec (St Andrew), *totum Fyshusum nostrum, a predicto Fishuso* (Joh. le Blekstere and his wife sell their fish house in St George Tombland) 1290 *ib, le Fishous* 1323 *R*

OE **fisc.** For *fish house, v.* MED s.v. *fish* 5. The forms quoted refer to more than one fish house. Their exact whereabouts have not been determined. Cf. Elmeswell Lane (earlier *Fishous Lane*).

GIRLS' HOSPITAL (lost)

Barons Hospital 1696 Cleer, *(The) Girls Hospital* 1746 B, 1830 M&M, *Girls Hosp* 1766 King, *Girl's Hospital* 1789 H

The Girls' Hospital, founded in 1649 with money left by Robert *Baron*, stood south of Golden Dog Lane. In 1802 it was united in one establishment with the Boys' Hospital in Fishergate (*v.* Blomefield IV 450 ff., White 127 f., NoRec II cxii ff.). The 1830 form above refers to the old building.

GREAT HOSPITAL

(*fundamus siquidem*) *Hospitale quod dicitur Beati Egidij* 1249 *Ch, Hospit(al)', Hospitale Sci Egidii* c. 1250 *et freq* to 1614 *NPD*, 1254-75 Val, c. 1270, 1296 *TophCh*, 1272-89, 1285 ChNCP, 1282, 1335, 1634 Phillipps, 1287 *et freq* to 1294 *R*, 1292, 1312 *OR*, 1310 *Ch*, 1327, 1340, 1483 *AddCh*, 1430 *NAR, the Hospytall of Seynt Gyle* (*Gile*) 1450 *NPD*, 1550 *CG, St Giles's or Old Men's Hospital* 1746 B, *St Giles Hospital* 1766 King, *St Giles's Hospital* 1789 H, *St Giles's Hospital commonly called the Old Men's Hospital* 1819 Stacy
(*Hospitale*) *Sancti Egidii in vico de Holmestrete* 1428 FA, *manntencionem Pauperum ... the hows of the pore people in vico de holmestrete* 1566 *NPD*
St Hellens Hospital 1696 Cleer

the Great Hospital formerly called St Giles Hospytal c. 1720 K, *Great
    Hospital* 1830 M&M, 1845 White, 1885 OS

Situated to the north of Bishopgate (the former Holmstrete).
Founded in 1249 by Bishop Suffield (*v.* the first quotation) 'to maintain
... all the poor and decrepit chaplains in Norwich diocese, who had not
wherewith to maintain themselves; and also to support thirteen poor
people to be lodged there, and have one meal every day' (cf.
Blomefield IV 381). Within two months of the accession of Edward
VI the Hospital came into the hands of the City (*v.* NoRec II xcix). It
was called the Old Men's Hospital (Blomefield, Stacy), although, in the
mid-18th century, it had fifty male and fifty female inmates (Blomefield
IV 377). The Hospital still continues as an old people's home and the
Hospital Church is still being used.   *v.*   St Helen (Norwich
Churches).

GREY FRIARS (lost)

fratribus minoribus (*de Norwico*) 1248 NoRec, 1272 *WillD,* (*ex opposito*)
    fratrum minorum 1289 NoLeet, *fratres minores* (*de Norwic'*)   1285
    K², 1290 NoLeet, (*longitudo chori ... navis*) *ecclesie fratrum sancti
    Francisci Norwici* 1479 Worcestre, *Fryeris Mynours* 1483 K²,   the
    chirche of St Frawncesse at the Fryers Mynours 1496 *ib*
The New Scite of the Minors or Grey Friers 1746 B

The Grey Friars, also called Franciscans or Friars Minor, settled in
Norwich in 1226. The donor of the site was John de Hastingford.
Their monastery was near the north end of King Street, between the
present St Faith's Lane and Rose Lane. After the suppression of the
friars, in 1539, the site, church, house, other buildings and possessions
of the Grey Friars of Norwich were granted to the Duke of Norfolk by
King Henry VIII. In Kirkpatrick's time (c. 1725) one gate of the
monastery could still be seen (K² 108). *v.* Blomefield IV 196 ff.

GUILDHALL

(*le*) *Gildehall*(*e*) 1407 NoRec, 1413 (3x) *NAR, atte Gyldehalle* 1415
    NoRec, *þe Gild Hall* 1447 *ib, the gyld-hall* 1462 (2x) Past, *þe
    gyldhalle in Norwyche* 1473 *ib, the Gelde Halle* Hy8 K, *the Gylde hall*
    1551 NoRec, *the Guyldhall* 1551, 1554 NoLeet, 1584 NoRec, *the
    Gwildehall* 1570 *ib, the Guylde Haule* 1579 *ib, the Guildehall* 1585
    AddCh, 1595 NoRec, (*the*) *Guild Hall* 1696 Cleer, 1830 M&M, 1845

White, *the Guild-Hall* 1746 B, *the Guild-hall* 1819 Stacy, *Guildhall*
1789 H, 1885 OS
Gilda Aula 1414 *NPD*
(*the*) *Guyhald* 1434 to 1506 NoRec, 1551 NoLeet, *Guihald* 1681, 1682,
     1692 *ib, the Guyhalle* 1511 NoRec
the Yeld Hall 1533, 1534 NoRec, *the Yeldehall* 1540 *ib*
Guldehalle 1535 VE

Built in 1407-13 at the north end of the Market Place (on the site of
the old Tollhouse), repaired in 1511-35 and restored in the 19th c. (*v.*
Pevsner 259).   Like its predecessor, the Tollhouse, the Guildhall was
not only a town hall but also a prison for several hundred years (Dunn
& Sutermeister 1 ff.).

The forms with initial *Y-* represent OE **g(i)eld, gyld** 'association
formed for mutual benefit', those with initial *G(u)-* may represent
MLG, MDu *gilde* 'guild', but derivation from ON **gildi** 'banquet,
guild' is also possible.

HIGH SCHOOLS OF NORWICH (lost)
ex opposito scolarum Norwic (*Norwyc*) 1279, ? 1285 *NPD, le*
     Skolhalleyerd 1361 K, *Skoleyerd* 1529 *NPD, Skooleyard* 1530
     Harrod, *the Skolehousyerd* 1536 *NPD*

This was the old school which was closed down at the Reformation
(Blomefield IV 376), when a new school was opened in the Charnel
House (*v.* Cathedral, Carnary College). Cf. World's End Lane.

HILDEBROND'S HOSPITAL (lost)
hospit. Hyldebrond de Cunegesford c. 1250 *Langley, Hospit.*
     Hildebrondi 1254-75 Val, 1268 *D&C, Hospital'* (*de*) *Hildebrond*
     1263 to 1330 *ib*, 1288 to 1302 *R*, 1347 *OR*, 1400 *NPD, hospital de*
     Hildebronne 1348 *OR*, (hospital called) *Hildebrand* 1385 Pat,
     (Hospital of St Mary Cunesford called) *Ilbrond* 1385 *ib, hosp' de*
     hildebrondes in Conisford 1416 *NAR*
hospit. Sce Marie in parochia sci Edwardi in Conesford 1308 *D&C*

Situated south-east of St Etheldred's Church, approximately where
King Street and Rouen Road now meet. The hospital was founded at
the beginning of the 13th century by Hildebrond the mercer (*H. le*
mercer in Cunesford 1289 *R*) and his wife Maud (Matilda). *v.* NoRec

II xciv.   Dedicated to the Blessed Virgin Mary, it was to give shelter and warmth to poor people and wayfarers.   At a later date the hospital was known as *Ivy Hall* (cf. *Hospital' de Hildebrond voc. Ivy-halle* 1448 K[2], *Chantry of Ivy-halle* 1482 to 1486 *ib*, *le Hospitall al' Ivewall* (sic) *in Norwici* 1535 VE).   The value in the VE of 1535 is only 14*s.*, which suggests that spoilation had perhaps already begun.   The hospital came to the City at the Dissolution. *v.* Blomefield IV 71 f.

HOSPITAL OF SAINT SAVIOUR (lost), *Hospital' Sancti Saluatoris in Coselanye* 1298 *R*, (*ad sustentacionem*) *unius Hospitalis ... in honore S. Saluatoris* 1306 NoRec. This hospital seems never to have come into existence for the testator's legacy was transferred to some other purpose in 1306 (NoRec II xciv and 17).

MUSIC HOUSE
the great messuage of Isaac the Jew in Conesford 1260 Lipman, *the great Messuage in St Audrey's Parish known by the name of the Musick House* c. 1720 K, *Isaac's Hall or the Musick House* 1746 B, *Music House* 1766 King, 1789 H, 1885 OS

Built c. 1175 for Jurnet the Jew, this house in King Street was the home of the Jurnet family for four generations (Lipman 112).   The undercroft of the original building is well preserved and now forms part of WENSUM LODGE (Pevsner 272).
On Cleer's Map (1696) *Isaakes Hall* has been added by hand. Isaac was Jurnet's son.   The name *Music House* does not occur until the eighteenth century.   E.A. Kent (NfA 28, 1942, 37 ff.) suggests that the Norwich Waits (an official band of musicians and singers maintained by the City) made use of the house for their rehearsals.   MUSIC HOUSE LANE, which connects King Street to Rouen Road, used to be part of Horns Lane.

NORMAN'S HOSPITAL or ST PAUL'S HOSPITAL (lost)
hospit' pauperum de Sco Paulo (*de Norwico/Norwyco*) Hy1, Steph
    Ch, 1121-33, 1135-40,1163-6 ChNCP, *hospit'* (*pauperum*) *Sci Pauli*
    (*de Norwico/Norwyco*) 1186-1200, 1199-1203 *et freq ib*, J *Ch*, 1262
    D&C, 1301 *CottR*, *hospit*(*al*)*' Sci Pauli* c. 1285 *et freq* to 1492
    D&C, *hospital' de Sco Paulo* 1301 *CottR*, 1312 to 1390 *OR*
Poulis Hospital 1415 NoRec

Normannespitel 1268 FF, *Normanspital, Normannesspitel* 13 *D&C,*
   Normanespitel 1286 *Ass,* 1315, 1322 *D&C,* 1322 *R, Normanspetil*
   1307 *ib, Normanspitel* 1305 QW, 1311, 1318 *R,* 1342 *AddCh,*
   Normanispetel 1403 *D&C (at) Normans in Norwich* 1482 Past
hospit' Normanni 13, 1313, 1314 *D&C,* 1324 K, (*magister*) *hospitalis*
   Noreman 1272-80 ChNCP
Ecclesia Sancti Pauli cum hospitali quod dicitur Normanyspytell 1368
   RAN, *Hospit' Sci Pauli voc' Normans* 1370 *D&C, hospit' Sci*
   Pauli voc' Normannys 1414 *ib, hospit' Sci Pauli Normanis* 1459
   ib, hospit' Sci Pauli Normann' 1459 (2x) *ib, the hospitall of Seint*
   Paule cleped Normannys 1428 Chichele
Scite of the Normans or St Pauls Hospital 1746 B, *site of Norman's*
   Hospital 1819 Stacy

The church and hospital of St Paul were founded in the time of
Bishop Herbert and finished under his successor, Bishop Eborard (the
middle of the 12th cent.).   The addition *Norman's* is from the first
master (on the origin of the name, *v.* Feilitzen s.v. *Norðmann,* 331 f.).
On the dissolution of the Priory, no more masters were appointed,
but the hospital remained for a short time as such.   In 1571 it
came to the City and was turned into a bridewell.   Blomefield IV
429 ff.; Stacy 198 f.; *v.* also Normans Lane and Spitellond.

NORWICH SCHOOL, *v.* Carnary College, Cathedral Close.

NORWICH UNION BUILDING, *v.* Surrey House.

POPINGAY INN (lost), *the Popingaye* 1626 BLR, *the Popingay Corner*
c. 1720 K, (a private residence, not an inn in the modern sense of the
word) stood at the west end of Ratton Row (Tombland).   It was
named after the Popingay family (cf. Roger *Papunjay* 1316 K, Robertus
Papungay 1376 *ib*).   Roger *Papinjay* owned the house in 1330
(Blomefield IV 117).   OF *papegai, papingay* 'parrot'.

PRINCE'S INN (lost)
tenement late the Princesin 1397 NoRec, *ten' vocat' le Prince Inne*
   1414 *NPD, þe Prince Inne* 1456 Past, *Prynces Inne* 1535 NoRec

The Prince's Inn was situated along the east side of the little
alley-way today called Plumbers Arms Alley, mentioned in K 61

('another Lane which ran North ..., between the Mess: called the
Princes Inn East and another Mess: West'). The Prince's Inn was
the private city residence of the Paston family (cf. Popingay Inn and
Segores Inn). The Pastons later moved to the house in King Street
which was to become the Ship Inn (*q.v.*).

ROME HALL (lost), (*mes' vocat'*) *Romehall*(*e*) 1349, 1360, 1394 *NPD*,
1530 Harrod, *Rome Hall* 1766 King, was a building situated east of St
Martin at Palace in the now lost World's End Lane (*q.v.*).   According
to Harrod (248) 'there are several instances of a large piece of land in
the neighbourhood of a monastery being called "Romeland" and houses
upon them being called "Romeland Houses".' Possibly the Grammar
School was actually housed in Rome Hall (Harrod *ib*, Knights 106).   Cf.
Rome Land Ess (*Roumelond* 1331 PN Ess 30), Romeland Hrt (*terra
voc. Roumland* c.   1275 PN Hrt 88) and Romeland at Billingsgate,
London, explained by Reaney as 'empty, unoccupied land' (PN Ess *ib*).
v. OE rūm[2] 'roomy, spacious'.   The modern form may be due to
popular association with Rome and Rome Hall due to ellipsis of
Romeland Hall, not uncommon in toponymical formation.

ROYAL ARCADE -- ARCADE STREET, *a grounde ... called the
Angell* 1535 NoRec, *Angel Inn* 1766 King,   1830 M&M, *Angel Yard* 1789
H, *Angel yard, now Royal Hotel street* 1845 White, *Royal Hotel* 1885 OS.
The Arcade runs from the Walk to Castle Street.   It was constructed in
1899-1900 on the site of the old *Angel Inn*, which had been renamed the
Royal Hotel in 1840 on the occasion of Queen Victoria's marriage
(Riddington Young 39 ff.).   Arcade Street, from Castle Meadow to the
back of the Arcade, is *Angel Street* on the 1885 OS Map.

SACK FRIARS (lost), *Fratres de Sacco* 1254-75 Val, *fratribus de Sacco*
1272 *WillD*. The Sack Friars, *fratres de penitentia* or *de sacco*, were
settled in Norwich, in the parish of St Peter Hungate, shortly after
1250.   Their area was increased but in 1307, when this order was
suppressed by order of the Pope, their site was taken over by the Black
Friars. *v.* Tillyard 6.

ST ANDREW'S HALL
the place late cald the Blacke Fryers, now cald the Common Halle 1542
   K[2], *the Com*(*m*)*on Hall* 1543 *et freq* to 1551 NoRec, *the Common-
hall* 1819 Stacy

the Hall late the Blak Freres 1548 NoRec
New Hall 1696 Cleer, 1766 King, *the Newhall & the rest of the Black
  Fryers Precinct* c. 1720 K
the Common-hall, called St Andrew's-hall 1745 B, *St Andrew's Hall* 1789
  H, 1845 White, 1885 OS, *St Andrews Hall and Chapel* 1830 M&M

This is the old conventual church of the Dominican, or Black, Friars,
situated on the north side of St Andrew's Plain. It is the second
Dominican church on this site, completed in 1470 according to Pevsner
(260). (The first was destroyed by fire in 1413.) When the monasteries
were dissolved, this church was converted into a city hall, sometimes
called the *New Hall* to distinguish it from the Guildhall in the Market
Place. The chancel (*the chapell of Saynt John* 1543, 1548 NoRec) was
separated from the nave when the steeple that connected the two fell
down in 1712. The chancel, which is now known as BLACKFRIARS
HALL, served for long periods as a Dutch church. *v.* Blomefield IV
339 ff.

ST GEORGE'S INN (lost), (*hospicium vocatum*) *le George Inne* 1501
et freq to 1526 NfRS 9, *the George Inne* 1529, 1530, 1531 *ib.* Property
in the parish of SS Simon and Jude near Fye Bridge owned by the Gild
of St George (NfRS 9:21).

SEGORES INN (lost), *tenementum vocat' Segores* 1568 *NPD,
Segores-inn* 1586 B. William *Segore* is known to have had a house in
the vicinity of Orford Hill 'next the Castle Dikes' R2 (K 20. A
tenement called *Segoresinn* was given in 1586 to St John's Timberhill
(Blomefield IV 129).

SHIP INN, *Ship Inn* 1885 OS. The Pastons moved from the Prince's
Inn (*q.v.*) to a house in King Street which was later to become the Ship
Inn (opposite the Music House). They took with them the 'sign' of the
Prince's Inn, a carved beam containing the name and Early
Renaissance decoration, and placed it as a lintel above the entrance to
their new home (Knights 23, Pevsner 272).

SHIRE HALL, *the Shire Hall* 1845 White, *Shirehall* 1885 OS, in
Market Avenue, to the east of the Castle. Built in 1822-3 in succession
to a shirehouse that adjoined the Castle on the north side. This old
shirehouse (built in 1578-9) had been destroyed by fire in 1746 and

rebuilt three years later on the same site (Stacy 86, White 90 f.). For
the medieval Curia Comitatus (south of the Castle), *v.* Norwich Castle
supra.

LE STERRE (lost), (*in hospicio, mesuagium vocatum*, etc.) *le Sterre*
1497 to 1516 NfRS 9, *the Stergrounde* 1532 *ib*, *the Sterre grounde* 1547 *ib*,
refers to property on Tombland owned by the Gild of St George which
the Gild had acquired before 1420 (NfRS 9:21).

STONE HOUSE (lost), (*de tenemento meo et domibus meis que*
    vocantur) *le stonhus* 13 *D&C*, (one house before the gates of the
    Monastery called) *le Stonhowse* R2 NoRec, (a Mess. formerly
    called) *Stonhall* c. 1720 K

The D&C document concerns a rent of 6*s.* paid by Simon de
Stonhus to the Cellarer of the Cathedral Priory. The Stone House
belonged to the Priory and Simon was the sitting tenant. It stood on
the site of the Earl's Palace, which Bishop Herbert had caused to be
pulled down in the last decade of the 11th century (*v.* NoRec I xii, 53
f.). Other entries *stonhus*, etc., in the records have not been included.

SURREY HOUSE (lost), *Surrey-house* c.1720 K, 1745 B, *Surrey House*
1766 King, 1845 White, 1885 OS. East of Great Newgate (*v.* Surrey
Street) the Poet Earl of Surrey had a palace built in the 1540s.
Nothing is left of it. The Norwich Union Building, erected in 1904,
stands on the site of the old palace (*v.* Pevsner 278 f.).

TOLLHOUSE (lost)
(*in*) *theolonio Norwici* 1274 NoRec, (*in prisona*) *tholonii Norwici* 1276
    ib, *Theolonium* 1287 K, (*ad*) *Teolonium* 1288 NoRec, (*in domo*)
    theolonii Norwici 1290 *ib*, (*dom'*) *Theolon'* 1295 to 1376 *NAR*, (*in*)
    tholonio 1368 NoRec
Tolboth 1250 K, 1286 NoRec, *Tolbooth* 1376 *ib*
Le Tolhus 1295, 1303 *NAR*, (*Le*) *Tolhous(e)* 1382, 1385 (2x) *D&C*,
    1386, 1387 *NAR*, Hy4 K

MLat *theoloneum, theolonium* 'toll'. This house stood on the site of
the present Guildhall. The latter building was erected soon after 1404
when Norwich became a county (Dunn & Sutermeister 1 f.). The
Tollhouse was not only used for fiscal purposes but was also a law court

and a prison (cf. the 1276 quotation).

WENSUM LODGE, *v.* Music House.

WESTWICK or APPLEYARD'S MILLS (lost)
dimidium molendini de Westwyk 1175-86 Holme, *inter molendinum de*
    Westwic et stratam pupplicam que iacet versus Hecham 1186-1210 *ib*
Westwic or Appleyerds Mills 1746 B

These mills were situated near Heigham Gate and can be traced
back to the 12th century. In the 15th century they belonged to the
Appleyard family; *v.* Blomefield IV 505 and Bridewell Alley.

WHITE FRIARS (lost)
fratribus de Carmelo 1272 *WillD, ex opposito fratrum Carmelitanorum*
    1288 NoLeet, *iuxta fratr' Carmlit'* 1413 *NAR, ecclesie fratrum*
    Carmelitarum 1479 Worcestre
The Priory 1696 Cleer, *Scite of the White Friers* 1746 B, *The Friery* 1766
    King

The Carmelites or White Friars had their monastery (founded in
1256) to the east of Cowgate (on the north bank of the river), on a site
given them by a Norwich merchant, Philip son of Warine (who
assumed the name *de Cowgate*). The house was suppressed in 1543,
whereupon it came into private hands. Now the Jarrold printing works
(a former yarn mill) stands on the site of the monastery (Pevsner 269).
v. Cowgate and Whitefriars Bridge. Blomefield IV 414 ff.

WORSTED SELD (lost)
le Worstedeceeld 1398 *NAR, worsted celd* 1416 *ib, le Worstedeceld* 1421
    ib, le Wurstedecelde 1430 *ib*

This was the northern part of Welbourn's messuage (along
Pottergate), bought by the municipality in 1384 (cf. Common Inn).
Blomefield (III 113) quotes an ordinance of 1388 which said 'that no
citizen should buy any worsteds of any country weavers, in the city
liberties, without they set their chests in the messuage late John de
Welbourn's, now called the Worsted-Celde'; *v.* also NoRec II xxxv f.,
233 ff., Campbell 15. *Worsted* was originally a fabric from Worstead
Nf; ME *seld* 'shop, stall', OE **seld** 'abode', a metathetic form of **setl**

'seat' (*v.* OED s.v.).

FIELDS, GARDENS, OPEN PLACES AND OTHER CITY
AREAS

ADAM and EVE GARDENS (lost), *ye Garden called Adam & Eves Garden* c. 1720 K, *Adam and Eve's Gardens* 1745 B, *Adam & Eve Gardens* 1830 M&M, 1885 OS. These Gardens (on the site of the Old Norwich Schools, *v.* World's End Lane) took their name from one of the oldest inns still in business in Norwich. It stands off Bishopgate.

ANGLIA SQUARE, a shopping precinct west of Magdalen Street, near the point where Botolph Street and Magdalen Street used to meet (Stump Cross).

BUTTER HILLS
(land which was) *John le Botelers* 1175-86 FK, (land at) *Botelers hill* 1175-86 *ib,* *Botelereshil* 1298 R, *Botelleres hil* 1299 *ib,* *Botylereshil* 1311 *ib, le Butelereshil* 1322 D&C, *Boteleris Hilles* 1361 K
Botylerehil 1304 R, *Butlerhilles or vulgarly Butterhills* 1521 *NPD, terr' voc' Butterhill'* 1537 *MinAcct, Butter Hills* 1711 ECC, 1746 B, 1766 King, 1789 H, *Butter Hill* 1830 M&M

Named after an ancient owner, John *le Boteler* (*v.* the first quotation, K 9, and Blomefield IV 68), the Butter Hills area originally extended from Carrow Hill in the south to Holgate, i.e. Mariners Lane, in the north (*v.* K 9). Now the name *Butter Hills* is restricted to the area south of Southgate Lane; north of Southgate Lane is RICHMOND HILL (1830 M&M, 1885 OS, 1920 OS 6" Map). A pub of that name stood near the remains of Ber Street Gate (Nobbs 10).

CHAPEL FIELD GARDENS, *v.* College of St Mary in the Field.

DOSIES DOLE (lost)
Dosies dole 1297 R, *dosyesdole* 1313, 1319 *ib, Dowzisdole* 1352 K, *Douzis del* 1357 *ib, Doses Dole Closse* 1626 BLR, *Dosys Dole* 1746 B, 1766 King

A piece of land near the site of St Benedict's Gate, north of St

Benedict's Street, within the ancient wall. *Dosi* is probably the ODan personal name *Dūsi; v.* DEPN s.n. *Dowsby,* Reaney s.n. *Dowsing. Dole* is OE **dāl** 'share'.

GILDENCROFT, *v.* Streets.

HORSEFAIR, *the Horse Fair* c. 1720 K, *Old Horse Fair* 1766 King, *Horse fair* 1845 White, *the Horsefair* 1885 OS, *Horse Fair Green* 1887 Knights, is a triangular patch of grass at the junction of St Faith's Lane with Cathedral Street. The horsemarket was probably moved here from Rampant Horse Street (*q.v.*). The livestock market south of the Castle (*v.* Cattle Market Street) started being used c. 1740, hence *Old* Horse Fair on King's Map.

JAMES STUART GARDENS, situated in the bend formed by St Faith's Lane and Recorder Road. *James Stuart,* a Cambridge professor of Scottish descent, married into the Coleman family and settled in Norwich towards the end of the nineteenth cent. He made additions to Carrow Abbey, where he lived, and also benefited the City in other ways.

JEWRY (lost)
in Iudaismo 1273 *OR, extra Iudaismum* 1273 *ib, in iudaismo Norwici*
    1276 NoRec, *in vico de Iudaismo* 1285 *R,* (*excepto*) *Iudaismo* 1285
    D&C, in Iudeismo 1288 NoLeet
la Jurye (p) 1288 NoLeet
[*h*]*ortus Scole Iudeorum* 1293 NoRec, *introitus Scole Iudeorum* 1293 *ib*

The Jews of medieval Norwich dwelt in the White Lion area. They chose this place because it was close to the Castle, in which they could take refuge in case of a pogrom. The *Scola Iudeorum,* their synagogue, was near the present Orford Place. MLat *iudaismus* 'Jews, Jews' quarter', AF *juierie* 'Jews, Jews' quarter'.

ST CATHERINE'S CLOSE
Seynte Katerynes Croft 1378, 1390 K, *St Katherine's Closse* 1626 BLR, *St*
    Catherine's Close 1746 B, 1766 King, 1830 M&M, 1885 OS, 1920
    OS 6" Map, *Little Chapply Field* c. 1720 K.

This was earlier a field between Little Newgate (St   Catherine's

Lane) and the City Wall (*v.* Surrey Street). Today *St Catherine's Close* is the name of a notable house in All Saints Green, built shortly after 1778 (Pevsner 266). It is used by the BBC as their East Anglia Centre.

ST PAUL'S SQUARE, between Willis Street and St Crispin's Road. On the east side of the square there is a playground, the former site of St Paul's Church, which was destroyed by enemy action during the 1939-45 war.

SCOLES GREEN (lost)
Skolds Green 1615 K, *Skouldsgreene* 1626 BLR, *Skoulds Green* 1628 K,
    Skowlds Green 1635 *ib*, *Skoldes-green* 1643 *ib*, *Scold's Green* 1746 B
Schole Green 1696 Cleer, *Scoles Green* 1766 King, 1789 H, 1830 M&M,
    1845 White, 1885 OS, *Scole's-green* 1819 Stacy
St Martin's Green 1638 K, 1746 B

An open space that was situated at the east end of the lost Rising Sun Lane (*q.v.*). Kirkpatrick (12 f.) derives the name from one William *Scoles* (Scole, from ON **skáli** 'hut', is a Nf village), who held property here in 1470, but this explanation does not account for the *d* of the earliest forms. The considerable time gap between the 1470 document and the first recorded instance of the place-name is another difficulty. This place was not far from St Martin in the Bailey.

SPITELLOND (lost)
Spitellond(e) 1277 ChNCP, 1294 *NAR*, 1477 NoRec, *Spitelonde* 1333
    SR, *Spitlond* 1424, 1473 NoRec, *Spitillonde* 1428 FA
Normanslond R2, 1442 (2x) NoRec, *Normansland* 1492 *ib*

This was the land within the precinct of St Paul's Hospital (*q.v.*), coextensive with the ancient parish of St Paul, bounded on the north and east by Cowgate, on the west by Tolthorp Lane (now Peacock Street - - Blackfriars Street) and on the south by Spiteldike. (Not to be confused with the place called Spitalfields between St James Hill and Ketts Hill, outside the old City Wall.)

WYKEREFELD (lost), *Wicherefeld* 1153-68 Holme, (*terram de*) *Wykerefeld* 1175-86 *ib*, (*terram de*) *Wykerfeld* 113 *ib*, occurs in grants of *molendinum de Westwyc* & *terram de Wykerfeld* and can be interpreted as 'the field of the dwellers or workers at the *wīc*', which one would assume refers to Westwick.   *v.* OE **wīc, feld**; cf. the pers.n. *Wicker* (Reaney s.n.).

MARKET PLACE

MARKET PLACE
Mannecroft 1141-6, 1175-86 Holme, 1210 FF, c. 1250 *Langley,* 1254
  Coxf, c. 1270 *NPD,* 1280 *Landsdowne Ch, Manacroft* 1211 FF,
  Manercroft 1214 ClR, *Manecroft* 1215 *ib,* 1223 HMC, 1254-75 Val,
  1257 *Ass,* 1285 *et freq* to 1298 *R,* 1288 NoLeet, 1333 *SR, Manecrofth*
  1269 *Ass, Manecrofte* 1269 *ib, Mancroft(e)* 1270, 1568 *NPD,* 1304 *R,*
  1428 FA, 1462 Ch
in foro Norwyc' 1199-1214 ChNCP, *Forum regale (Norwici)* Hy3, 1294
  K, *magnum Forum Norwici* 1250 *ib*

Mancroft was the site on which the new market was laid out after the Norman Conquest.   The Anglo-Saxon civic and commercial centre had been at Tombland.   Once the name of one of the four leets or wards into which medieval Norwich was divided, *Mancroft* now only survives in the name of the great parish church to the south of the Market Place, St Peter Mancroft. OE **(ge)mǣne** + **croft** 'common enclosure, common land'.   *Mancroft* is recorded as a field-name in Bole Nt, Chieveley Brk, Much Hadham Hrt, Olveston Gl (Field 133) and Beeston-next-Mileham Nf (Carthew III 31).   The long vowel is preserved in *Mean Croft,* Hambledon Ha, Holme We (Field 135) and in *Mene Crofte,* Earley (PN Brk 95) and *Menecroft,* Ashampstead (*ib* 510). In view of this field-name material, Schram's suggestion 'Manni's croft' (148) cannot be considered plausible.

   The medieval tradesmen's stalls have been listed   below   in alphabetical order. They are of course all lost today, like the Murage Loft, where the tolls and the customs of the market were collected.

APOTHECARY MARKET
Forum Unguentor' Hy3 K, *Forum Ungwentor'* 1290, 1319 *ib, in foro*
  vnguentar' 1290 *R*
Apothecaria 1316, 1329, 1332 K, *Apotecaria* 1328 *R, Appothecaria* 1329
  NoD
  MLat *unguentum* 'ointment', *unguentarius* 'one who prepares

ointments'.   It is doubtful if the Apothecaria was in the Spicers' Row, as K seems to imply (32).   Hudson thinks the evidence rather points to the western 'Rengea' of the Forum Carnium (K 38 note 6).

BARLEYMARKET, *Venditores Ordei* 1454 K; MLat (*h*)*ordeum* 'barley'.   The sellers of barley had their stalls by the Guildhall, next the Women's Prison there (*coram Prisonam ordinatam pro faeminis* 1454 K); *v.*   K 39.   Prior to 1397 the Barleymarket had been in Barleymarket Yard (*q.v.*), behind the Upper Market.

CHEESEMARKET, *Forum Casei* 1333 K, *Chesemarket* 1345 *OFB*, 1365, 1368 K, *le Marche de furmag'* c. 1350 NoRec, *Oldechesemarket* 1390 K; MLat *caseus,* OF *formage* 'cheese'. The cheesemongers had their stalls to the south-east of St Peter's churchyard (K 37, NoRec II xxv).   *Oldechesemarket* 1390 would seem to indicate that by then they had moved elsewhere.

CLOUTMARKET, *Cloutmarket* 1381 K; ME *clout* 'a patch (of cloth or leather) for mending' (MED).   Kirkpatrick hesitatingly suggests the meaning 'cloth market' (38), but identity with *le Cobellere rowe* is also possible.   Cf. ME *cloutere* 'cobbler, patcher' (Fransson 132).   The *Promptorium Parvulorum* (1440) gives: *Clowter* or *cobelere*: Sartorius, rebroccator (MED).

COBBLERS' ROW
(*le*) *Cobel*(*l*)*ere rowe* 1287 to 1313 *R, Cobiller rowe* 1312 K, *Coblererowe*
    1312, 1332 NoD, 1345 *OFB*, 1346 NoRec, *le Coblere rouwe* 1318 K,
    Cobblere rowe 1326 *ib, the Cob*(*e*)*lerrowe* 1397 (2x) NoRec
Cobeleria 1311 *R*

ME *cobellere* 'mender of shoes', of uncertain derivation (Fransson 132).   The cobblers had their workshops along the east side of St Peter's churchyard in what later became, and still is, Weavers' Lane (*q.v.*). A word *cobeleria* 'shoemenders' quarter' does not seem to be on record.

CORDWAINERS' ROW
Calceria 1278, 1302, 1314 K, 1286 *et freq* to 1290 *R*.   1315 NoD,
    Cord(*e*)*waneria* 1280 K, 1285 *et freq* to 1331 *R, Cordewanria* 1286,

1318 K, *Caligaria* 1290, 1301 *R*, *Caligeria* 1305 NoD, *Allutaria*
1310 K
Cordwanrowe 1317 K, *(le) Cordewanerrowe* 1329 *AddCh*, 1345 *OFB*,
1346 NoRec, *Cordewanerowe* 1331 *R*. *le Cordeweiner rowe* 1370 K, *Le
Cordwaner Rowe* 1370, 1399 *ib*, *le Cordener Rowe* 1401, 1480 *ib*
le Hosiere Rowe 1320, 1351, 1354 K, *Hosieres Rowe* 1325 *ib*

MLat *calcearius, calceator* 'shoe-maker' are on record (LathamD),
but not *calcearia* for 'shoemakers' quarter'. For MLat *cordewaneria*
'cordwainers' quarter', *v*. LathamD *s.v. cordubanaria*. ME *corde-
waner* 'one who makes shoes of cordwain, shoe-maker' (MED,
Fransson 130 f.). MLat *caligaria* (from Lat *caliga* 'military boot')
usually denoted 'hosiers' quarter' (LathamD), but in this case it would
seem to have referred also to the shoe-makers' stalls. Cf. MLat
caligarius 'hosier', but also 'boot-maker' (LathamD, Niermeyer). MLat
al(l)utarius 'tawyer, cordwainer, shoe-maker' is known to LathamD and
Niermeyer, but not *allutaria* for 'shoe-makers' quarter'. Cf. Hudson in
K 26 note 3. ME *hosier* 'maker or seller of hose' (MED), here
probably 'shoe-maker' (cf. Fransson 115).

According to Hudson (K 93), the *Cordewaneria* was situated north
of the street now called White Lion Street (formerly Sadelgate), along
the present Gentleman's Walk.

DRAPERY
(vicus de) Draperia 1256 to 1319 K, 1286 *et freq* to 1307 *R*, *Le Draperi(e)
Rowe* 1355, 1369 K, *le Draperierowe* (2x) 1368 NoRec

Mlat *draperia* 'clothmarket, drapery'. The Drapery was immediately to the north of St Peter's churchyard, on both sides of a lane
running parallel to the churchyard. In 1368 the churchyard was
enlarged northwards (*v*. NoRec II xxv, 228; K 33) and the Drapery was
moved to a site south of the church (K 29). The following forms refer
to the latter site: *Forum Draperie Norwici* 1376 K, *le Clothmarket* 1483
ib, *Le Cloth market* 1483 *ib*.

By the time Kirkpatrick wrote his monograph (c. 1720), this place
had become the Haymarket; *v*. Hay Hill.

FISHMARKET
Forum Piscatorum Hy3 K, *in foro piscat'* 1366 *MinAcct*
Piscaria in magno Foro 1251 K, *Forum Piscenariorum* 1260 *ib*, 1305,

1306, 1307 *R, Forum Piscium* 1286 to 1298 *R,* 1302, 1303 *NPD,* 1330 NoRec, 1385 *NAR*
Fresfismarket 1251, 1272 K, *Freshfishmarket* 1288 (2x) *R,*
   Freschfischmarket 1288 (2x) *ib, Fresh Fischmarket* 1288 NoRec,
   Freschfishmarket 1292 *R*
le Marche de pessoun c. 1350 NoRec, *the Fysshemarket* 1584 *ib*

MLat *piscator* 'fisherman', *piscaria* 'fishmarket', *piscenarius* 'fish-monger', *piscis* 'fish'; OF *pesson, pessun* 'fish'. The Fishmarket was immediately to the south of the Tollhouse (Guildhall) and to the west of the Meatmarket (K 31, 36).

GIRDLERS' STALL, *Stallum Fraternitatis Zonatorum* 1286 K, *stallum Societatis Zonatorum Norwici* 1292 NoRec; MLat *zonator* 'girdle-maker'. This guild possessed a single stall in the Needlers' Row; it is only heard of in connection with this stall and about this date (NoRec II xxii).

GLOVERS' STALLS, *Forum ubi Cirotece venduntur* 1294 K; MLat *chirotheca* 'glove, gauntlet'. Kirkpatrick (35) describes the situation of the glovers' stalls as 'the South ends of the Nedler rowe'; this would seem to imply the southern half of the lane that ran along the Needlers' Row (*commune iter infra Nedelererowe* 1292 NoRec).

HATTERS' ROW, *le Hattere Rowe* 1313 K, *Hatters Row* 1766 King, was the north end of the Market Place (now Guildhall Hill), west of Holtor (now Dove Street). There were also hatters' stalls along the east side of Holtor (K 26; Campbell, Map 6). ME *hattere* is a derivative of OE **hæt(t)** (Fransson 115 f.).

IRONMONGERS' ROW
le Yrenmongererowe 1288, 1294, 1296 *R, le Yrenmonger rowe* 1288 K,
   Irynmongere rowe 1291 *R, Yrinmongere rowe* 1294 K, *Irenmongger rowe*
   1296 *ib, Yrynmongere rowe* 1296 NoD, *le Irynmongerowe* 1302 *ib,*
   Irynmongererowe 1303 *R, Irunmongererowe* 1307 *ib, Irenmoggererowe*
   1307 *ib, Iren mongeres rowe* 1324 K, *Iren monger(e) rowe* 1326, 1348
   ib, Ironmongererowe 1330 NoD, *Irenmongger rowe* 1485 K
Forum fabrorum 1405, 1416 K

The Ironmongers' Row was north and south of the Murage Loft and

east of the Meatmarket (K 36).   MLat *faber* 'smith, dealer in hard-
ware'.

LEEKMARKET
Lekmarkette 1290, 1297 K, 1291 *R, Lekmarket* 1291 NoD, *Lecmarket*
   1295 *R, Le Lekmarket* 1297 K
le Erbere 1397 NoRec

'The market of the dealers in leeks, the herbalists' market'; OE **lēac**.
Cf. Fransson, s. nn. *Lekman* and *Leker* (69).   In ME *lek* was used for
herbs in general.   The *lekmen* may have provided the apothecaries with
herbs for pharmaceutical use.   According to Hudson (K 38 note 6),
their stalls were in the same row as the Apothecaria, i.e. the West Row
(Rengea Occidentalis) of the Meatmarket.   Cf. also a rental of the year
1346:   '... a certain common place near the meat stalls ... which was
William Lekman's' (NoRec II 366).
   According to the editors of NoRec (II 242 n.), /h/*erbere* could mean
'leek or vegetable market'. This sense is not recorded in OED (*s.v.*
arbour) or MED (s.v. *herber*), however, nor is it recorded for ME
herberi (*v.* MED, *s.v.*).   But OF *herberie* could actually mean 'herb-
market' (*marché aux herbes*); *v.* Godefroy, s.v.

LINEN DRAPERY (1)
Lindraperia 1286 *et freq* to 1308 *R, Lyndraperia* 1304 *ib, Le Lyndraperie*
   Rowe 1369 K

The northern row of the Drapery (*q.v.*) was a double row (called *le*
Mid(d)elrowe 1288, 1298 *R*), of which the Linen Drapery was the north
side. OE **līn** 'flax'; cf. Fransson s.n. *Lyndraper* (91).

LINEN DRAPERY (2)
Lyndraperia Norwici 1263 to 1335 *R, Lindraperia Norwici in Superiori*
   Neweport 1303 *ib, Lindraperia* (on the Overrow) 1304, 1306 *ib,*
   (*quondam vocat'*) *Lyndraper rowe* 1357 *ib*

These stalls were in the Overrow (St Peter's Street), on both sides of
the entrance to Barleymarket Lane. They extended as far south as Over
Newport (Bethel Street) and into Over Newport itself, as is apparent
from the 1303 quotation (cf. K 30). The quotations also show that the
drapers had to move from here some time between 1335 and 1357.

MALTMARKET, *Forum Brasei* Hy3 K, *Forum Brasii* 1386, 1398, 1399 *ib*; MLat *brace, bracium, braceum*, etc., 'malt'. At the end of the fourteenth century the Wheatmarket was transferred to a site near the Tollhouse and the Maltmarket was transferred to where the Wheatmarket had been, viz. a place opposite the south-west corner of St Peter's churchyard (K 39).

MEATMARKET
Bucheria Norwici 1256, 1267, 1305 K, 1268 *AddCh*
Forum Carnium 1280 K, 1286 *et freq* to 1306 *R*, 1330 (2x) NoRec, 1385
    NAR
Forum Carnificum 1273 NoRec, 1315 K

MLat *bucheria* 'butchers' quarter', *caro* 'butcher's meat', *carnifex* 'butcher'. The Meatmarket was situated east of the Fishmarket and south of the Tollhouse, the present Guildhall (K 31, 36).

MIDDLEROW
the Myddyl Rowe 1508 K, *Midyl Rowe* 1524 *ib*, *Myddyll rowe* 1541 *ib*,
    Middle Rowe 1626 BLR
the Murage Rowe 1627 K

These spellings all refer to a row which was identical with the Ironmongers' and Ropers' Row (K 37). The double row north of the churchyard of St Peter Mancroft which contained the Drapery and the Linen Drapery also went by the name *Middlerow* (K 32). OE **middel**.

MURAGE LOFT
Domus Muragii 1300, 1308 K, (*ad hostium*) *domus Murag'* 1304 *NAR*,
    (*iuxta ostium*) *Murag'* 1376 *ib*, *the Muragehus* 1309 *R*, *the Moragehous*
    1309 *ib*, *le Muragehous* 1324 *NPD*, *le Murage hous* 1346 K
Merage lofte 1390, 1409 K, *Morageloft(e)* 1395 to 1419 *NAR, Murage*
    Loft 1480, 1541 K
solar' recepti 1379 NoRec, *Murage Soler* 1379 K

MLat *muragium*, OF, ME *murage* 'toll exacted in a town for repairing the walls'; OE *solor, soler* (Lat *solarium*) 'loft, upper room', in ME perhaps readopted from AN *soler, solair* = OF *solier* (OED). The Murage Loft was situated in the middle of the Ironmongers' Row (*v. supra*), near the Market Cross (*v.* K 36). This was where 'the supervisors of the affairs of the commonalty met every market day, to collect the tolls and customs of the market, as the market-committee doth at this day in the Gild-hall' (Blomefield IV 234).

NEEDLERS' ROW

Acuaria 1288 K

(*le*) *Nedelererowe* 1288 *et freq* to 1312 *R, Nedlere Rowe* 1288 *ib,* (*le*) *Nedlererowe* 1292, 1301 NoRec, 1294 NoD, 1306 K, *le Nedelerrowe* 1294 *ib, Nedlerrowe* 1298 *R, Nedelerowe* 1299, 1338 NoD, *Niedlerowe* 1380 K

Nedleres rowe 1317 NoD, 1351 K, *Nedeleresrowe* 1321 NoD

MLat *acuare, acuaria* 'needle-case' (LathamD) could apparently be used for 'needle market, needlers' quarter'. MLat *acuarius* 'needler' and *acuarium* 'needle-case' are also recorded in LathamD. For ME *nedelere* 'needlemaker', *v.* Fransson 148.

OATMARKET, *Forum Avenarum* 1416 K; MLat *avena* 'oats', often plur. (LathamD). The location is not known.

OMANSETEROW

Omancete market 1277 *NPD, Omansete Market* 1278 *ib*

(*le*) *Omanseterowe* 1288, 1316 *R,* 1308, 1315 K, 1323, 1324 NoD, 1346 NoRec, *Oman(n)esseterowe* 1290 to 1301 *R, Onemanseterowe* 1306 K, *Omaneseterow(e)* 1308 (2x) *R,* 1323 to 1334 *NoD, Homanseterowe* 1309 *R, Omansetterowe* 1309 *ib, Omanneseterowe* 1323 NoD, *Omanserowe* 1324 *ib*

ME *oman(nes)sete* 'cloth made on a loom worked by one man' as opposed to *to-manny-shete* 'cloth made on a broad loom worked by two people' (*v.* Hudson in K 31 note 4 and Wilhelmsen 42 f.). MED (s.v. *omanneshete*) tentatively defines the word as 'a sheet of a width suitable for covering one person'. *Omanseterow* was west of St Peter's Church.

PARMENTER ROW

Peleteria 1285, 1307 *R*

Parmenter Rowe 1286, 1291 K, 1290 *R*

Pelliparia 1300, 1301 K, *Vicus Pellepariorum* or *Vicus Pellipar'* 1300 to 1356 *ib*

Parchemyners Rowe 1368 *D&C*

MLat *pel(l)eteria* 'peltry, skins (coll.)' and *pelliparia* 'peltry, pelterers' quarter' (Latham) apparently both referred to the 'place where skins and furs were sold'. Cf. *pelliparius* 'pelterer, skinner'. ME *parmenter* 'tailor, furrier' (MED). OF *parcheminier* 'maker or seller of parchment' (Fransson 128 f.) in the 1368 name of the row suggests that there was a connection between parmenters and sellers of parchment, as Hudson suggests (K 41 note 8). The parmenters, like the cobblers, had their stalls east of St Peter's Church, in the present Weavers' Lane. Cf. Mountergate.

POULTRYMARKET, *forum Gallinarum* 1294 *R, Forum Pulterr'* 1380 K, *Old Pultre market* 1421 K, seems to have been next to the south side of St Peter's churchyard, from where it was later (c. 1379) removed to the north side (by the Overrowe), hence the *Old Pultre market* 1421 (K 37). Lat *gallina* 'hen'; ME *pultrie* 'place where fowls are sold for food', from OF *pouletrie* (SN 186); MLat *pulterius* 'poulterer' (Latham), ME *puleter* 'dealer in poultry' (Fransson 75 f.).

PUDDINGMARKET, *Pudding Stall* c. 1250 K, *Le Puddyng market* 1406, 1483 *ib*; ME *pudding* 'bowels, entrails', when sold as food 'stuffed pig's intestines, a kind of sausage' (OED s.v.); cf. Pudding Lane and the two Pudding Lanes in the City of London (SN 102 f.).

ROPERY, *the Ropery* 1537 K, *Ropars Row* 1565 *ib*. The ropers' stalls occupied the place which had earlier been held by the ironmongers, east of the butchers' stalls. It was decreed in 21 R2 (1397-8) that the sellers of ropes should have their shops in this place and nowhere else (*v.* K 36). ME *ropere* 'ropemaker', a derivative of OE **rāp** 'rope' (Fransson 85).

SCUDDERS' ROW
le Scouderesrowe 1161 K, *Scouderesrowe* 1314 NoD; *le Scouthere rowe*
    1303 (2x) *R, Scoudhererowe* 1308 *ib*
Scouthere market 1300 K, *Scoudheremarket* 1308 *R*

ME *scoudere* 'leather dresser' is peculiar to Norwich. Reaney says, '*Scudder*, who appears to have been a dresser of white-leather, has been noted only in Norwich' (ReaneyO 354). This noun is to be connected with ModE *scud* 'remove remaining hairs, dirt, etc., from skins with a hand-knife' (OED s.v. *scud* v.[3], earliest instance 1788, as a tanning term 1880). These tradesmen were also known as *whittawers*; Hudson (K 40 note 7) identifies *Scouthererowe* with *Quittowere-market*. *v.* Whittawers' Market.

SHEEPMARKET - - NEATMARKET
Shep-market c. 1240 K
Net market 1311, 1317 K, *le Nete market* 1365, 1393 *ib*
Forum Bestiarum Ed3 K

South of St Peter's churchyard, towards the present William Booth Street (earlier Gun Lane and Church Street). OE **scēap, scēp** 'sheep', **nēat** 'ox', MLat *bestia* 'farm animal'.

SKEPPERS' ROW, *Skepper rowe* 1480 K. Kirkpatrick (41 f.) locates the skeppers' (or basket-makers') row between the Murage Loft and the Market Cross. ME *skepper* 'basket-maker'. This is a derivative of late OE *sceppe* 'a dry measure' (ModE *skep* 'basket', also used as a measure), from OScand *skeppa* (Björkman 124).

SOAPERS' LANE, *Seperia* 1223 K, *le Soperes Lane* 1306 *ib*, *le Sopere Lane* 1346 *ib*. The soap-makers had their stalls in the immediate neighbourhood of the glovers and the needlers. MLat *seperia* 'place where soap is sold', from *sepum* (older *sevum, sebum*) 'hard animal fat, tallow, suet'. OE **sāpere** 'soapmaker, soap-dealer', ME *sopere* (Fransson 71).

SOURBREADMARKET, *Suyrbredmarket* 1298 *R*, *Surbredmarkette* 1305 *ib*, *Surbredmarket* 1305 *ib*, *Surbred Markette* 1312 NoD, *Sourbred market* 1343 K; ME *surbred* 'leavened bread'. The different breadmarkets seem to have been in the same area, in the western part of the Market Place, along the northern half of the Overrowe. OE **sūr**, ME *brēd* 'bread'.

SOUTER ROW, *Mercatum Sutorum* 1268 K, (*in*) *foro sutorum* 1289 *R*, *forum sutorum* Hy3, 1318, 1379 K; MLat *sutor* 'shoemaker'. Probably identical with Cordwainers' Row, i.e. Gentleman's Walk (q.v.).

SPICERS' ROW
Speceria 1288 to 1308 *R*
Le Especerierowe 1306 *R, le Spicerierowe* 1320 *ib, le Spicerie rowe* 1322
   K, *Specerowe* 1312 *R, Le Specer rowe* 1312 K, *le Spicer rowe* 1342 *ib*
le Spiceres rowe 1341 K, *le Spiceris rowe* 1369 *ib*

   The Spicery was north of the Drapery. It ran from west to east and
was thus parallel to the Drapery. MLat *speceria* 'spicery, spice-shops';
ME *specer, spicer* 'dealer in spices, apothecary, druggist', from OF
espicier, especier (Fransson 68 f.). *v.* Worsted Row *infra.*

TALLOWMARKET, *Taleth market* Hy3 K, *the Market for Tallow* 1315
ib; ME *tal(u)ʒ* 'tallow'. The location is not known. The *th*-spelling for
the voiceless velar fricative is worthy of note.

TANNERS' MARKET, *Forum Tannatorum* 1285 to 1360 K, 1292, 1298
R; MLat *tannator* 'tanner'. These stalls were immediately east of
Needlers' Row. Kirkpatrick knew this spot as *Honey Hill* (35).

WASTELMARKET, *Wastelmarket* 1302 NoD, 1303 (2x), 1311 *R*, 1314
K; ME *wastel* 'bread made of the finest white flour', from AN *uastel*
(cf. OCF *guastel*). At the outset, many grades of bread were baked.
Later legislation brought them under three headings ('wastel bread',
'bread of whole wheat' and 'bread treet'); *v.* H.W. Bailey and Alan S.C.
Ross in EGS 6 (1957) 23 ff., and E.P. Kuhl in PQ 2 (1923) 302 f. The
Wastelmarket was identical with the Whitebreadmarket. The bakers'
stalls seem to have been along the northern half of the Overrowe (St
Peter's Street).

WHEATMARKET
(*Le*) *Qwetemarket* 1287 *R*, 1290 K, *Old Whetemarket* 1347 *ib, Locus
   dudum vocatus Qwetemarket 1361 *ib*
Forum Frumenti 1398, 1481, 1492 K

   OE **hwǣte** 'wheat', MLat *frumentum* 'grain'. The original place for
this market was opposite to the south-west corner of St Peter's
churchyard. According to Kirkpatrick (39) it was transferred to a
place immediately south of the Tollhouse in 22 R2 (1398-9) and the old
site was allotted to the sellers of malt. From the quotations of 1347
and 1361 *supra* one would have thought that the transfer took place

well before 1347.

WHITEBREADMARKET
Whitbredmarket 1250 K, *quitbred market* 1258 *ib, Qwitbred market* 1275
   ib, Qwytbredmarket 1303 *R, Quytbredmarket* 1312 *ib*
Forum Pistorum 1255 to 1408 K
Forum Panis 1286 *R*

OE **hwīt** 'white' and ME *brēd* 'bread'; MLat *pistor* 'baker', *panis*
'bread'.   Identical with the Wastelmarket *(q.v.)*.   For the *Qu-,*
Qw-spellings, a characteristic feature of the Norfolk dialect, *v.* Seltén
149.

WHITTAWERS' MARKET, *Qwittowermarket* 1298 *R, Qwyttowere-*
market 1300 *ib, Qyttoweresmarkette* 1302 *ib, Qwittoweremarket* 1302 *ib*;
ME *whittaw(y)er* 'one who taws skins into whitleather'.   The first
element is OE **hwīt** 'white', the second is a derivative of OE *tāwian*
'make ready, prepare'. Identical with Scudders' Row.   The whittawers
had their stalls west of Needlers' Row (together with soapers, glovers
and worstedweavers).   For the *Qw*-spellings, *v.* Whitebreadmarket.

WOODMARKET, *Le Old wodemarket* 1397, 1421 K; OE **widu, wudu**
'wood'.   These stalls were in the middle of the Haymarket (Hay Hill),
not far from the Sheepmarket (K 37, 39).

WOOLMARKET
Forum lane 1298 K, *(de) Foro Lanar'* 1385 *NAR, (in) foro Lanar'* 1399
   K, 1416 (4x) *NAR*
Wollemarket 1357 K

OE **wull**, MLat *lana* 'wool'.   It is possible that *lanar'* stands for
lanariorum (the gen.pl. of *lanarius* 'wool-merchant') rather than
lanarum, as Kirkpatrick would have it (35). Similarly, *Forum Avenarum*
(*v.* Oatmarket *supra*) should perhaps be *Forum Avenariorum* 'the
market of the sellers of oats'.   *Pellipariorum* (the gen.pl. of *pelliparius*
'skinner') is known to have been abbreviated *pellipar'* (*v.* K 33, line four
from bottom).

WORSTED ROW
Merceria 1266 K, 1286 *R, Merceria super le Especerierowe* 1306 *ib*

Worthstederowe 1331 NoD, *Worstederowe* 1334 *ib*, *Worstede Rowe* 1352
K, *Worthstede Rowe* 1369 *ib*.

Worsted Row would seem to have been in close proximity to the
Spicery (cf. the 1306 quotation and K 33).   It is possible, however,
that *Merceria* refers to the Drapery, south of the Spicery.   MLat
merceria 'mercery, cloth trade, mercer's shop(s)'; *worsted* (yarn and
cloth) has its name from Worstead, a Nf village.

NORWICH STREET-NAMES

ABBEY LANE, *Cockey-lane* c. 1720 K, *Cockey Lane* 1766 King, 1845
White, 1885 OS.   St Clement's Church was situated immediately south
of this lane, off the east side of King Street (*v.* Norwich Churches).   It
was known as St Clement at the Well, from 'a cistern that was near it'
(Blomefield IV 77).   *Cockey* in the early forms of this name probably
referred to this cistern, which was used as a depository for mud and
refuse (*v.* K 7); the dialect word *cockey* was synonymous with 'sewer'
(cf. the Great Cockey).   The modern name may possibly be due to the
fact that, before 1456, the Abbot and Monks of Wendling Abbey (Nf)
had the right to appoint the incumbent of St Clement's. They also
owned the Old Common Staithe and some houses in Abbey Lane (*v.*
Blomefield IV 77 f. and NoRec II 244).

ALAN ROAD, a small street on the west side of King Street, opposite
Carrow Road and south of Stuart Road, with which it is connected by a
footpath.

ALDERSON PLACE, *Alderson's buildings, St Catherine's plain* 1845
White, *Alderson's Street* 1885 OS.   On the 1885 OS Map Alderson's
Street is on the south side of Finkelgate (then *Finket Street*), along the
churchyard of St John Sepulchre.   The original Alderson Buildings
have been replaced by corporation housing (Nobbs 6).

ALL SAINTS GREEN
Swynemarket 1253 to 1266 *NPD*, *Swinemarket* 1254, 1255 (2x) *ib*, 13
      Holme, Svynmarket 1269 *Ass*, (*All Saints in*) *Swynmarket* 1285 NoD
Holdswynemarket 1276 NoRec, *Oldswinemarket* 1278 NoLeet,

Holdeswynesmarket 1299 *R, Holdswynesmarket* 1299 *ib,*
Oldeswynnemarket 1304 NoD, *Oldswynemarket* 1305 *R, Old*
Swynmarket 1306 *ib, Holdeswynemarkette* 1313 *ib, Olde Swyne*
Markette 1313 K, *Holdswynmarket* 1316 *R,* 1326 K, *Old Swynmarket*
1428 FA
(*vetus*) *Swynemarket* 1290 to 1293 *R, vetus Swynemarkette* 1293, 1310 *ib,*
vetus Swynemarket 1304 K
regium Forum vocat' Tymbermarket 1346 to 1384 K, *le Tymbermarket*
1350 *D&C,* (*de*) *timbermarket* 1364 *NPD,* (*apud*) *Tymmermarket* 1372
ib
Alhalowe Greene 1553 K, *Ould Swynemarkett, now Allderhollow* 1626
BLR, *Alderhallen Green* c. 1720 K, *Alderby-holland- green* 1745 B
All Saints Green or Old Swinemarket 1746 B, 1766 King, *All Saints*
Green 1789 H, 1885 OS, *All Saints Plain* 1830 M&M, *All Saints'*
Church yard and green 1845 White

According to extant evidence the swinemarket in front of All Saints
Church had been transferred to what is now Orford Hill *(q.v.)* by 1270.
It was replaced by a timbermarket. The name *Timbermarket* in turn
gave way to *Alderhallen Green* from the church (OE *ealra hálgena*
cirice). In due course *Alderhallen Green* became *All Saints Green,*
which is now the name of the street that extends from All Saints
Church to Queen's Road, the site of the ancient Brazen Doors. This
street has gone by the following series of names:
Old Swynemarket Street 1303 NoD
Brason Doors Lane 1696 Cleer
Winalls or St Winewaloys Street 1746 B, *Winnalls Street* 1766 King
Upper Surry Street 1789 H, 1830 M&M, *Upper Surreystreet and now*
more commonly Rodney-street 1819 Stacy, *Rodney street now Upper*
Surrey street 1845 White, *Upper Surrey Street* 1885 OS
All Saints Green 1920 OS 6" Map

The Iron or Brazen Door was originally not a proper city gate but a
postern (*v.* Gates). Formerly Surrey Street ended at its junction with
All Saints Green, its continuation on the eastern side of the Green
being known as St Catherine's Lane or Surrey Road. It was therefore
quite natural for the Green or a part of it to be regarded as an
extension of Surrey Street, hence the name *Upper Surrey Street.* The
Church of St Winwaloe (later re-dedicated to St Catherine) stood by
the junction of present-day Surrey Street with Queen's Road (St

Catherine's Plain).   In view of the church's situation, the name
Win(n)all's Street ought first to have applied to St Catherine's Lane.

ALMSHOUSE LANE (lost), *Almeshouse Lane* c. 1720 K. This lane
ran along the west and south sides of the (lost) church of St Crouche
(*v.* under School Lane).   There was an almshouse immediately south of
it (K 59).

ALMS LANE
Almes house Lane 1626 K, *Ammys Lane* c. 1720 *ib*, *Alms House Lane*
    1766 King, *Almshouse Lane* 1789 H, *Alms house lane* 1845 White,
    Alms Lane 1885 OS

Runs from St George's Street westwards into Muspole Street.
Named from almshouses in Muspole Street, 'given by Alice Crome, in
1516, for the residence of seven poor widows of the parish of St
George Colegate' (White 136).   As Alan Carter pointed out (private
communication), an almshouse is recorded in St George Colegate as
early as 1311 (*super qu'dam domum Elemosinar' R* 6:7d).   Cf. the
almshouse near St Crouche's Church (*v.* Almshouse Lane).

ANNE'S WALK, off the west side of Magdalen Street, provides an
approach to Anglia Square.

ARCADE STREET, *v.* Royal Arcade.

ARGYLE STREET, *Argyle Street* 1885 OS, 1920 OS 6" Map. This
street leads from Southgate Lane to Rouen Road. It used to link up
with Burleigh Street, which has been incorporated into Rouen Road.

BACK OF THE INNS -- CASTLE STREET
(lane called) *Cokeye* 1340 K, 1473 *Beecheno,* (*super*) *venellam de*
    Cokeye 1402 *R, in Cokeye* 1458 *Beecheno, in Kokey* 1494 *ib*, *Cokeylane*
    1536, 1539, 1546 *ib, Cokeilane* 1536 *ib, Cokkylane* 1546 *ib, Cokkey*
    lane 1551 *ib, Cockey lane* 1570 to 1659 *ib, Cockey lane or back lane*
    1670 *ib*
the Backside of the Inns c. 1720 K, 1746 B, *Back of the Inns* 1766 King,
    1789 H, 1830 M&M, *Back of the Inns -- Castle Street* 1845 White,
    1885 OS

This medieval lane followed much the same line as 'the common *Cokey(e)*', which passed along the western side of the Castle (*v.* Great Cockey). The later Back(side) of the Inns is so called from the former Angel, Bear and King's Head inns along the Walk. Today it runs from White Lion Street to London Street. Since the middle of the last century the name *Back of the Inns* has been restricted to the southern part (now open to pedestrians only); the rest is Castle Street. *v.* Beecheno 84 f.

BALDERSTON COURT. Formerly the Old Meeting House could be approached from Calvert Street via this alley, which is now a cul-de-sac. It was named after Bartholomew *Balderstone*, who in 1761 left money for the foundation of a charity school (White 126). In 1845 this school was kept in a building in Old Meeting House Alley (or Yard), off Colegate. Nobbs (8) calls the benefactor *Matthew* Balderston. One *Timothy* Balderston (died 1764) has a monument in St George Colegate (Pevsner 240).

BANK PLAIN
Motstowe 1257 *Ass*, 1288, 1290 K, 1289 *Holme*, *Mothstowe* 1342 K
Redwell Plain c. 1720 K, 1789 H
Bank place 1819 Stacy, 1845 White, *Bank Plain* 1885 OS

BANK STREET
Blue Boar Lane 1766 King, 1789 H
Bank-street 1819 Stacy, *Bank Street* 1830 M&M, 1845 White, 1885 OS

Bank Plain today extends from the east end of London Street to Agricultural Hall Plain; Bank Street runs from Bank Plain to Upper King Street.
OE **(ge)mōtstow** 'place where assemblies are held'. It is reasonable to assume that the meeting place of the burgesses was near St Michael at Plea Church, *alias* St Michael de *Motstow*. Hudson argues that St Michael de Motstow was built to take the place of St Michael on Tombland, which Bishop Herbert had caused to be pulled down at the end of the eleventh century, and that the new church did not only take over the dedication of its predecessor but also the appellation 'de Motstow'. According to Hudson, then, Tombland, and not a spot somewhere in the Bank Plain/Red Well area, was the original meeting place of the Anglo-Saxon burgh (K 105 f.). However, Bishop Herbert

is known to have had a chapel built as a replacement for the demolished Tombland church, not on the site of the present St Michael at Plea, but east of the river, to the north of St Leonard's Priory (*v.* NoRec I 54, and Campbell Map 4).

Redwell Plain, v. Red Well Street. *Blue Boar Lane,* named from a tavern sign, was a street which corresponded to the present Bank Street and Bank Plain. *Bank Plain* and *Street* are so called from Barclays Bank, a monumental building erected in 1929-31, which occupies the entire west side of the Plain.

BARLEYMARKET LANE (lost)

communis introitus a foro regio usque in Barlimarketyerd 1293 K
Barly market Lane 1407 K

This was a short lane that led from the west side of the Market Place (now St Peter's Street) to the ancient Barleymarket. Just north of it ran Cosyn's (or Herlewyne's) Lane (*v.* Wounded Heart Lane). Later there was another approach to Barleymarket Yard which led out of Upper Newport, i.e. Bethel Street (*v.* Blomefield IV 234): *Barley Market Lane* 1746 B, 1766 King.

BARLEYMARKET YARD (lost)

(*Le*) *Barlikmarketyerd* 1282 *Phillipps,* 1283, 1287 K, 1293, 1329 *R,*
    Barlimarketyerd 1287 to 1316 *ib, Barlemarketyerd* 1303 *ib, Barly*
    market yerd 1303 K, *Barleymarketyerd* 1304 *R, Barlikmarketycherd*
    1308 *ib, Barlicmarketyerd* 1316 *HarlCh, Barly- marketesyerd* 1397 K,
    Old Barlymarket 1401 K
Barlicbachusyerd 1318 K, *Barlibachusyerd* 1318 *ib*

Behind the Upper Market (the west side of the Market). The OE adjective **bærlic** (ME **barlich**) replaced the noun **bere** in colloquial use. In 1397 the barleymarket was removed from Barleymarket Yard to the north side of the Tollhouse (Blomefield IV 234 note 8), hence *Old* Barlymarket in the 1401 quotation. John Cosyn and John le Blekestere had bakeries here in Edward II's time (K 30; cf. the 1318 quotations). Whether a reference to *curia pistrini* 'the bakery court' 1288 *R* belongs here is doubtful.

BARRACK STREET

regia via que tendit apud Pokethorp 1298 K, (*in*) *vico vocato Pokethorp*

1428 FA, *Pockthorp Street* c. 1720 K
Bargate Street 1746 B, 1766 King, 1798 H, 1830 M&M
St James's street 1819 Stacy, *Barrack Street* -- *St James' Street* 1845
White, *Barrack Street* -- *St James Street* 1885 OS

This street used to run from Peacock Street to the Kett's Hill roundabout, but the stretch between Peacock Street and Cowgate has been incorporated into St Crispin's Road (*v.* Normans Lane). After the Horse or Cavalry Barracks (*Horse Barracks* 1819 Stacy, *Cavalry Barracks* 1885 OS) had been put up in Pockthorpe in 1792-3 (*v.* Campbell 21 and Pevsner 283), *Bargate Street* (*v.* Pockthorpe Gate) was changed into *Barrack Street* (east of the old gate) and *St James Street* (west of the gate). These barracks were demolished in the nineteen-sixties. St James Church stands near the roundabout on Cowgate - - Whitefriars.

BARGATE COURT, north of Barrack Street, consists of council flats.

BARWELL'S COURT, *Barwell's Court* 1845 White, 1885 OS, runs out of Malthouse Road into St Stephen's Street opposite Surrey Street. Messrs. Barwell & Sons, wine merchants, had their premises here from c. 1760 (Wicks 55).

BEDDING LANE
Baddinges Wente 1287 *R, Baddingeswente* 1288 *ib, Bandrigglane* 1302 *ib,*
Baddings Lane 1766 King, 1789 H, 1830 M&M, 1845 White, 1885 OS
three privy Lane c. 1720 K

Leads from Palace Street to Quay Side. The name is a reminder of someone surnamed *Badding,* cf. Walter *Badding* 1288 NoLeet, 1303 *NPD,* John *Baddyng* 1413, 1414 NoRec, 1433, 1436 *NPD.* See further Reaney s.n. *Badcock. v.* ME **wente.** *The Three Privies* was probably the popular name of a pub. The number 'three' is not unusual in names of pubs; cf. the Three Kings (Three King Lane), the Three Tuns (the Tuns Corner, i.e. St Stephen's Plain), the Three Mariners (Mariners Lane), and the Three Pigs (Pigg Lane).

BEDFORD STREET, *Bedford Street* 1885 OS, is a late differentiation of a section of Pottergate (east of Exchange Street). The name derives from a public house, the *Bedford Arms*, which formerly (*v.* the

1885 OS Map) stood here.   Off Bedford Street is OLD POST
OFFICE YARD.

BELL AVENUE, *Bell Avenue* 1920 OS 6" Map, is the prolongation of
Orford Street across the Old Cattle Market to the junction with Market
Avenue.   It is indicated on the 1885 OS Map, but without a name;
named from the nearby *Bell Hotel* (disused), said to have been the Blue
Bell originally (*Bell Inn* 1766 King,   1845 White, *Bell Hotel* 1885 OS;
Wicks 48 ff., Riddington Young 15 f.).

BER STREET
Berstrete 1135-54 BM, 1239 *Holme*, 1248 *et freq* to 1540 *NPD,* 1285 *et*
       freq to 1322 *R,* 1428 FA, *Berchestrete* 1140-5 (p) *NCR,* c. 1150 K,
       Berestre(e)t(e) 1181 (p) P, 1207 (p) FineR, 1250 (p), 1257, 1269 *Ass,*
       c. 1280 *Langley,* 1295 (p), 1583 (3x) *NPD, Bergstrete* 1262 (2x) *D&C,*
       1265 to 1279 *NPD,* c. 1280 *Langley, Berstrette* 1294 (2x), 1309, 1313 *R,*
       Berystrete 1438, 1444 K, *Bredstrete or Berestrete* 1547 Pat, *Bear Street*
       1696 Cleer, 1711 ECC, *Burgh Street or Berstreet* 1746 B, *Bear or Berg*
       Street 1766 King, *Berg Street* 1789 H, *Ber-street* 1819 Stacy, *Ber Street*
       1830 M&M, 1845 White, 1885 OS

OE (WSax) **beorg,** (Angl) **berg** 'hill, mound'.   The street runs
from the site of Ber Street Gate to Timber Hill along the top of a
ridge.   From the second element *street,* which is exceptional in
Norwich street-names, Hudson argues that Ber Street was once a
Roman road (K 104 f.).   Alternatively it has been suggested that a
Roman road running north to south through Norwich followed
approximately the line of Magdalen Street - - King Street.   There
is, however, no archaeological evidence for either route (Green &
Young 9).
       Red Knappe Closse 1626 BLR is recorded in Ber Street. **rēad,**
cnæpp, clos.

BETHEL STREET, ST GILES STREET
Neuport c. 1200 *D&C,* 1258 *NPD,* 1268 *NfD, Neweport* 1240, 1254 *Coxf,*
       1303, 1308 *R, forum Regium quod vocatur Neweport* 1312 *ib*
Superior Newport 1276 NoRec, 1428 FA, *Superior Neweport* 1285 *et freq*
       to 1307 *R, Superior Neuport* 1291 to 1306 *ib, Overeneweport* 1295 *ib,*
       Overneweport 1304 *ib, Overneuport* 1313 (2x) *ib, Upper or Over*
       Newport 1746 B; *Committee Street* 1696 Cleer, c. 1720 K;

Bedlam-street 1745 B, *Upper Newport or Bedlam Street* 1766 King,
   Bethel Street 1789 H, 1819 Stacy, 1830 M&M, 1845 White, 1885 OS
Inferior Neuport 1268 K, 1284, 1329 *D&C,* 1296 K, 1285 to 1314 *R,*
   Inferior Neweport 1285 *et freq* to 1311 *ib,* *Neweport inferior* 1355
   AddCh, Netherneweport 1285 *NPD,* 1304 *R,* *Nethere Neweport* 1302 to
   1314 K, 1313 *R,* *Nether Neuport* 1315, 1348 K, *Nether Newporte* 1392
   ib, *St Giles's Street* 1570 K, *St Giless Street* 1696 Cleer, *Lower
   Newport or St Giles's Street* 1746 B, *St Giless Street or Lower Newport*
   1766 King, *St Giles's Broad-street* 1819 Stacy, *St Giles Broad Street*
   1830 M&M, *St Giles Street* 1845 White, 1885 OS

v. **nīw e, port**[2]. If, as has been maintained, the meaning of *Newport*
was 'new town', then it must be assumed that the name was originally
given to the French settlement that was formed west of the Castle in
the years following the Conquest (cf. NoRec I ix). This is a plausible
theory, for names of districts are known to have become street-names
in Norwich (e.g., Needham and Westwick) and elsewhere (*v.* SN 201
f.). ME *port* referred especially to 'a town with market rights'. In the
extant documents, however, Newport would seem to refer to either of
the two streets that are now called Bethel Street and St Giles Street.
St Giles Street (*Nether,* or *Inferior,* Newport) runs almost due west
from the Market Place; the more southerly Bethel Street (*Over,* or
Superior, Newport) runs west-north-west from the Market Place and
eventually joins St Giles Street. There are street-names ending in
-*port* in other towns and in Lincoln there is a suburb called Newport
(PN L 30). It seems that, in OE, *port* could mean a street lined with
tradesmen's stalls (*v. Studies*[2] 180 ff.). That in the course of time the
second element of the Norwich Newports came to be understood to
mean 'market' is suggested by the quotation *forum regium* ... from *R*
under the year 1312 *supra.* Apparently the main market place had
become too crowded and business had spread into the adjoining
streets. On the sense development of *port, v.* also Sawyer 230 f.
   The name *Committee Street* arose through ellipsis of *Committee
House Street.* The Committee House was blown up in a riot in 1648.
The names *Bedlam Street* and *Bethel Street* are due to the *Bethel* or
Bedlam Hospital (q.v.) south of the street, on the site of the Committee
House. A part of Nether Newport passed along the wall of St Giles
churchyard, which explains the late name *St Giles's (Broad) Street.*

BISHOPGATE

Holm(e)strete 1107-16, 1277 ChNCP, c. 1250 *et freq* to 1705 *NPD*, 1257
   Ass, 1285 (3x) *D&C*, 1292 *AddR*, 14 *Binh*, 1307 *R*, 1333 *SR*, 1336
   NoD, 1349 *NAR*, 1428 FA, 1575 *AddCh, Holstrete* 1269 *Ass,*
   Holmystrete 1333 *NPD, Holmestreet* 1647 *ib*
Bishops Gate Street 1696 Cleer, 1746 B, *Bishopsgate Street* 1789 H,
   Bishop-Gate Street or vulgarly *Bishop-street* c. 1720 K, *Holm or Bishop*
   Gate Street 1766 King, *Bishopgate Street* 1830 M&M, 1845 White,
   1885 OS
Hospital Lane 1766 King, 1789 H, 1830 M&M
Tabernacle Street 1789 H, 1830 M&M, *Tabernacle Row* 1845 White

   v. **holmr, hulm**. A thoroughfare from Bishop Bridge westwards to
St Martin at Palace Church. The oldest name, *Holmestrete*, is from
Cowholme (*Couholm* 1253 K, R2 NoRec). *Holme* signified 'water
meadow' or 'flat ground' generally and is to be derived from ODan
holm (*v.* Hald 99 f.).   Beside Ber Street and Tombland, Holm-
strete/Bishopgate is one of the oldest streets in Norwich.   Very
probably it was at one time part of an east-west Roman road through
what was later to become Norwich (Green & Young 8).   The name
Bishopgate (*Street*), of fairly late introduction, is due to the city gate
which used to be at the west end of Bishop Bridge (*la porte sur le pount*
le Evesqe 1343 NoRec; *v.* Bishop Gate).   As a street-name,
Bishopgate is to be explained as due to analogy (cf. *Colegate, Cowgate,*
etc.)
   The section from the eastern entrance of the Cathedral Close to the
Adam and Eve public house was called *Hospital Lane* (from the Great
Hospital) and the section from the Adam and Eve to St Martin at
Palace was known as *Tabernacle Street* (from the Methodist Tabernacle
that stood at the east end of this part of the street, on the site of Rome
Hall).

BLACKFRIARS STREET, *v.* Peacock Street.

BLEXTEREHOLE (lost)
Blekestereshole 1292 to 1312 *R*, 1319, 1329, 1342 K, *Le Blecksteres hole*
   1297, 1303 K, (*Le*) *Blekesteres hole* 1297, 1347 *ib, Blexsterehole* 1306
   R, Blexterhole 1308 *ib, Blexterehole* 1308 K, *Blekstere hole* 1308 *ib,*
   Blekesterehole 1317 *R, Blekesterys hole* 1342 K, *Blekstereshole* 1347 *ib,*
   Le Blextere rowe 1344 *ib*

This street ran from Charing Cross along the west side of the former Duke's Palace to the river.   Several men surnamed . *le Blekestere* occur in the records; one William *le Blekestere* had a messuage on the west side of this lane in the thirteenth century (K 56 f.).   ME *bleikstere* 'one who bleaches cloth', from ON *bleikja* 'to bleach' (*v.* MED and Fransson 109).   Fransson makes a distinction between ME *blextere* and *bleykestere*, assigning to the former the meaning 'one who blackens'. But the only evidence for the sense 'one who blackens' is the *Promptorium Parvulorum* (c. 1500), which explains *blextere* as *obfuscator* 'slanderer'.   As an occupational term *blekestere/blextere* is here no doubt a spelling for *bleikstere* 'one who bleaches cloth' (*v.* OED and MED).

BOTOLPH STREET - - BOTOLPH WAY

St Buttolph's commonly called Buttle-street 1745 B, *St Botolph's Street* 1766 King, *Botolph Street* 1789 H, 1845 White, 1885 OS, 1920 OS 6" Map

All that remains of the old Botolph Street is a stretch of roadway and footpath from St Augustine's Street to Anglia Square. The Anglia Square end is called Botolph Way.   The original Botolph Street linked up with Magdalen Street at Stump Cross. St Botolph's Church stood north of the junction of Botolph Street and Magdalen Street (*v.* Churches). What used to be the northern part of St George's Street has been regarded as part of Botolph Street since St George's Street was bisected by St Crispin's Road (*cf.* Botolph Street - - St George's Street *infra*).

BOTOLPH STREET - - ST GEORGE'S STREET

Merholt 1278, 1377 K, 1288 to 1303 *R*, 1298 *OR, Mereholt* 1287 (2x), 1294, 1307 *R*, 1316, 1333 *NPD, Merheholt* 1288 *R, Marholt* 1491 K, *le Marreholde* 1506 *ib*
Gildenegate 1273 *D&C,* 1275, 1301 K, *Gilden Gate* 1766 King, 1789 H, *Gildengate Street* 1845 White
S: Georges Street 1696 Cleer, *St George's Street or Gilden Gate Street* 1746 B, *St George Street* 1920 6" Map
Middle Street c. 1720 K, 1885 OS, 1887 Knights, *St Georges Middle Street* 1830 M&M
Neubriggate Ed1 K, *Blackfriers Bridge Street* c. 1720 *ib*, *Black Friers Bridge Street* 1746 B, *Blackfirars Bridge street* 1845 White, *St George's*

Bridge Street 1766 King, 1789 H, 1830 M&M, 1845 White, *Bridge Street* 1885 OS

Black Friers Street 1746 B, 1766 King, *Black Friars Street* 1789 H, 1830 M&M

Mer(e)holt referred to a wood at the northern end of the street. The first element is OE **(ge)mære** 'boundary' rather that OE **mere** 'pool', which has been suggested as an alternative (Campbell 25). The second element is OE **holt** 'wood'. The boundary of Taverham Hundred as well as the boundary of Blofield Hundred was once close to Mereholt.

The first element of *Gildenegate* is probably OE **(ge)gilda** (*gildena* gen.pl.) 'member of a guild'. The street's connection with guilds is not clear. Knights (71) suggests that guilds used this street for their processions. *St George's Church* stands by the junction of St George's Street with Colegate. *Middle Street* may originally have applied only to the middle portion of the stretch 'beyond the water'.

St George's Street now runs from St Andrew's Plain to St Crispin's Road (the Inner Link Road). The continuation to the north of St Crispin's Road used to be part of St George's Street but has been renamed *Botolph Street.* The portion from St Andrew's Plain to Blackfriars Bridge was anciently *Neubriggate,* later *Blackfriars* (*Bridge*) *Street;* the section from the Bridge down to Colegate was anciently *Neubriggate,* later *Blackfriars Bridge Street* or *St George's Bridge Street* (*v.* Blackfriars Bridge); the rest was *Gildengate,* or *St George's* (*Middle*) *Street,* or *Middle Street.*

BRIDEWELL ALLEY
Seint Andreu Lane 1397 K, *St Andrews Lane* 1766 King
Bridewell c. 1720 K
Bridewell Alley 1789 H, 1830 M&M, 1845 White, 1885 OS

Runs from St Andrew's Street to Bedford Street, along the west side of St Andrew's churchyard. *Bridewell* refers to a building which began as a private house about 1370 and was the home of William Appleyard (first Mayor of Norwich 1404, died 1419). In 1585 this house became a *Bridewell,* i.e. a place of correction for 'vagabonds and minor delinquents' (NoRec II cv). The name derives from the London penal institution which stood near St Bride's (or Bridget's) Well, not far from Fleet Street (*v.* OED s.v. and SN 160).

BRIGG STREET
Over Wastelgate 1395 K
Market Lane n.d. K, 1696 Cleer
Brigg's Lane c. 1720 K, 1746 B, *Briggs Lane* 1766 King, 1789 H, 1830
   M&M, *Briggs's-lane* 1819 Stacy, *Briggs Street* 1845 White, 1885 OS

For *Wastel-*, *v.* Wastel Market (Market Place). The name
Market Lane is due to the fact that it provided an approach from
the Horsemarket (now Rampant Horse Street) to the Market Place.
The street was called *Briggs's Lane* from Augustine *Briggs* the Elder
(died 1684) and the Younger (died 1704), who had a messuage
here. Both were aldermen and mayors (K 17, Blomefield IV 217
ff.).
About 1810 a subscription was started by the Rev. William D'Oyley
for the widening of Briggs Lane (*v.* Stacy 50). The work was not finally
carried out until c. 1850, long after D'Oyley's death (note the change
from *lane* to *street*). Further widenings were undertaken at the turn of
the century and during the last war (Nobbs 14).

BULL CLOSE, *Bull Close* 1766 King, 1830 M&M, 1845 White, 1885
OS, links Cowgate to Bull Close Road. On King's Map, Bull Close is a
field bounded by Magdalen Street, Cowgate (All Saints Street),
Bargate Street and the Wall. An inn called the Bull stood in Bull
Close Road, on the corner with Bull Close (Riddington Young 65).

BULL CLOSE ROAD, *Bull Close Road* 1885 OS, 1920 OS 6" Map,
runs from the site of Magdalen Gates to the bottom of Silver Road.

BULL LANE, *Bull Lane* 1845 White, 1885 OS, 1920 OS 6" Map, used
to run from All Saints Green to St Stephen's Street but now only the
southern section remains (south of the Bus Station). The pub stood on
the corner with St Stephen's Street. The Bull was a popular sign; in
1845 there were five Bull inns in Norwich (White 190).

CALVERT STREET
Snayl(e)gate Ed3 K, 1397, 1520, 1536 *NPD*, *Snailgate* 1492 *ib*, *Snail
   Gate* 1766 King, 1789 H
Snackegate Street Eliz1, c. 1720 K, *Snackgate wey* Eliz1 *ib*, *Snackstrete*
   1620 *ib*
Doughty's Hospital Street c. 1720 K, *Doughtie's Hospital street* 1725 K[2]

St George's Street or Preachers Street 1746 B
Calvert Street 1819 Stacy, 1830 M&M, 1845 White, 1885 OS

Connects Colegate with St Crispin's Road; it used to run further
north but was truncated in the construction of the Inner Link Road.
OE **snægl** 'snail' is on record as a 13th-century surname; Reaney (s.n.
Snail) adduces two instances: Hamelin *Sneyl* 1221 (Sf), Geoffrey *Snayl*
1277 (C). The absence of a genitive-*s* in *Snaylegate* does not
necessarily tell against the first element being a personal name; from
the 14th century on, it became increasingly common for -*s* to be dropped in street-names beginning with a personal name (*v.* SN 8 ff.).
Snackegate, etc., is a corruption of the original name.

The buildings of *Doughty's Hospital* are east of Calvert Street and
north of Golden Dog Lane. The name *St George's Street* on
Blomefield's Map is surprising; cf. Botolph Street -- St George's
Street *supra*. According to Stacy (68), Calvert Street 'was named
from a noble house, built by a counsellor Calvert'. Cf. John *Calvert*
(sheriff of the City 1741, died 1744), who has a monument in St George
Colegate (Pevsner 240).

CARROW HILL -- CARROW ROAD, *New Road* 1830 M&M,
Carrow New road 1845 White, *Carrow Road* 1885 OS, is a street on the
southern extremity of the Butter Hills (*q.v.*). A road was built in 1817
to provide an approach from Ber Street to the old Carrow Bridge
(Stacy 63). With the building of the new bridge (*v.* Carrow Bridge) it
was partly laid out differently, and the section west of King Street was
named Carrow Hill.

CARROW VALE is a recent development east of Carrow Hill.

CASTLE MEADOW. Since the late nineteenth century (1885 OS)
this is the name of the thoroughfare from Orford Place to Agricultural
Hall Plain. It follows the line of the old Inner Bailey to the west and
north of the Castle and is not to be confused with the original Castle
Meadow (*v.* Norwich Castle).

CATHEDRAL STREET, *Cathedral Street* 1885 OS, 1920 OS 6" Map,
leads from Prince of Wales Road to the Horsefair (now a mere strip of
grass in St Faith's Lane). Like St Vedast Street (formerly South
Cathedral Street), Cathedral Street was created as part of the Prince of

Wales Road scheme in the 1860s.

CATHERINE WHEEL OPENING, runs from the north end of St Augustine's Street, on the east side, and links up with Magpie Road (Nobbs 16). The *Catherine Wheel* pub (1845 White, 1885 OS) stands at the St Augustine's Street end of the Opening. St Catherine of Alexandria (or of Mount Sinai) was tortured between spiked wheels before being beheaded (*v.* Wicks 93).

CATTLE MARKET STREET
Beomont Lane 1696 Cleer, *Beaumont's Hill and Lane* 1766 *Beecheno*
Common Pump Street c. 1720 K, *Common Pump Street - - Beaumont*
   Hill & Lane 1766 King, *Common Pump Street - - Beaumonts Hill* 1789
   H, *Buff Coat Lane* 1793 Beecheno, *(the) Common Pump Street* 1819
   Stacy, 1861 *Beecheno, Common Pump Street - - Buff Coat Lane* 1830
   M&M, *Pump Street - - Beaumont's hill, now called Buffcoat lane* 1845
   White
Cattle Market Street 1885 OS

   Runs from Rose Lane to Golden Ball Street along the east side of the Old Cattle Market. Kirkpatrick (K 12) gives the name Common Pump Street to the entire stretch of road from Ber Street (Timber Hill) to Rose Lane. The pump, according to him, stood where Golden Ball Street now joins Cattle Market Street. Beecheno, however, places it where Rose Avenue joins the latter. King and most map-makers and compilers of directories after him assign the name *Common Pump Street* only to the northern half of what is now Cattle Market Street. The name of the southern half is variously given as *Beaumont's Hill* or *Buff Coat Lane*. Cf. 'Father' *Beamont*, inn-keeper, 1564 NoRec, Thomas *Beamonde*, alderman, 1571 *ib.* The *Buff Coat* was an inn on the east side of the street, not far from the entrance to the present Rouen Road.
   The ditches on the south side of the Castle were levelled c. 1740, and a livestock market was held there every Saturday right up to the early 1960s, when it was moved to Hall Street, Harford (*v.* Blomefield IV 124, Stacy 280, White 149, Pevsner 283).

THE CHANTRY, *Chantry* 1845 White, *Chantry Lane* 1885 OS, off Theatre Street, along the east side of the Assembly House, leads to the site of the Chantry Chapel of the College of St Mary.

CHANTRY ROAD, *Chantry Road* 1920 OS 6" Map, runs from Chapel Field East to Malthouse Road, to the south of the Theatre and the Assembly House. It was named from the former chantry of the College of St Mary and is indicated, but nameless, on the 1885 OS Map.

CHAPEL FIELD EAST, CHAPEL FIELD NORTH, *Chapel Field East, Chapel Field North* 1920 OS 6" Map. These streets skirt Chapel Field Gardens to the east and north.

CHAPEL LOKE, *Chapel Loke* 1885 OS. This narrow by-way, situated between Surrey Street and Ber Street, provides an approach to the undenominational Surrey Chapel. *Loke* is an East Anglian dial. word (Nf and E Sf, according to EDD) meaning 'a lane, a short, narrow, blind lane, a cul-de-sac', to be derived from OE **loc** or **loca** 'fold, enclosure'. Cf. Dunstan's Lock PN L 23.

CHARING CROSS
(*in vico de*) *Tonsoria* 1286 *et freq* to 1308 *R*
(*vicus de*) *Tunderie* 1289, 1298 K
le Scherereshil 1309 K, *Sherershil* 1309 *R, Scherer hil* 1351, 1355 K,
    Sherereshille 1367 *ib, le Schererys hill* 1404 *ib, Sherehill* 1626 BLR
Sherergate 1312, 1321 *R, Sheregate* 1316 *ib*
Sherererowe 1317 K, 1319 *R, Shereresrowe* 1329 *ib, Shereman rowe* 1362
    K
Sherill Cross 1494 K, *Shering Crosse, Shereman Crosse* 1626 BLR,
    Charing Cross 1696 Cleer, 1728 Hoyle, 1766 King, 1789 H, 1830
    M&M, 1885 OS, *Sharing Cross* c. 1720 K, *Sherew or Charing Cross*
    1746 B

    This is a stretch of road from the St Andrew's Street - - Duke Street crossroads to St Benedict's Street. MLat *tonsoria*, OF *tonderie* 'workshop where woollen cloth is shorn'; ME *sherere, sherman* 'one who shears woollen cloth'. The 18th-century (and modern) form is an imitation of the London street-name. The Cross was removed in 1732 (Stacy 280).

CHARLTON ROAD connects Cowgate and Bull Close Road.

CHATHAM STREET, *Chatham Street* 1885 OS, 1920 OS 6" Map,

connects Sussex Street with Gildencroft, Jenkins Lane and Quakers Lane. The nearby Pitt Street (*q.v.*) was thought to allude to William Pitt the Younger; hence *Chatham Street*.

CHERRY LANE

Cherry Ally 1696 Cleer, *Cherry Alley* 1746 B, 1766 King, 1789 H, 1830
    M&M, *Cherry Lane* 1845 White, 1885 OS
St Olaves Lane c. 1720 K, *St Tooley's-lane* 1745 B

Runs from Pitt Street to Botolph Street, south of Cherry Tree Opening. This lane was known to Blomefield as *Cherry Alley* or *St Tooley's-lane* (IV 475). *Cherry* refers to a pub called the *Cherry Tree*. *Tooley* was of course due to misdivision, the *t* of *Saint* having been attached to *Olave*; cf. Tooley Street (London, Southwark), which was known to John Stow (1598) as *St Olaves Street* from the local parish church (PN Sr 33; cf. also Field GL 127).

CHERRY TREE OPENING

the quondam Churchyard of St Olave, now called the Cherry ground c.
    1720 K, *Cherry tree yard* 1845 White, *Cherrytree Yard* 1885 OS

After the demolition of St Olave's Church (not long after 1546), the churchyard was leased out by the Dean and Chapter (Blomefield IV 475). A public house, the *Cherry Tree*, was built on the site (Riddington Young 51).

CHURCH STREET

(the) Gun(n) Lane 1696 Cleer, 1746 B, 1766 King, 1789 H, 1830 M&M,
    1845 White
Church Street 1885 OS

This street leads from Rampant Horse Street to Hay Hill. The first name derived 'from the Sign of a Wheel Gun or Cannon at an Alehouse there' (K 18). The name *Church Street*, from the churches at either end, St Stephen and St Peter Mancroft, has recently been changed to WILLIAM BOOTH STREET, which, of course, refers to the founder of the Salvation Army.

COBURG STREET, *Cobourg street* 1845 White, *Coburg Street* 1885 OS, off the west side of St Stephen's Street, used to lead to Chapel

Field East but now ends at the south end of Malthouse Road. It is
blocked at both ends by factory gates. The name commemorates the
house of Saxe-Coburg-Gotha (cf. Field GL 151).

COCKEY LANE (lost), *communis venella vocat Cokeye* 1346 K,
Cokeye Lane 1390 *ib*. This lane would seem to have followed the
upper course of the Great Cockey, i.e. from Jack's Pit northwards
between Magna Newgate (Surrey Street) and Swyne Market (All Saints
Green). *v*. K 16.

COLEGATE
Colegate c. 1220 Bodl, c. 1300 to 1501 *NPD*, 1431 FF, 1766 King,
    Colgate 1254-75 Val, 1287 *et freq* to 1313 *R*, 1380, 1547 Pat, 1448 to
    1492 *NPD*, 1535 VE, 1696 Cleer, *Collegate* 1292 to 1309 *R*, 1428 FA
street, formerly called Colegate, now the Black Boys' street c. 1725 K²
St Mile's or Colegate or St Clement's street 1746 B
Colegate Street 1789 H, 1830 M&M, 1885 OS

    The first element of *Colegate* is either the OE font-name *Cola* (gen.
Colan), alternatively Scand *Kol*(*i*), or the family-name *Cole*, which
derives from either of those. *Cole* could also be a hypocorism for
Nicolaus (*v*. ELPN 78). Cf. Colkirk (Nf) and *Colechurch Street*, now
Old Jewry, in the City of London (SN 96). The family-name *Cole* is
well evidenced in Norwich, e.g. Henry *Cole* of Wroxham 1278 *et freq*
to 1313 NoD, Walter *Cole* of St Faith's 1303, 1304 *ib*, Richard *Cole* of
Wymundham 1306 to 1336 *ib*. The *Black Boys* pub is still (1981) in
business. It stands opposite the south end of Calvert Street (*v*.
Riddington Young 58). The Church of St Michael or Miles (disused)
stands at the west end of the street (at the junction with Coslany
Street), that of St Clement at the east end (at the junction with Fye
Bridge Street).
    Off Colegate is OLD MEETING HOUSE ALLEY (*Old
Meeting-house alley* 1845 White). The Congregational Meeting House,
built in 1693, received the distinguishing addition *Old* when its
neighbour, the Unitarian Octagon Chapel, was built in 1756.

COSLANY STREET -- OAK STREET
Coslania 1146-9, 1175-86 Holme, 1287 *R*, *Choselanie* c. 1250 *Langley*,
    Coslane 1254-75 Val, 1269 *Ass*, *Coslanie* c. 1255, 13 *Coxf*, *Coslayne*
    1258 *ib*, *Coselany(e)* 1285 NoD, 1286 *et freq* to 1312 *R*, 1288 NoLeet,

1381 Pat, 1385 (p) *NPD, Koselanye* 1287 *R Coselanie* 1287, 1289 *ib*, 1293, 1322 NoD, *Coslanye* 1287, 1298, 1312 *R*, 1299 Wals, 1340 Pat, 1428 FA, *Coselayne* 1293 *R*, 1354 Pat, *Coselaine* (p) 1303 *R*
St Martins Street 1696 Cleer, *Coselany or St Martin at the Oak Street* 1746 B, *St Martins at Oak or Coslany Street* 1766 King, *Coslany Street -- St Martins at Oak Street* 1789 H, *Coslany Street -- St Martin at Oak Street* 1830 M&M, *Coslany street* 1845 White, *Coslany Street -- St Martin's Street* 1885 OS, *Oak Street* 1920 OS 6" Map

The earliest forms refer to a city area, *Coslania* , which occurs as the name of a subleet (*v.* Leets). The original Coslany seems to have been an island amid riverside marshes (*v.* Carter Fig. 8), so the final element may well be OE (Angl) **ēg** 'island'. The second element is more difficult. It cannot very well be *land*, seeing that there are no *d*-spellings. Formally it seems possible to suggest OE **lane, lanu** 'lane', which could mean 'the course of a river in meadowland', as it still does in Scottish dialects (EDD). Cf. the river Asland (PN La 126). Since there are reasons to believe that *Coslany* is a name of considerable antiquity, such a suggestion would not seem unwarranted. If it were not for the total absence of *r*-spellings, one would be tempted to posit Brit **cors** 'reed; bog' (ERN 95) as the first element, the first part of the name being a British-English hybrid *corslane* 'a stretch of the river with plenty of reeds'. From a topographical point of view this would not seem an unreasonable meaning. Although formally unobjectionable, an OE pers.n. **Cosa* or **Cossa* seems a less convincing alternative, assuming we are dealing with a river name + *ēg*. Other place-names possibly containing the element *cors* 'reed; bog' are Crossfield (PN C 144), Cosford (PN Wa 107) and Corsham (PN W 95 f.), though Corsham is rather doubtful.

Today *Coslany Street* is the name of the southern part of the street which is otherwise called *Oak Street*. (Coslany Street extends from St Miles Bridge to Colgate; the rest is Oak Street.) Cf. St Martin Coslany Church, also known as *St Martin at the Oak*.

COTMAN FIELDS, a new housing-development off Bishopgate (east of the Gt Hospital), named after John Sell *Cotman*, the painter, who moved to Norwich in 1806.

COWGATE

Kugate c. 1250 K, 1300 *D&C, Cugate* 1289, 1307 (2x) *R, Cougate* 1307,
 1316 *ib*, 1327 K, *Cowegate* 1391 *ib*, 1626 BLR, *Cowgate* 1485 K, 1533
 to 1538 *NPD*, 1746 B, 1766 King
Cowgate Street 1789 H, 1845 White, 1885 OS, 1920 OS 6" Map, *Cow
 Gate Street* 1830 M&M
Alhalwen Lane 1397 K, *All Saints Street* 1746 B, 1766 King, 1789 H,
 1830 M&M, 1845 White, *All Saints' street, now more commonly called
 Little Magdalen-street* 1819 Stacy
Carme Strete 1391 K, *St James's Street* 1746 B, *White Friars' street* 1819
 Stacy, 1845 White

OE **cū** 'cow'. Schram (148) suggests that dairymen lived here, but
the name may just as well refer to cows having been driven to and from
pasture in Cowholme along this street (cf. SN 106). The street led
from Whitefriars Bridge to Magdalen Street but is now divided into
two by the roundabout close to St James's Church.
    Alhalwen Lane and *All Saints Street* referred to the part leading to
Magdalen Street, north of St James's Church. This name was due to
the lost All Saints Fyebridge Church, which also lent its name to
Alderhalwen Welle 1378 K, some distance to the south.
WHITEFRIARS STREET, formerly *Carme Strete* and *St James's
Street*, is the southern part of the street, from St James's Church to
Whitefriars Bridge. The Carmelites or White Friars had their friary
east of the street.

COW HILL, *St Giles's Hill* 1789 H, *Cow Hill* 1830 M&M, 1845 White,
1885 OS, between Pottergate and Upper St Giles Street; anonymous on
the early maps; also nameless in Kirkpatrick (50), where it is referred
to as 'a very broad Street on the Ascent of a Hill S ... along the West
end of ye Churchyard [of St Giles] into Newport'. The modern name
is from an eighteenth-century public house, the Red Cow (Wicks 120,
Riddington Young 25).
    WATLING'S YARD (Charles *Watling*), CHESTNUT COURT and
COW YARD run off the west side of Cow Hill. Cow Yard, by St
Giles Parish Hall, is where the old pub stood.

CROSS LANE, *Tubbis Lane* 1766 King, 1789 H, 1830 M&M, *Cross
Lane* 1845 White, 1885 OS; a lane which links St George's Street with
Calvert Street. Cf. the surname *Tubby* (Ed. *Tubby* 1676 NoRec), of

Scand origin; ODan, ON *Tubbi* DGP I 1479, Feilitzen 388. Lind (1043) explains it as a pet form of ON *Þorbjǫrn*. *v.* also Reaney s.n. *Tubb(s)*. There was also a *Tubby's Yard* off Muspole Street (1845 White, 1885 OS).

At the junction of this lane with Calvert Street there stood a cross, which in Elizabeth I's time was called the Stumped Cross (the truncated cross). By the time Kirkpatrick wrote his memoir (c. 1720), this cross had been demolished for a long time (K 79). Later in the eighteenth century, however, a new cross was erected, which came to be known as *Cow Cross* (1766 King, 1789 H, 1830 M&M). According to tradition, the city cow-herd used to gather the citizens' cows here and drive them to the *Town Close*, which was outside St Stephen's Gates, in the common: *communitatem* (correctly *communam*) *Norwici* 1391 NoLeet, *ye comon* 1555 *ib*, *the Town-close* c. 1720 K, *Town close, Ipswich road* 1845 White, *the Town Close* 1891 NoLeet.

CROWN ROAD, *Crown Road* 1920 OS 6" Map, used to connect Agricultural Hall Plain with Cattle Market Street, but the north end was blocked in 1981-2 when the former Agricultural Hall (Anglia House) was connected with the former *Crown Bank*/General Post Office (built in 1866, *v.* Pevsner 262).

DAVEY PLACE, *Davey Place* 1830 M&M, 1845 White, 1885 OS, is a passage from the Market Place to Castle Street and, via DAVEY STEPS, to Castle Meadow, named after Alderman Jonathan *Davey*, who, in 1813, had the King's Head hostelry on the Walk pulled down to establish a direct communication with the Castle Ditches (Stacy 51). The inn was given new premises at the Castle Street end of the alley-way (Riddington Young 39).

DOVE STREET
Holdtor 1287 NoRec, 1296 to 1318 *R*, *Holdthor* 1287, 1288 *ib*, 1308, 1321 K, *Holthor* 1287 K, *Holtor* 1287, 1312 *R*, 1301 NoD, 1346, 1397 NoRec, *Oldtor* 1311, 1313, 1319 K, *Holter* 1543 NoRec, *Halter Way, now the Dove Lane* 1626 BLR
Smalegate 1290, 1294 *R*
St John's Lane 1546 K
Dove Lane 1696 Cleer, c. 1720 K, 1789 H, 1830 M&M, *Holtor or Dove Lane* 1746 B, *Dove Lane or Holtor* 1766 King, *Dove Street* 1885 OS

This street runs northwards from Guildhall Hill to Pottergate; on the other side of Pottergate it becomes St John Maddermarket. We assume that the second element of *Holdtor* is ME *tor(r)* 'tower'. It is doubtful whether this word was a survival of OE **torr**, since OF had also *tor* beside *tur*. The occasional *th*-spellings *(Holdthor)* are no doubt due to AN influence (Zachrisson 39 ff.).

It seems that a tower was put up here at an early date for some unspecified purpose (K 48, Blomefield IV 227). Kirkpatrick and Blomefield think that the first element is 'old', but as the spelling *Holdtor* is earlier and more frequent than *Oldtor*, the *H-* may be regarded as etymological. The first element is probably ME *hold* 'place of imprisonment, jail', (*v.* MED s.v. *hold* n. 2, 4 c). It is possible that the Holdtor was a predecessor of the Tollhouse, which, in turn, was succeeded by the Guildhall. *Smalegate* means 'the narrow street' (OE **smæl**). *St John's Lane* refers to the neighbouring St John Maddermarket Church, *Dove Lane* to 'the sign of the Dove at a Tavern' (K 48).

DUKE STREET, *Duke Street* 1830 M&M, 1845 White, 1885 OS, is the prolongation of Pitt Street from St Crispin's Road to Charing Cross. The stretch from St Mary's Plain to Charing Cross was constructed in the early 1820s. Pitt Street used to extend as far south as St Mary's Plain, but after the construction of St Crispin's Road the southern end was incorporated into Duke Street. Work on the Palace of the Dukes of Norfolk (on the south bank of the river, close to the bridge) was started c. 1602; most of it was pulled down little more than a century later (1711).

EBENEZER PLACE, (row of houses called) *Ebenezer Terrace* 1885 OS; this is a cul-de-sac that runs off Sussex Street, opposite Chatham Street. It used to connect Sussex Street with St Martins at Oak Wall Lane. *Ebenezer* is a biblical term, often adopted by dissenters for their congregation or a particular chapel (*v.* OED s.v.).

EDWARD STREET. The northern half of this street, which describes a curve from Magpie Road to Magdalen Street, is on the 1920 OS 6" Map, where it is nameless, however.

ELMESWELL LANE (lost)
Mustard man's Lane 1339, 1355 K

le Fishe Lane 1349 K, *Fishouse Lane* 1361 *ib*, *Fyss houslane* 1377 *ib*
Ermeswelle lane 1354, 1358, 1365 K, *Elmeswelle lane* 1378 *ib*,
   Elmeswellys Lane 1390 *ib*, *Ermeswelles Lane* 1395 *ib*, *Elmeswell or*
   Fishouse Lane 1746 B

This lane ran west from the Market Place, north of Wounded Heart Lane. *Mustard man's Lane* is 'from one William Mustardman, formerly owner of Houses here' (K 30), perhaps identical with Will. le *Mustardman* 1329 NoD (cf. Fransson 65). A *fishhouse* was a building for storing fish (*v.* Buildings). John de *Elmeswelle* (1312, 1320, 1324 NoD) was a taverner who had a messuage on the north side of this lane (K 30). Cf. Elmswell in the East Riding of Yorkshire (PN YE 154).

ELM HILL
Elm Lane 1696 Cleer, *the Friers or Elm Lane* 1746 B
the Elm Ground c. 1720 K, *Elm Hill and Elm Hill Street* 1789 H

Elm Hill was named from elm trees which stood here, two as early as Henry VIII's and Elizabeth I's times (K 60). The *Elm Ground* and *Elm Hill* originally referred only to the small open place, of triangular shape, from which the two streets Elm Hill and Waggon and Horses Lane fork out. On Hochstetter's Map the name *Elm Hill* also covers the short stretch between Prince's Street and this open place. *v.* Prince's Street.

ESDELLE STREET, *Esdelle Street* 1920 OS 6" Map, a post-1885 street (not in the Ordnance Survey of that year) that links St Augustine's Street to Edward Street and Magpie Road.

ESPERANTO WAY/LADY LANE
The Chapelle of the felde Lane 1451 K
Ladys Lane c. 1720 K, 1789 H, *Ladies Lane* 1746 B, *Lady's Lane* 1830
   M&M, 1845 White, *Lady Lane* 1885 OS

Runs from Bethel Street to Theatre Street in front of the Norwich Central Library. It was called *Ladys Lane* 'because it was made upon the Land of the College of Our Lady St Mary in the Fields, and lead to it' (K 22). According to Blomefield (IV 235), the original Lady's Lane, *Old Ladies-lane*, was sealed off, and *New Ladies-lane* was laid out in its stead more to the west. The name *Esperanto Way*, introduced in 1962 on completion of the Library, did not find general acceptance, and the name plate now reads 'Esperanto Way formerly Lady Lane'.

EXCHANGE STREET
Exchange Street (upper half only) 1830 M&M
Exchange street (upper half), *Museum street, now Post office street*
  (lower half) 1845 White
Exchange Street (upper half), *Post Office Street* (lower half) 1885 OS

Runs from Gentleman's Walk to St Andrew's Street. The section from the Walk to Lobster Lane - - Bedford Street (upper part) was the first to be built (1829). On the 1830 map the lower part of Exchange Street is indicated and labelled 'Intended New Street'. Exchange Street got its name from the Corn Exchange of 1828 in Bedford Street. A second, rather more stylish Exchange, built on the same site in 1863 (Pevsner 270), was pulled down in 1964.

On its completion in the early 1830s, the lower half of Exchange Street was at first briefly known as *Museum Street*, from the Norfolk and Norwich Museum (situated across St Andrew's Street, on the site of the Duke of Norfolk's Palace), then as *Post Office Street*, from the main Post Office at the south end of the street (White 158).

FARMERS AVENUE, *Farmers Avenue* 1920 OS 6" Map, skirts the south side of the Old Cattle Market; named from the *Jolly Farmers' Inn* (1845 White, 1885 OS, Wicks 26, Riddington Young 94).

FINKELGATE
Fenkelstreet 1506 K, *Fenkelgate* 1508 *ib, Finkel Street* 1746 B, *Finket*
  Street 1766 King, 1789 H, 1830 M&M, 1845 White, 1885 OS

It connects Ber Street with St Catherine's Plain. The name is a common one in Scandinavian England. Lindkvist derives Finkle Street in York from the OScand personal name *Finnkell* (LindkvistY 366). Smith suggests (PN YE 286 and EPNE I 169 f.) that the first element is either ME **fenkel**[1] 'fennel' or ME **fenkel**[2] 'corner, bend'. Schram (148) favours the interpretation 'fennel street', probably because the Norwich Finkelgate has no bend in it (unless one looks upon it as part of Surrey Street).   Ekwall (Studies[3] 47 ff.) thinks Lindkvist's suggestion worthy of consideration; the other two theories he rejects. Instead he suggests that there may have existed a ME verb **finkle* 'cuddle, pet' and that the name was originally an indecent one for 'lovers' lane'. Discussing Finkle Street in Lincoln, Cameron accepts Ekwall's suggestion as the most plausible (PN L 66).

FISHERGATE

(*St Edmund in*) *Fischergate* 1285, 1297 (2x) NoD, *Fischeregate* 1287 to 1312 *R*, 1332, 1365, 1381 K, *Fisscheregate* 1291 *R*, *Fissheregate* 1291, 1310 *ib*, 1302, 1358 K, *Fhisscheregate* 1297 *R*, *Fisshergate* 1301 NoD, 1322 *AddCh*, *Fhischeregate* 1306 *R*, *Fyscherrigate* 1308 K, *Fisheregate* 1312, 1314 *R*, 1337, 1354 K, *Fyssheregate* 1324 *ib*, *Fisherigate* 1324 *ib*, *Fishergate* 1326 *ib*, *Fysshergate* 1337 Pat, 1383 K, *Fychergate* 1341 *ib*, *Fysshereygate* 1385 *ib*

Fisher Gate Street 1746 B, *Fishers Gate or Fishgate* 1766 King, *Fish Gate Street* 1789 H, 1830 M&M, 1845 White, 1885 OS

St Edmunds Street 1696 Cleer, *the old ... Fish-gate is now known by the same name as the parish* 1819 Stacy

This street runs from Fyebridge Street to Whitefriars (Cowgate), along the north bank of the Wensum. In medieval times there was a concentration of fishermen (OE **fiscere**) in St Edmund's parish. The fish was landed at St Edmund's Quay (cf. Hansard Lane).

Off the north side of Fishergate is a blind alley called THOMPSON'S YARD (1885 OS). West of Thompson's Yard is THOROUGHFARE YARD (1885 OS), which connects Fishergate with Magdalen Street.

FISHERS LANE

Smalegate 1285 *et freq* to 1316 *R*, *Smalelane* 1307, 1312 *ib*, *Le Smale lane* 1324, 1351, 1380 K, *Smal lane* 1383, 1421 *ib*, *Smale Lane alias St Lawrence Lane* 1626 BLR

S[l]opereslane 1306 *R*, *Sloperes Lane* 1355 K

Seyn Laurence Lane 1378, 1389 K, *St Laurence lane* 1585 *AddCh*

Fishers Lane 1696 Cleer, 1746 B, 1766 King, 1789 H, 1830 M&M, *Fisher's Lane* 1845 White, 1885 OS

This is a continuation of St Laurence's Lane, southwards from Pottergate to St Giles. *Smalegate*, etc., signifies 'the narrow lane'; OE **smæl**. *Sloperes Lane* is from a man surnamed *Sloper*; Richard le *Slopere* held a messuage here in 1286 (K 49), to be compared with Ric. *Sloper'* 1332 and Adam le *Slopere* 1291 (Fransson 114). A *slopere* was a maker or seller of slops, i.e. 'outer garments that were "slipped" on' (for this etymology *v.* LöfvenbergC 42; Fransson 114). *Fishers Lane* is probably from a property holder in this street.

FRELANE (lost), *Frelane* 1356, 1386, 1402 K, led from Oak Street westwards to the river. According to Kirkpatrick (K 73) it was near Water Lane[2] (*q.v.*).

FRIARS' QUAY, *Freris lane* 1394 K. The medieval *Freris lane* is not identical with the present street but it was not far from it and the name-giving factor seems to be the same. According to Kirkpatrick (K 76), *Freris lane* belonged to the Black Friars, who used it for transporting goods from the river to their first establishment (*v.* Black Friars).

FYE BRIDGE STREET - - MAGDALEN STREET
Fibrigestrete c. 1200 *D&C, Fibrigge Strete* 13 *ib; Fibriggat(e)* 1200 *et freq* to 1535 *NPD*, 1266 to 1368 *D&C*, 1285 to 1304 *R*, 1288 NoLeet, *Fibbriggate* 1233 *Phillipps, Fibrigate* 13 *Coxf*, 13 *D&C*, 1256, 1260 *NPD, Fibriggegate* 13 *Holme*, 1262 *AddCh*, 1275 RH, 1289 *R, Fifbriggate* 1266 K, *Fiuebriggegate* 1285 *NCReg, in vico de Fybrig* 13 *D&C, in vico de Fibrigge* 13 *Phillipps, in vico vocato Fibrigg* 13 *NPD; Fybriggate* 1235, c. 1270, 1538 *NPD*, 1257, 1331 *D&C*, 1297, 1309 *R*, 1428 FA, 1447 *NPD; Fibrigge gate ex opposito Crucis* 1538 *ib, Fybryggate strete* 1550 K, *Fybrigg Streete to Stumpe Cross* 1626 BLR, *Fibriggate streete* 1627 *D&C, Fibridgate Street* 1673 *ib*
Magdalen Street 1696 Cleer, *Magdalen Street vulgo Maudlin Street* c. 1720 K, *Fibridge-gate now Stumpcross or Magdalen Street* 1746 B, *Fye Bridge Gate* (south of Stump Cross) - - *Magdalen Street* (north of Stump Cross) 1766 King, *Magdalen Street* 1789 H, 1819 Stacy, 1830 M&M, 1845 White, *Fyebridge Street* (south of Colegate) -- *Magdalen Street* (north of Colegate) 1885 OS

v. Fye Bridge. Fye Bridge Street originally extended from Tombland to the City Wall, but the section south of the river soon became known as *Cookrow (v.* Wensum Street) while, north of the bridge, the name Magdalen Street (from the chapel and hospital of St Mary Magdalen outside the City Wall, on the road to Sprowston) all but ousted the old name. Today the name *Fye Bridge St.* applies only to the stretch from the bridge to St Clement's Church.

Stump Cross ('the broken cross'), which stood approximately where St Crispin's Road now crosses Magdalen Street, is mentioned in documents of 1500 and 1538 (K 83). Demolished in the late 16th cent., it was re-erected in 1640 only to be taken down again four years later (K 83). The place where it stood went by the old name as late as 1885 (OS Map), if not later.

GENTLEMAN'S WALK ("THE WALK")
Le Nether Rowe 1363 to 1513 K, *the Nethe(r)rowe* 1397 NoRec, 1508 K,
  the Netherowe alias Souter Rowe 1480 K, *Le Nedyr rowe* 1491 *ib*
Gentlemen's Walk c. 1720 K, *Nether Row or Gent. Walk* 1766 King,
  Gentleman's Walk 1845 White, 1920 OS 6" Map, *The Walk* 1885 OS

This thoroughfare extends along the bottom (east) side of the Market Place, from White Lion Street to London Street. *Netherrowe* 'the lower row' (OE **neoðera, niðera**) is in contrast to the *Overrowe* (*v.* St Peter's Street). In 1480 it is called *the Netherowe alias Souter Rowe* (*v.* Souter Row in the Market Place). Kirkpatrick, explaining *Gentlemen's Walk*, says that 'on Saturdays, at Sessions time & other occasions, when the Gentlemen of the Country resort to yᵉ City, this is the usual place of their walking for their divertion & having discourse together, as it is also for the Principal Citizens' (K 28).

GILDENCROFT
Gildencroft c. 1260, 1428, 1498 *NPD*, 1291, 1294, 1315 NoD, 1296
  TophCh, 1299, 1301 *R, Gildene croft(e)* 13 *Coxf,* 1287 *et freq* to 1319
  R, c. 1290, 1337 *NPD, Gyldenecroft* 1296 *TophCh, Gildennecroft* 1310,
  1313 *R, Gyldencroft* 1466, 1574 K, *Gyldyncroft* 1515 *ib, Gyldon Crofte*
  1547 Pat, *Gilding Croft* 1696 Cleer, *Gilden Croft* 1746 B, 1766 King,
  1789 H, 1885 OS, *the Gilden-croft* 1819 Stacy, *Gilden croft lane* 1845
  White

Once a large open space between Jenkins Lane and the City Wall, it is now a street that links Chatham Street with St Augustine's Street, running along the south side of St Augustine's churchyard.

OE *gildenacroft* 'the guild brethren's croft', OE **(ge)gilda, croft** (so already K 82). The Anglo-Saxons do not seem to have had any trade or craft guilds, but social-religious fraternities of guild brethren are known to have existed from the first half of the 11th cent. (*v.* Loyn 123 f., Unwin xxiii ff.). In this connection it is perhaps worth noticing that inscriptions on rune-stones at Bjälbo (e11th c.) and Törnevalla (somewhat later) testify to the existence of merchants' guilds in Sweden (province of Östergötland) in the last period of the Viking age (v. ENS 118). Two rune-stones found at Sigtuna (l11th c.) show that there was a guild of Frisians, clearly merchants, in this city (ib). Trade guilds were for a long time discouraged in Norwich (cf. K 36 note 3), but they grew steadily stronger despite the prohibition of the King and the Bailiffs. There was a *Gildenecroft* in Writtle parish (PN Ess 37). For a discussion of this type of name, v. PN Wo 124-6.

The north-west corner of the original croft was called *Justyngacre* 1523, 1525 K, *Justing Acre* 1626 BLR, *Justyng Acre* 1746 B, *Justings Acre* 1766 King (*just* or *joust* 'engage in single combat on horse-back'). In or near Gildencroft there was also an observation hill, *Tothille* 1291 K, *Tythille* 1364 ib, *Tothylle* 1397 ib, *Tote Hill* 1626 BLR, *Tut Hill* 1746 B (OE **tōt-hyll** 'look-out hill').

GOAT LANE, LOWER AND UPPER

Stongate 1268, 1277 NfD, 1286 *et freq* to 1367 *NPD*, 1286, 1290, 1298 *R*,
  Stonegate 1276 *D&C*, 1311, 1314 *R*, *Stonegate Lane* 1568 K
Magna Stongate 1313 *R*, *Stanegate magna* 1345 K, *Micle Stongate* 1375
  ib, *Stonegate Magna* 1561 *NPD*, 1626 BLR, 1746 B; *Est Stongate* 1450
  ib; *Goat Lane* 1696 Cleer, *Lower Goat Lane or Stongate Magna* 1766
  King, *Lower Goat Lane* 1789 H, 1830 M&M, 1845 White, 1885 OS
Parva Stongate 1313 *R*, *Stongate parva* 1314, 1351, 1361 K, 1746 B,
  Inferior Stongate 1323, 1324 K, *Litel Stongate* 1375, 1380, 1385 *ib*, *Lytel
  Stongate* 1386 *ib*, *Huvere Stongate* 1329 *R*, *Overstongate* 1332 *ib*, *Over
  Stongate* 1380, 1391 K, *Newe Stongate* 1450 *ib*; *Blynd Stongate* 1473 *ib*,
  Blinde Stongate or Little Stongate 1626 BLR; *Goat Lane* 1696 Cleer,
  Back Goat Lane c. 1720 K, *Upper Goat Lane or Stongate Parva* 1766
  King, *Upper Goat Lane* 1789 H, 1830 M&M, 1845 White, 1885 OS

These parallel streets lead out of Pottergate and end in St Giles Street and Guildhall Hill. Cf. Stonegate in York, which Smith interprets as 'the stone-paved street' (PN YE 298). Orders for paving certain Norwich streets are not known to have been passed until 1428-9; the earliest extant orders are those of 1467 (NoRec II cxxix, 97). Thus *Stonegate* is more likely to have meant 'the stony street' than 'the stonepaved street' (OE **stān**). *Stone* is also evidenced as a personal name: cf. Johannes *Ston* and Adam *Ston* 1288, 1292 NoLeet, Roger *Ston* 1290 *R*, possibly a locative surname, although it may also derive from a font-name, OE *Stān* (*v.* SNPh 40, 1968, 11). The first element *blinde* usually referred to a street where there was no thoroughfare; *v.* **blind**. According to Kirkpatrick, *Inferior Stongate* actually refers to Upper Goat Lane (*Over Stongate*). *Goat Lane* is from the sign of an inn which stood here (K 49).

GOLDEN BALL STREET

Golden Ball Alley 1696 Cleer, *Golden Ball Lane* c. 1720 K, 1766 King, 1789 H, 1819 Stacy, 1830 M&M, *Golden Ball Street* 1845 White, 1885 OS

Woolpack Street 1696 Cleer

The name derives from an inn 'at the N.W. corner House next the Castle Dikes' (K 12). In connection with alterations to the Castle Hill in 1862 the name was transferred to the western part of Pump Street (*v.* Cattle Market Street). Hudson thinks that the original Golden Ball Street, which extended as far as the Castle Bridge, was identical with *Barningham Stile*. This identification has not been accepted by later scholars (*v.* King's Arms Lane). The Woolpack was a pub opposite St John Timberhill Church.

GOLDEN DOG LANE

Brent Lane Hy8 K, 1566, 1571, 1572 *NPD*, *Brentlane* 1580 *ib*
(the) Golden Dog Lane 1696 Cleer, c. 1720 K, 1789 H, 1830 M&M, 1845 White, 1885 OS
Brent Lane now Golden Dog Lane 1746 B, *Golden Dog or Brent Lane* 1766 King

This lane, which connects Calvert Street with Magdalen Street, is mentioned in 1287 and 1294 'but by no proper Name, only called the common Lane which leads from the Church of St Mary the burnt to the King's Way' (K 79). The name *Brent Lane* was probably elliptical, *(St Mary the) Brent Lane* (*v.* **brende, brente**). The church stood at the Magdalen Street end of the lane. An *NPD* document of 1558-9 describes the lane as a footpath (*quandam viam pedisequiam*) through the north side of the churchyard (cf. Blomefield IV 450). Kirkpatrick, on the other hand, places the lane south of the church (K 79). The modern name is from the *Golden Dog* alehouse, which is known to have existed in 1626 (K *ib*) but seems to have closed down not long afterwards. A later pub by the same name and at the same place (on the corner of Magdalen Street) survived until comparatively recently (Riddington Young 56).

GOOSE HILL (lost)
Gosehil 1267 K, 1287 to 1306 *R*, *Gosehill* 1287, 1289, 1303 *ib*, *Cosehil*
    (sic) 1291 NoRec, 1326 K, *Gosehyl* 1303 *R*, 1318 K, *Goshil* 1306, 1307,
    1322 *R*, *Gosil* 1309 K, *Gosehille* 1360 *ib*, *Gooshille* 1487 *ib*
Gosehill hall 1288 *R*, *Gosehilhalle* 1290 *ib*, *Gosehillhalle* 1746 B, *Aula
    de Gosehil* 1289 (2x) *D&C*
Goshill land R2 (1450) NoRec
Gose Hill Lane 1746 B

In the late fourteenth century *Goshill land* is described as 'belonging to the Prioress of Carrowe lying from Consford gates to Berstret gates' (NoRec I 57 f.), a description which fits in better with the Butter Hills. *Gosehill* was also the name of a street that ran southwards from Skeygate (now Horns Lane) to Holgate (now Mariners Lane).

OE **gōs** 'goose'; geese were perhaps kept to feed here (K 11).   *Gos* is, however, attested as a medieval surname, also in Norwich: William *Go(o)s* 1329, 1336 NoD, Edmund *Goos* 1414 NoRec, John *Goos* 1453 *ib*, 1457 *NPD*.   In 1290 Thomas de Heltheton, knight, granted his messuage called *Gosehilhalle* to Henry de Norwich, clerk (cf. the list of forms *supra* and Blomefield IV 76, NoD I 34, NoRec I 247).

GRAPES HILL
St Giles' hill 1845 White, *St Giles Hill* 1885 OS, *Grapes Hill* 1920 OS 6"
    Map

Grapes Hill is immediately outside the Wall.   It extends from the footbridge at Upper St Giles Street to St Benedict's Street. There are some remains of the Wall at the northern end (between Grapes Hill and the parallel Wellington Lane).   The hill has been levelled to make room for the Inner Link Road. The *Grapes* pub (now closed) used to mark the boundary of the parish of Heigham (Wicks 117).

GREYFRIARS ROAD, *Cooks Lane* 1766 King, 1789 H, 1830 M&M, *Cooke's lane* 1845 White, *Greyfriars Lane* 1885 OS, runs from King Street to Rose Lane.   For only a small portion of its length does the present Greyfriars Road follow the line of *Cooks Lane/Greyfriars*

Lane. Cook's Hospital originally stood in Rose Lane. The ancient Grey Friary stood between the present St Faith's Lane and Rose Lane.

GRIFFIN LANE (lost), *Griffin Lane* 1789 H, 1819 Stacy, 1830 M&M. From a sharp bend in St Faith's Lane there used to meander a lane south-west into King Street at a point opposite the site where the Crown Bank was later built (cf. Crown Road). The north-east end with its sharp turns was known as *Crinkle-crankle Lane* c. 1850 (K 5 note 1). *Griffin Lane*, from the *Griffin* alehouse on the corner of King Street (White 192, Wicks 71), would seem to refer especially to the King Street end of this lane.

HANSARD LANE
Lane leading to St Edmunds key (caium Sci Edmundi) 1313, 1338 K
St Edmunds Watering c. 1720 K
Fishers Gate 1746 B, *Fishers Gate Staithe* 1766 King
Water Lane 1845 White, 1885 OS

This street used to lead out of Fishergate along the west end of St Edmund's churchyard down to where the fishing-boats landed. In the eighteenth century there was a watering place for horses here (cf. K 86). Present-day Hansard Lane does not reach the river. The name *Hansard Lane* commemorates Luke Hansard, who in the late eighteenth and early nineteenth centuries printed William Cobbett's unofficial accounts of parliamentary debates. Hansard was born in Norwich (St Mary Coslany) in 1752.

HAY HILL/HAYMARKET
the Haymarket c. 1720 K, *Hay Market* 1746 B, 1766 King, 1789 H, *the old haymarket* 1819 Stacy, *Old Hay Market* 1830 M&M, 1845 White, *Haymarket* 1885 OS
Hay Hill 1920 OS 6" Map

Today *Haymarket* is only the name of the bottom (or east) side of the sloping square that is called *Hay Hill;* formerly it was the name of the whole piece of land. In the early nineteenth century the haymarket was moved to the Castle Ditches (Stacy 52 note), hence the use of the distinguishing epithet *Old* for a number of years. Cf. Drapery (Market Place).

HOBROUGH LANE, *Briggs Lane* 1696 Cleer, c. 1720 K, *Briggs Staith(e)* 1766 King, 1789 H, 1830 M&M; a lane off the east side of King Street, just north of Abbey Lane (formerly Cockey Lane), which, like Abbey Lane, no longer reaches the river. *Briggs Staith(e)* is actually printed along the lane on the maps quoted (1766, 1789, 1830). For *Briggs, v.* Brigg Street and St Julian's Wharf.

HORNS LANE
Caua via de skeydegate 1258 *NPD, Skeythegate* 1291, 1298 (2x, p) *R, Skethegate* 1296 K, *Skeygate* 1310, 1322 *R,* 1766 King, *Skeygate Lane* 1746 B, *Sky-gate 1789 H*
Fregate 1310, 1370 *R*
St Bartilmews Wente 1364 K, *Saynt Bartylmewes Lane* 1551 NoLeet, *St Bartylmews Lane* 1577 K, *St Bartilmews Lane* 1578 *ib, St Barthelmews Lane* 1583 *NPD*
Adcock Lane 1696 Cleer
Horns Lane c. 1720 K, *Sky-gate or Horns Lane* 1830 M&M, *Horn's Lane* 1845 White, 1885 OS

Horns Lane runs downhill off Ber Street. Like the nearby Thorn Lane it originally led to King Street. As regards the earliest forms, cf. *Skygates Farm* (Warter) PN YE 171. The Norwich *Sky-gate* and the Yorkshire *Skygates* have this in common that they both climb a steep ridge. The Norwich *Sky-gate* is on the eastern slope of the ridge that divides the City south of the Wensum into a western and an eastern part.

OScand **skeið** 'something that separates (and thus forms a natural boundary)', such as, for instance, a ridge. *v.* Falk-Torp, s.v. *Skei.* The most recent discussion of this element is by Stå hl in NSFL 388-91. In both cases, therefore, *Skygate* can be taken to mean 'the road on the ridge'. Kirkpatrick (11) makes mention of a reference in an Obedientiary Roll of 1478 to a field called *Skeygate* in Swardeston parish (Nf): 'cultura quae vocatur *Skeygate*'. This field probably derived its name from a track or way that separated it from another field (cf. Falk-Torp *l.c.* and George Flom, MLN 39, 1924, 208).

Fregate was the name of the eastern part of the street, in the parish of St Julian. It looks like an adjectival compound, 'the free street'. *St Bartilmews Wente*, etc., from St Bartholomew's Church (now in ruins), seems to have applied only to the western part (*v.* Campbell Map 6). *v.* ME **wente**. *Adcock*, a diminutive of Adam, is attested as a medieval surname in Reaney s.n. *Horns Lane* is from 'the sign of a pair of Bucks Horns' (K 10).

JENKINS LANE

Ienkins Lane 1696 Cleer, *Jenkins Lane* c. 1720 K, 1746 B, 1766 King,
1789 H, 1830 M&M, *Jenkins's Lane* c. 1720 K
Jenkin's lane 1845 White, *Jinkin's Lane* 1885 OS

This lane turns east out of Oak Street and leads to Chatham Street and Quakers Lane. Only a few feet wide, it is one of the narrowest passage-ways in Norwich. There are no nameplates. On the north side are the backs of some houses, on the south, a brick wall. It is mentioned in 1472 as 'a lane which leads from the field of Gildencroft into the said street [of Coslany] which was streightened by the buildings newly erected by Greg: Clerk in the Southside, and by the Master of St Giles's Hospital on the North side' (K 73). It must have been considerably wider then, or it could not possibly have been 'streightened' (i.e. 'narrowed'). It is not known who Jenkins was, but he probably inhabited this alley. *Gos Lane* is given as an alternative name by Blomefield.

KING'S ARMS LANE (lost)

Baryngham Stile 1354 K, *Bernyngham Style* 1421 *NPD*, *Bernyngham Stile*
1506 K, *Baringham Stile* 1613 *ib*, *Barningham Stile* 1766 King
(*the*) *King's (Kings) Arms Lane* c. 1720 K, 1746 B, 1819 Stacy

This lane ran off the south side of London Street (west of Redwell Plain/Bank Plain) into what was then Castle Meadow (now Agricultural Hall Plain). The inn called the King's Arms stood at the London Street end of the lane (K 46).

Beecheno and Campbell (Map 6) identify *Barningham Stile* with King's Arms Lane. This agrees with King's Map. Hudson identified it with the original Golden Ball Street (K 12 note 4, 46 note 6). *Barningham Stile* probably derives from a surname (cf. Walter de *Berningham* 1296 NoLeet, Robert *Bernyngham* 1441 K). Barningham is a Nf village.

KING'S HEAD LANE, *Kingshead Yard* 1885 OS, is a walk-way between Calvert Street and St George's Street (north of Cross Lane). The King's Head inn was on the corner of St George's Street.

KING STREET

Cunesford(e) 1147-9, 1168-75 Holme, 1205 *Coxf,* 1220 (p) Cur, c. 1250
   HMC, c. 1250 to 1323 *NPD,* c. 1250 to 1330 *D&C,* 1257 *Ass,* 1280 (p)
   LansdCh, 1289 to 1307 *R,* 1290 NoLeet, *Cung(g)esford(e)* 1165 *R,*
   1175-86 Holme, *Cunegesford* (p) 1166-70 P, c.   1250 *DC,* 1254 Val,
   1267 *AddCh, Cunegeford* 1171-4 P, *Cuningeford* 1173-5 *ib, Cuningesford*
   1175-86, 1190-1200 Holme, *Cunigefordia* 1183 *ib, Chunigesfort* c. 1200
   St Will, *Cunungesford* 13 *D&C,* 1225 K, *Cunghesford* 13 NfD, 1225 K,
   Cunewesford c.   1240 *Holme, Kunesford* 1250 *Ass,* c. 1260 *D&C,*
   Cunesfort 1257 *NPD, Cunungeford* c. 1260 *D&C, Cunisford* c. 1260 *ib,*
   Cunsford(e) 1300 to 1582 *NPD,*   1371 Pat, *Cunisforthe* 14 *Binh,*
   Cunesfordh 1323 *NPD*
Conesford(e) 1250 *et freq* to 1507 *NPD,* c. 1250 *et freq* to 1481 *R,* 1257
   Ass, 1289 to 1423 *D&C,* 1324 Ipm, 1348, 1357 *Phillipps,* 1391 to 1455
   NPD, 1428 FA, 1462 Ch, *Conyngesford* 1269 *Ass, Consforde* 1333 *SR,*
   Conysforde 1550 Pat
Cunsfordmedewe 1275 RH, *Conesforhte Medowes* 1535 VE,   *Consforthe*
   Place (site of late Augustinian friars) 1548 Pat
Superior Cunesford 1286 to 1299 *R,* 1315 *D&C, Superior Conesford(e)*
   1286 to 1313 *R,* 1289 to 1548 *NPD, Conesforth Superior* 1481 *ib,*
   Conisford Superior 1611, 1614 *ib; Longe Conesford* 1289 *R; Ouere*
   Cunesford 1297 *R; magna Conesford* 1308 *NPD, Magna Cunesford*
   1308   *ib,* 1313 *R, Magna Conesford* 1312 *ib*
Conesfordgate 1330 to 1331 *D&C, Confur Streete* 1599 Nashe,
   Coneysford Street 1696 Cleer, *Conisford Street* 1746 B, 1766 King
King Street 1789 H, 1819 Stacy, 1830 M&M, 1845 White, 1885 OS

   The earliest forms quoted above refer to the leet of Conesford (*v.*
Leets). *v.* ODan **kunung,** OE **ford.** Since the second element is
English, ODan *kunung* 'king' may possibly have replaced an earlier OE
cyning. Cf.   Coney Street in York (*Cuninge(s)strete,* etc., 12th c.   PN
YE   285).   The whereabouts of this ford is not easy to determine (cf.
K 2).   Hudson places it near the modern Foundry Bridge, which would
agree with the situation of the medieval Leet of Conesford (K 2 note
4).   Recent research favours a site near Bishop Bridge or Fye Bridge
(Green & Young 10).·   If so, the name has migrated south as a
district- and street-name in the course of the centuries.   It is worthy
of note that there was an old timber road across the river where Fye
Bridge was later to be built (NfA 13, 1898, 217-32).   *Superior*
distinguished this street from *Inferior Conesford,* i.e. Mountergate - - St

Faith's Lane (*q.v.*).

The southern part of King Street would seem to have been called *Southgate* at one time. According to Hudson (K 3 note 6), Southgate is found in the existing records almost exclusively in connection with the church situated here, St Peter Southgate (*v.* Churches). Cf., however, also *Bartholomeo de Soudgat* 1324 OR and *mes. in Suthgate* 1329 *R*.

LILY TERRACE, on the east side of Ber Street, facing Finkelgate. It commemorates the *Lily* tavern (1885 OS), which was pulled down in the early 1960s (Nobbs 39).

LITTLE BETHEL STREET, *Bethel street open* 1845 White, *Short Bethel Street* 1885 OS. This connection between Bethel Street and Chapel Field North was opened in 1792 (Nobbs 39).

LITTLE LONDON STREET
Hosyergate 1290, 1306 K
Smithes Rowe 1357, 1365 K, *Smethes Row* 1359, 1362 *ib*, *Smythes Rowe* 1384, 1389 *ib*
Smythy Rowe 1389 K, *Smythyrowe* ?1397 NoRec, *Smythe Rowe* 1391, 1400 K, *Smithy Rowe* 1467 *ib*, *Smethi Rowe* 1484, 1492, 1503 *ib*, *Smythey Rowe* 1626 BLR
Smithy Lane 1746 B, 1766 King
Cockey Lane c. 1720 K, *Little Cockey Lane* 1830 M&M
Little London Street 1845 White, 1885 OS

Together with Hole in the Wall Lane (School Lane) this alley once formed a route from London Street to St Andrew's Street along the line of the Great Cockey. The earliest name, *Hosyergate*, usually referred to London Street (*q.v.*). When Little London Street was called *Smithy Lane*, because of a concentration of blacksmiths here (K 48), London Street was called *Cocky Lane* (1696 Cleer) and *London Lane*. Whether *venella vocat' Cokeye* 1396 *NPD*, *le Cokeye* 1418 *ib* refer to this street or the neighbouring London Street or School Lane (*q.v.*) we have not been able to find out. OE **smið**, ON **smiðr** 'smith' and OE **smiððe** 'smithy'.

LITTLE WATER LANE, *v.* Water Lane[1].

LOBSTER LANE, *Lobster Lane* 1830 M&M, 1885 OS, is the name of a small section of Pottergate, between St John Maddermarket and Exchange Street. Lobster Lane originally included Bedford Street (*v.* the 1830 Map). According to King's Map (1766) the *Lobster Inn* stood on the north side of what is now Lobster Lane.

LONDON STREET

le Oserie 1223 K, *Hosyergate* 1258 to 1307 R, *Hosiergate* 1268 D&C, 1295 *et freq* to 1303 *NPD, Hosieregate* 1291, 1294 (2x) R, *Hosieryegate* 1299 *ib, Vicus olim vocatus Hosieregate* 1362 K

le Coteller Rowe 1247 D&C, *le Cotelerrowe* 1277, 1378, 1388 *NPD,* 1419 *NAR, le Cotillerrowe* 1399 *ib, Cuttlerrowe* 1527 (2x) *NPD, Cutlerrowe* 1388, 1527 *ib,* 1535 NoRec, *Cutler Rowe* 1626 BLR

Aurifabria 1287 (2x), 1294 R, *Goldsmytherowe* 1372, 1401, 1408 K

Latonerowe 1334 NoD, *Latone Rowe* 1339 K

Cocky Lane 1696 Cleer

London Lane c. 1720 K, 1766 King, *Cokey Lane or Cutlers Row or London Lane* 1746 B, *Cockey Lane or London Lane* 1789 H, *London-lane* 1819 Stacy, *London Street* 1830 M&M, 1845 White, 1885 OS

The north side of the Market Place towards its eastern end was called *Aurifabria* 'the goldsmiths' row', which was continued some way into the neighbouring street, i.e. *Hosyergate* (ME *hosiere* 'maker of stockings'), which here led out of the Market Place towards the east. By the middle of the fourteenth century the hosiers had been replaced by cutlers (ME *cuteler*) and latteners (ME *latoner*). Cutlers made knives, daggers, etc., latteners were workers in latten, an alloy of copper, zinc, lead and tin. *v.* Fransson 115, 137, 153. *Cockey Lane* is from the Great Cockey (*q.v.*). That part of the street which is east of Swan Lane was the first to be called *London Lane*, 'possibly from the number of Shops of all Trades & the great traffic and passage of Peoples Horses, Carts, Coaches, &c, through it' (K 45).

The corner next to the Market (at the west end of this street) was called *Cornera de Hosiergate* 1287 K, *Geneys Corner* 1406 *ib, Ginnys Corner* 1626 BLR; cf. John *Geney,* 'one of the Baillives in Edw. 3d time' (K 27), John de *Gedeney,* clerk of the Lord King 1386 NoRec, John *Godeneye* 1414 *ib* (Gedney is in Lincolnshire).

LONG LANE (lost)

Craketayleshole 1305 to 1317 *R*, 1482, 1498, 1520 *NPD, Craketayles hole*
  1329, 1346 K, *Craketailes hole* 1319 *R*, 1345, 1355 K, 1520 *NPD,*
  Craketailleshole 1350, 1379 K, *Craketayl hole* 1378 *ib, Craktayleshole*
  1390 *ib*, 1498, 1515 *NPD, Craktaylehole* 1515 *ib, Crayketaileshole* 1520
  ib; Craketayles Lane 1317, 1391 K, *Craketayleslane* 1482 *NPD,*
  Crayketaileslane 1520 (2x) *ib, Craketail Lane or Fullers Hole* 1746 B

Le Fulleres holes 1323, 1328, 1332 K, *Le Fulleris hole* 1344 *ib, Fulleres*
  lane 1351 *ib, Le Fulleres hole* 1378, 1390 *ib, Fullerys hole* 1406 *ib,*
  Fuller hole 1457 *ib, Le Fullers hole* 1469, 1516 *ib, Fullers holelane*
  1515 *NPD, Fullershole* 1520 *ib, Fullers hole* c. 1720 K; *Fullers Lane*
  1766 King, 1789 H, 1830 M&M

Long Lane 1845 White, 1885 OS

This lane ran northwards from Charing Cross to the river. It is still
indicated on the 1920 OS 6" Map (nameless).   The name of the fuller
William *Craketayle* is on record in documents of 1273 (NoRec I 217),
1290, 1298, etc. (NoD).   It has been explained as an indecent one: OE
cracian 'crack, break' + OE *tægl* 'tail, vulva, penis' (Seltén N 7). *Fuller*
is OE *fullere* 'one who cleanses and thickens cloth', though the OF
word is similar, *fouleor, foleur* (cf. Fransson 100).

OE **hol**[1], ON **hol**. The use of *hole* for a narrow passage seems to
have been more or less confined to this area; cf. *Blexterehole* and
Smaleberghes hole. In the mid-18th century the name *Fullers Hole* was
also given to an area west of St Martin's Road (beyond the site of St
Martin's Gates), now St Martin's Close (*v.* King).

MAGDALEN STREET, *v.* Fyebridge Street -- Magdalen Street.

MALTHOUSE ROAD

the Common Lane which runs along the Back of the Houses on the W.
  side of Nedham c. 1720 K

Nedham Back Street or Row 1746 B, *the Back of St Stephen's* 1766 King,
  1789 H, 1830 M&M, *St Stephen's Back street* 1845 White, *St Stephen*
  Back Street 1920 6" Map

Malthouse Lane -- St Stephen's Church Lane 1885 OS

This street runs from Rampant Horse Street to Coburg Street.   The
section north of the present Chantry Road (and east of St Stephen's
Church) is mentioned in documents of 1287, 1304 and 1306, but only as

communis venella, a common lane; the southern part is mentioned in
a document of 1317 as *communis semita*, a common footpath (K 17
f.).

The 1746, 1766, 1789, 1830, 1845 and 1920 quotations all refer to the
southern part.   On the 1885 Map, *Malthouse Lane* also refers to the
southern part.   There were numerous malthouses in nineteenth-century
Norwich, but Malthouse Lane boasted two, one on each side.

MARINERS LANE
Hollegate 1288 *R*, 1290 (p) NoD, *Holgate* 1317 K, 1789 H, *Hollewent*
1331, 1360 K
Bliburghes Lane 1391 K
St John Lane 1578 K, *Holgate, Holwent or St John Street* 1746 B,   *Holgate
or St Johns Street* 1766 King
the 3 Mariners Lane c. 1720 K, *Holgate or Mariners Lane* 1830 M&M,
Mariner's Lane 1845 White, 1885 OS

It leads out of Ber Street down the hill-side.   Now a cul-de-sac, it
once extended as far as King Street.   The earliest name meant 'the
hollow street, the street in the hollow'; OE **hol**[1], ON **hol**, OE **hol**[2], ON
holr.   Rain-water flowing down the ridge-side hollowed the street.
Skygate/Horns Lane, north of Holgate/Mariners Lane, is referred to
as *cava via* in early documents.   Cf. Ten Bell Lane (formerly
Hollegate).   For **wente**, cf. Horns Lane.   The *Bliburghs* had a messuage
south of the street, next to St Etheldreda's Church.   They presumably
hailed from Blythburgh in Sf.   Cf. Seman and John de *Blitheburgh*
(father and son) 1289-90 NoLeet.   The latter may be identical with the
John de *Bliburghe* who flourished in 1316-7 (K 10).

St John Lane is from the church of St John Sepulchre in Ber Street,
The 3 Mariners Lane, 'from the Sign of a publick House' (K 10).

MARKET AVENUE, runs from Golden Ball Street to Agricultural
Hall Plain.

MOUNTERGATE -- ST FAITH'S LANE
Inferior Cunungesford 13 *D&C, Inferior Cunesford* 1262 *ib*, 1296 *NPD*,
Inferior Cunesfforde 1328 *R, Inferior Cunesforth* 1337 *NPD, Inferior
Conesford* 1289 to 1313 *R*, 1298 *et freq* to 1542 *NPD*, 1321, 1466
D&C, Inferior Conisford 1332 *ib*, 1611, 1614 *NPD, Inferior Consford*
1339 *NPD*

Nethercunesford c. 1250 *D&C*, 1285 *NPD*, 1290 *R*, *Netherecunesford*
   1285 *NPD*, *Netherconesford* c. 1250 *et freq* to 1340 *D&C*, 1287, 1290
   R, *Nether Conesford* 1295 *R*, 1322 *NPD*, *Neyere Conesford* 1295 *ib*,
   Neyerconesforth(e) 13 *D&C*, 1331 *NPD*, *Netherkonesford* 1329 *D&C*,
   Netherconesforth(e) 1329 *ib*, *Neȝerconesforth* 1331 *ib*, *Neyerkonesforȝe*
   1331 (3x) *ib*
Freres-went 1364 K
Seynt Vayst Lane 1549 K, *St Fastes Lane* 1567 *et freq* to 1613 *NPD*, *St
   Fasts Lane* 1572 K, *St Fasse lane* 1609 *ib*, *St Faiths lane* 1613 *NPD*, c.
   1720 K, *St Vedast or St Faiths Lane or Neither Conisford* 1766 King,
   St Faith's Lane 1789 H, 1845 White, 1885 OS, *St Faiths Lane* 1830
   M&M
Mountergate Street 1889 K, 1920 OS 6" Map

For the name *Cunungesford*, *v.* King Street. *Inferior* refers to the
situation in relation to King Street, which was *Superior Cunesford*. The
original St Vedast's (or Faith's) Lane must have been the present Rose
Lane, for St Vedast's Church stood there (*v.* the earliest form of Rose
Lane). After the demolition of the church in 1540 (Blomefield IV
105), the name migrated to the nearby thoroughfare from the present
King Street to Tombland, now known as Mountergate (from King
Street to Prince of Wales Road) and St Faith's Lane (from Prince of
Wales Road to Tombland). The dedication of the church is to two
Flemish saints, St Vedast (Vaast) and St Amand. The name of St
Vaast was confused with that of a better-known saint, St Faith the
Virgin. This saint will have been well-known because the Church of
Horsham was dedicated to her (*fundata est ecclesia sanctæ Fidis de
Horsham* 1102 Oxenedes 42). ST VEDAST STREET, which leads out
of Rose Lane into Prince of Wales Road opposite Wales Square and
Cathedral Street, is a rather late development; it was at first known as
South Cathedral Street (OS 1885).

   Mountergate derives from *Parmentergate* (*v.* the Church of St Peter
Permountergate), which may originally have been the northern part of
Conesford Superior; the fact that St Peter *Parmentergate* Church stands
west of King Street, the former Conesford Superior, speaks in favour of
this assumption. Note, however, that in the extant records
Parmentergate is never used except in connection with the church (K 3
note 6). *Inferior Conesford/St Faith's Lane* was not named
Mountergate until the 1880s (K 4 note 3). The first syllable of *Parmentergate* probably came to be regarded as a preposition and was

eventually dropped.   OF *permentier* signified 'a furrier, robe trimmer' or
'a tailor'; *v.*   Fransson 111 and Latham s.v.   *par(a)mentarius.*   The
Austin Friary south of Inferior Conesford explains the name
Freres-went in the 1364 document.

MUSPOLE STREET

Muspol(e) 1250 (p), 1251 (p) K, 1313 *NoLeet,* 1352 *NPD,* 1505 *AddCh,*
    Musepol 1298 K, c. 1300 *Wals, Mosepol* 1351 *NPD, Mospole* 1397 *ib,*
    Muspoole 1442 Chichele
Musepolstrete 1288 *R, Muspolgate* 1289 K
Muspole or Pit Street 1746 B, *Muspole* 1766 King, *Muspole Street* 1789
    H, 1819 Stacy, 1830 M&M, 1845 White, 1885 OS

This street runs from St George's Plain (in Colegate) to Duke
Street.   At the south end there was at one time a considerable spring
or pool with an eastern outlet.   The spellings suggest OE **mūs**
'mouse', but OE **must** 'must, juice of grapes', which is found as a
river-name denoting 'a muddy stream' or the like, is also possible, i.e.
'the muddy pool'. *v.* ERN 197 (Must), PN C 7 f. (Muscat).
    The Duke Street end of Muspole Street (and the east end of St
Mary's Plain) formerly went by the name of *Soutergate: Souter(e)gate*
1323, 1355 K, *Soutergate Street* 1789 H; *Southergate* 1766 King,
Southergate Street 1830 M&M, *Southgate street* 1845 White.
    Even if this stretch of the street was not specifically assigned to
shoemakers and cobblers, some practitioners of the craft must have
lived in this area; cf. Ranulph de Kesewyk, *sutor,* in St Michael in
Colgate 1298 NoD, Mess: Ranulph de Keswyk *Sutoris* in St George
Colgate 1320 K, Geoffrey *le Soutere* in St Mary of Coselanie 1339 NoD.
The 18th- and 19th-century quotations (except H) show corruption to
South(er)gate (*v.* also St Mary's Plain).   St George Colgate Church
was sometimes called *de Mospole* and the like (*v.* Churches).

NEUGATE (lost), *Beugate* R2 *Binh, Neugate* R2 NoRec, was situated
between the cemetery of St Cuthbert and the Franciscan monastery
according to the only document where the name occurs, a relation
concerning the foundation of the Cathedral extant in the Norwich Book
of Pleas and in the Binham Cartulary.   It ran from east to west and
was thus parallel to the southern end of Tombland. Kirkpatrick (K[2]
109) thinks that this was the street near the monastery that was
enclosed by the friars in 1285 (*Fratres Minores de Norwic. de Venella*

prope mansum includend.).

NEW MILLS YARD
Newemylles 1492 NfRS 9, *The new milles* 1558 Cuningham, *the New(e)
   Mylles* 1579, 1584 NoRec, (*the*) *New Mills* c. 1720 K, 1746 B, 1766
   King, 1789 H, 1819 Stacy
the Mill Bridges c. 1720 K, *New Mills Bridge* 1845 White
the Mill-yard 1661, c. 1720 K, *New Mills Lane* 1789 H, *New Mill Yard*
   1830 M&M, *New Mills lane and yard* 1845 White, *New Mills Yard*
   1885 OS

New Mills Yard is actually a road running from Westwick Street
across the river to Oak Street. The original corn mills were new as
long ago as 1430 (NoRec II 66 f.), but the name has stuck. There were
older mills a little higher up the stream; *v.* Westwick or Appleyard's
Mills.
A conduit, conveying water from the New Mills to the Market
Cross, was constructed in 1582 (NoRec II 392 ff., Stacy 274). A water
works was erected here in 1699 (Stacy 278), rebuilt in 1710 (White
146), and improved and extended between 1790 and 1800 (White 147).
This water works (*the New Mill water works* 1819 Stacy) continued to
serve the City with water for a long time; a disused late Victorian
pumping station is still standing.

NORMANS LANE (lost)
Normanes lane 1288 *R*, *Normanneslane* 1290 (2x), 1292 *ib Normannes
   Lane* 1382 K, *Normans Lane* 1766 King, 1789 H, 1830 M&M
S. Pauls Street 1696 Cleer, *St Paul's Street* 1845 White, 1885 OS

St Crispin's Road east of Peacock Street follows the line of the old
Normans Lane, which took its name from St Paul's or Norman's
Hospital (*q.v.*).

OAK STREET, *v.* Coslany Street.

OLD BARGE YARD, *Old Barge Yard* 1885 is a lane between King
Street and the river (opposite St Julian's Alley). It was named from an
old inn in King Street, no longer in business. (*v.* Pevsner 272).

OLD POST OFFICE COURT
Half Moon 1766 King, *Half Moon, 9 Gent's walk* 1845 White
Old Post office yard 1845 White, *Post Office Court* 1885 OS

Despite the appellation *court* this is a narrow thoroughfare (for pedestrians) from the Market Place to Castle Street. It was once the yard of the *Half Moon* pub. The post office here was probably the predecessor of the one in (Lower) Exchange Street (*q.v.*), which in turn was succeeded by the one in Prince of Wales Road. (*v.* Crown Road).

ONE POST ALLEY, *One post passage* 1845 White, *Stocking's Alley* 1885 OS. This lane, described by K (15) as 'very narrow and uphill', leads out of St Stephen's Street into Malthouse Road. It is mentioned in deeds of Edward I's and Edward III's times, but only as *Communis venella*.

OPIE STREET
Gropecuntelane 1305, 1308 *R*
Turpis Vicus 1333, 1468, 1490 K, 1346, 1397 NoRec, 1415, 1426 *OR*
Opie Street 1885 OS

This is a thoroughfare from London Street to Castle Meadow. Kirkpatrick's references to the vernacular form of the name (from OE *grāpian* 'grope' + ME *cunt* + **lane**) were suppressed by Hudson (*v.* K 59 note 6). The name was a common one in medieval England. We have not been able to verify the names *Evil Whore's Lane* and *Devil's Steps* mentioned by Nobbs (46). The present name commemorates Amelia *Opie* (1769-1853), a novelist. She had a house near the Castle; it no longer exists.

ORFORD HILL
Swynemarket 1285 to 1307 *R*, *Swynnemarket* 1307 *R*, *Suynesmarket* 1334 K
Swynemarkettehil 1312 *R*, *Swynmarkethil* 1317 *ib*, *Swinmarkethil* 1346 NoRec, *Suynmarket hil* 1364 *NPD*
Sygars Hill 1494 K, *Sigars hille* 1497, 1500, 1504 *ib*
the Hog market 1660 K, *the Hogge Markett* 1662 *NPD*
Hog Hill 1696 Cleer, 1746 B, 1766 King, 1789 H, *the Hoghill* c. 1720 K
Orford Hill 1830 M&M, 1845 White, 1885 OS

The swinemarket was removed from All Saints Green to this place in the late thirteenth century. The name *Siger/Segore* is attested in Norwich from the thirteenth to the fifteenth century: Roger *Syger* Hy3 K, Silvester *Siger* 1288 to 1290 NoLeet, 1299 NoD, William *Segore* R2 K, 1397 NoRec, Thomas *Segore* 1445, 1447, 1448 *ib.* For a discussion of the name *Siger, v.* Seltén II 144. Feilitzen (359 f.) reckons with Scand origin, 'in most cases probably ON *Sigarr.* A possible base is also OE *Sigegār*'. On *e* for *i, v.* Feilitzen 50. The modern name commemorates the *Orford* family. In the words of his memorial plaque, George Walpole, third Earl of Orford (1730-1791), 'gave generously to public subscriptions for planning improvements made in his time'.

ORFORD PLACE
Wastilgate 1369, 1379 K, *Wastelgate* 1490 *ib,* Little *Orford Street* 1845
    White, 1885 OS
Ramping Hors Lane 1696 Cleer, *Ramping Horse Lane* 1746 B, 1766
    King, *Rampant Horse Lane* 1789 H, 1830 M&M, *Rampant Horse Back*
    Street 1885 OS

At the north end of Red Lion Street, on the west side of the road, there was formerly a triangular patch on which stood the bell foundry of Robert Brasier, who was an alderman in 1492 (NoRec I 112), and his descendants. Later the foundry was converted into a brewery (K 19, Blomefield IV 166). The place continued to be known under its old name, however. John and Charles Wesley, on their first visits to Norwich in 1754, 'preached at a place called the Foundry, near Orford Hill' (Wicks 49); cf. also *Foundery* 1766 King. In the early part of this century it was known as the *Tram Centre* (Wicks 48).

The triangle was bounded by two converging streets which, united into one, provided an approach from Orford Hill and Red Lion Street to Brigg Street. *Wastilgate,* etc., was the northern branch of the fork, *Ramping Horse Lane,* etc., the southern. The modern Orford Place does not exactly correspond to either.

For the etymology of the name *Wastelgate, v.* Wastel Market (Market Place). *Ramping/Rampant Horse Lane* is from a coaching inn south of the lane; cf. Rampant Horse Street. For the name *Orford Place, v.* Orford Hill.

ORFORD STREET

in vico Curia 1286, 1292, 1307 *R, Iter Regium quod ducit in Curiam*
  Comitatus 1287 NoRec, *Via in Curiam Comitatus* 1306 K²
Pyeslane 1486 *Beecheno*
Rochesters Lane c. 1720 K, *Rochester Lane* 1766 King
Gt. Orford Street 1845 White, *Orford Street* 1885 OS

This street leads from the south-east corner of Orford Hill to Bell
Avenue. Formerly it led to the old Shire House (*v.* Castle). In 1457-8
Thos. *Pye*, Corayour ('currier, one who dresses and colours leather',
Fransson 123), held property on the south side of this lane (Beecheno
79). Thos. *Rochester* had property on its south side in 1584-5 and John
Rochester in 1626-7 (Beecheno *ib*). For the present name, *v.* Orford
Hill.

PALACE STREET

White Horse Street 1696 Cleer
St Martin's Street 1746 B, 1819 Stacy, *St Martins Street* 1766 King, 1789
  H, 1830 M&M
Palace Street 1845 White, 1885 OS

K (67) mentions this street but does not give it a name: 'From the
N.E. Corner of Tomland a Street runs N.E. by E. into the void place
now called St Martin's Plain'. The White Horse was a very common
inn sign; at one time there were no fewer than nine White Horses in
Norwich (Riddington Young 21). St Martin's Church owes its latter-day
distinguishing addition, *at Palace*, to the Bishop's residence south of the
Plain (cf. St Martin at Palace Plain).

PALACE YARD, *common Lane leading to St James's stath* (*ad Kayum
Sci Jacobi*) 1313 K, *Seint James Went* 1345 Pat, *St James Palace* 1845
White, 1885 OS; a lane on the south side of Barrack Street which, like
the nearby River Lane, once reached the river. *v.* ME **wente.**

PARCHEMYNERS' ROW (lost), (*via que vocat'*) *parchemyneres rowe*
1368 *D&C*, unidentified. The document is filed under St Michael at
Plea in NfRO (no. 774). Sellers of parchment are known to have
resided in this area. In a document of 1290 concerning a messuage in
St Michael at Plea, Robert de Lincoln and Simon le Derham are
described as *parcamenarii*. In 1293 the latter is called Simon *le*

Parcheminer in a document concerning another messuage in the same parish (K 41 note 8).

PEACOCK STREET -- BLACKFRIARS STREET
Tolthorp Lane 1388 to 1500 K, *Tolthorplane* 1447 to 1500 *NPD, wey called Thorplane* 1535 *ib*
Cowgate Lane 1518 K
Rotten Row 1696 Cleer, c. 1720 K, 1789 H, 1819 Stacy, *Rotten Row or Tolthorp Lane* 1746 B, *Rotton Row or Tolthorp Lane* 1766 King
Rotten Row or Peacock Street 1830 M&M, *Peacock street* 1845 White, *Back Lane* (northern half) *and Peacock Street* 1885 OS

This street used to run from Cowgate to Fishergate but has been cut in two by St Crispin's Road (the Inner Link Road). According to K (88) the earliest known name derived from a certain Sir Gilbert de *Tholthorpe* (cf. Blomefield IV 454), who had a messuage here in 3 Ed3 (1329-30). Sir Gilbert got his surname from the manor of Tokethorpe or Tolthorpe (*Thoketorp'* 1203 Cur, *Toketorp'* 1203 *ib*, *Tholetorp* 1249 FF, *Tolthorp* (p) 1302, 1316, 1346 FA), which at one time included most of Gildencroft. Blomefield (IV 453 f., 478, 491) identifies it with the village of *Toketop* mentioned in DB II 145b (*v.* also Campbell 4 f.). *Toke* held this place in the time of Edward the Confessor. The first element, OScand *Tóki*, was later replaced by OScand *Tóli*.
Cowgate Lane is self-explanatory. Kirkpatrick (K 88) ascribes the name *Rotten Row*, evidenced from the late seventeenth century, to the fact that there were 'several old cottages on the East side of this lane towards Fishergate'. *Rotten Row* is not an uncommon street-name, used in a derogatory sense (EPNE II 81). The spellings point to derivation from ON **rotinn** 'rotten', but cf. the lost Ratton Row. In 1845 White (193) lists only two Peacock inns in Norwich and neither was situated in this street, so it would seem that the name *Peacock Street* was due to a resident.

PELLOUR LANE (lost)
a street which leads to Luuelestathe 13 *D&C, a lane leading to a quay (Cayum) called Nouelstathe* 1350 *ib*
Pellour Lane 1475 K

This lane used to run from the Horsefair (*q.v.*) at the junction of St

Faith's Lane with Cathedral Street to the lost Rushworth Staithe. *Pellour* is a shortened form of *appellour* 'an accuser, one who makes a formal charge against somebody' (MED). Cf. the lost Pelours Place in Lincoln (PN L 32) and Pelloures Medwe under Norwich Castle *supra.*

PIGG LANE
Normannes Lane 1288 to 1483 K, 1302 *R, Norman(n)eslane* 1290 NoRec, 1290 to 1316 *R*, 1335 NoD, *Normanslane* 1310 *R, Normanis Lane* 1346 K, *Normannes Lane als' dict Hornynges Lane* 1496 *ib Norman's Lane* 1626 BLR
Harpelees Lane R2 K
Hornyng(g)es Lane 1390, 1415 K
Wateryng Lane 1480 K
Piggs' Lane 1626 BLR, *Piggs lane* 1638 *NPD, Pigs Lane* 1696 Cleer, *the Piggs Lane* c. 1720 K, *Pigg Lane or Normans* 1746 B, *Pig or Normans Lane* 1766 King, *Pig Lane* 1789 H, 1830 M&M, 1845 White, 1885 OS

It runs from Palace Street to Quay Side. The different names, except *Wateryng Lane*, derive from people who held property here: Robert *Norman* (Piscator) Hy3; Laurence *de Maners de Harpele* (Clerk) Ed2 or Richard *de Harpelee* R2 (Harpley parish); William *de Hornyng* (Clerk) 1358, etc. (Horning parish); Henry *Pigge* (Chief Constable of E. Wymer 1514). There was a place for watering horses at Fybrigge Key (now Quay Side), mentioned in 1458 and 1546, hence *Wateryng Lane.* The reason for the def. article in the 1720 quotation was that an alehouse sign showing three pigs had lately been put up (K 68).

PITT STREET
St Olave's Street 1543 K
S. Austins Street 1696 Cleer
(*the*) *Pit Street* c. 1720 K, 1819 Stacy, *Pitt Street* 1789 H, 1830 M&M, 1845 White, 1885 OS
St Olave's or Tooley's Street and Pitt Street 1746 B, *St Olives or Tooleys Street & Pitt Street* 1766 King

Pitt Street once extended from St Augustine's (or Austin's) Church in the north to St Mary at Coslany in the south; today it does not extend further south than the roundabout on St Crispin's Road. *St*

Olave's Church, demolished at the middle of the sixteenth century, stood on the east side of this street. For the form *Tooley's Street*, cf. *St. Tooley's-lane* under Cherry Lane. According to Kirkpatrick, the pit that gave rise to the name *Pit(t) Street* was at the west end of St Olave's churchyard (K 77). Seeing, however, that on Blomefield's Map (1746) *Pit Street* is also an alternative name of Muspole Street, it seems possible that the pit originally alluded to was the pool at the junction of Muspole Street with Colegate. If so, the name migrated north.

PLUCLINGIS WENTE (lost), *Pluclingiswente* 1316 K, was a lane somewhere on the east side of King Street, named from the family of Will. *Plucling* 1344 and John *Plukling* (who had a messuage on the north side of this lane) 1337 (K 8). *v.* ME **wente**.

PLUMBERS ARMS ALLEY, *ye Princes Inn Yard* c. 1720 K, *Princes Inn lane* 1845 White, runs between Prince's Street and Waggon and Horses Lane; mentioned as a common alley in documents of 1324, 1394 and 1415 (K 61). The *Plumbers Arms* stood on the corner of Prince's Street (White 193).

POTTERGATE
Potter(e)gate Hy2 to 1380 K, c. 1250 to 1374 *D&C*, 1260 *et freq* to 1615
    NPD, 1285 *et freq* to 1315 *R*, 1357 *Binham*, 1626 K, 1766 *King*,
    Poterregate 13 *D&C*, *Poter(e)gate* c. 1260 *NPD*, 1261 *D&C*, 1289 to
    1313 *R*, 1357 *Binham*, *Poterrgate* 1293, 1306 *R*
Potteresgate c. 1250 *D&C*, c. 1260 K, *Potterisgat(e)* 1348, 1349 *NPD*
Potters Gate Street 1696 Cleer, *Pottergate Street* 1746 B, 1789 H, 1819
    Stacy, 1830 M&M, 1845 White, 1885 OS

Pottergate (Street) used to extend all the way from Heigham Road (outside the Walls) to London Street; today this stretch of road is divided into Pottergate, Lobster Lane and Bedford Street. OE **pottere** (possibly in the gen.pl. *pottera*) 'pot-maker'; cf. Fransson 184, Tengvik 266. Remains of earthenware have been found in the area immediately north-west of the Castle, in the vicinity of Bedford Street. This suggests that the name *Pottergate* migrated along the street in a westerly direction. By the thirteenth century there were no longer any potteries in Norwich, so Pottergate preserves the name of an activity that came to an end centuries ago (*v.* Campbell 4).
    A cul-de-sac off the west end of Pottergate is called COPEMAN

STREET, where we also find DAMOCLES COURT.

PRINCE OF WALES ROAD, *Prince of Wales Road* 1885 OS, 1920 OS
6" Map, was built as a result of the growing importance of railways.
Construction began in 1860. Prior to that date, and for some time
after, Rose Lane was the only approach to (the first) Thorpe Station
(built in 1844). Off the north side of Prince of Wales Road (west of
Cathedral Street) is WALES SQUARE (1885 OS), whose Victorian
houses were pulled down in the early 1970s (Nobbs 75).

PRINCE'S STREET
Hundegate 1257, 1269 *Ass*, (*via regia que vocat'*) *Hundegate* 1277 *D&C*,
    Hundegate 1278 to 1403 K, (*in vico de*) *Hundegate* 1287 to 1296 *R*,
    Hundgate c. 1300 *D&C*, (*apud*) *Hondegate* 1333 *NPD*,
    Hound(e)gate 1393 K, 1395 Bodl, *Hungate* 1453 K
Hungate Street 1746 B, 1789 H, 1819 Stacy
Princes Street 1830 M&M, 1845 White, 1885 OS

   The street from the old Dominican Friary (now St Andrew's Hall)
to Tombland was called *Hundegate*, according to popular tradition
because the Bishop's hounds (OE **hund**) used to be kept there
(Blomefield IV 329 and K 55 note 9). The name *Hundegate* was
earlier also given to three other streets in the area, namely the present
Redwell Street, Waggon and Horses Lane and Elm Hill. Some of the
early forms quoted above may refer to the church and parish of St
Peter Hungate (*q.v.*).
   Hungate is also found among field- and minor names in other parts
of Nf: *Hungate* in Aylsham (N. Erpingham Hundred), *Emneth
Hungate* and *Hungate Fm* and *Rd* in Emneth (Freebridge Marshland
Hundred), *Hungate Common* and *Fm* in Weston Longville (Eynsford
Hundred). For a discussion of the streetname *Hundegate, Hungate, v.*
Fellows-Jensen in OUA1979, 44-51. The name *Prince's Street* derives
from the *Prince Inne*, from which *Prynce Inne Lane* also got its name (*v.*
Waggon and Horses Lane).

PUDDING LANE, *Pudding Lane* c. 1720 K, 1766 King, 1845 White; a
footpath from St Peter's Street to Weavers' Lane and Gentleman's
Walk, along the north side of St Peter Mancroft Church. It has no
name on the current Norwich maps and routefinders. It is doubtful
whether this passage has anything to do with the medieval Pudding

Market (K 40).

QUAKERS LANE
Gildencroft Lane 1615, 1658, 1689 K, *Gilden Croft Lane* 1766 King, 1789
    H, 1830 M&M
Quakers Street 1746 B, *Quaker's Lane* 1845 White, *Quakers' Lane* 1885
    OS

    This lane runs north from St Crispin's Road and joins Jenkins Lane
at a point just south of Gildencroft. The Friends' Meeting House and
Burial Ground are to the east. The Meeting House was built in 1699
(*the Quaker's Meeting house* c. 1720 K) and was destroyed in an air raid
in 1942. A new building, more or less along the lines of the old one,
was erected in 1958 (Pevsner 254).

QUEEN STREET
Red Well Street 1766 King, 1789 H
Queen Street 1819 Stacy, 1830 M&M, 1845 White, 1885 OS

    Where Queen Street, Redwell Street and Bank Plain meet there was
a pump over a well, which was the reason for the name *Red Well Street*.
On King's and Hochstetter's Maps this name refers to the present
Queen Street. The present Red Well Street (*q.v.*) was at that time
called St Michael's Street.

RAMPANT HORSE STREET
Forum Equorum Ed1 and Ed2 K
Hors(e)market 1288 to 1311 *R*, 1288 K, *Le Horsmarket* 1294 to 1334 K,
    (*the*) *Horse Market* 1746 B, 1766 King
S Stephens Street 1696 Cleer
(*the*) *Rampant Horse Street* c. 1720 K, 1789 H, 1819 Stacy, 1830 M&M,
    1845 White, 1885 OS

    This street extends from St Stephen's Church to St Stephen's Plain.
It was once the City's horse market. The thirteenth-century *Rampant*
(or *Ramping*) *Horse* inn stood on the north side of the street and took
its name from the market; it was closed down c. 1900 (Riddington
Young 15).

RATTON ROW (lost)
in vico de ratunrowe 1288 NoLeet, *Ratun(e) rowe* 1288, 1291, 1303 K,
  Ratunrowe 1303 *NPD*, 1303 ChancWarr
Ratonerowe 1302 NoD, 1303 *R*, 1337 K, ?1397 NoRec, *Ratonrowe* 1309
  NPD, *Ratonesrowe* 1327, 1328 K, *Rattonrowe* 14 Binham. *(le)* *Raton*
  rowe R2 (3x), 1422 (2x) NoRec, 1456 K, *Ratten Rowe* 1626 BLR

   This was the south end of Tombland. Rat-infested rows of houses
were sometimes referred to as *Ratton* (or *Rotten*) *Row*, the first
element being ME, OF **rato(u)n** 'rat'. Cf. Peacock Street *supra* and
Ratones Lane in the City of London (SN 104). According to
Blomefield (IV 117) Ratton Row consisted of four buildings, two of
which were the *Stone House* (or *Stone Hall*) and the *Popingay Inn* (*v.*
Buildings).

RECORDER ROAD, *Recorder Road* 1920 OS 6" Map. Starting by the
James Stuart Gardens in St Faith's Lane, it runs towards the river but
turns abruptly south before reaching it and joins Prince of Wales Road.
The name may be due to association with a holder of the office of City
Recorder.

RED LION STREET
Wastelgate 1332 to 1475 K, 1340, 1343, 1380 *D&C*, 1391 NoLeet,
  Wastelgate alias *Baxtergate* 1404 K, *Wastel Gate Street* 1746 B, *Lower*
  Wastlegate 1766 King
Red Lyon Lane 1696 Cleer, *Red Lion Lane* c. 1720 K, 1745 B, 1789 H,
  1830 M&M, *Red Lion Street* 1845 White, 1885 OS

   Red Lion Street is the prolongation of St Stephen's Street north of
Rampant Horse Street/Westlegate. For *Wastel-, v.* Wastel Market
(Market Place). *Baxter* is OE **bæcestre** 'baker'. The modern name is
from an inn which was still in business in 1845 (White 194) but is not
indicated on the Ordnance Survey Map of 1885. One or two of the
medieval forms above may refer to the street called Westlegate today,
or to a street which used to link Red Lion Street with Brigg Street (cf.
Orford Place), or to Brigg Street.

RED WELL STREET, *St Michael's Street* 1789 H, *Red Well Street* 1830
M&M, 1845 White, 1885 OS, runs north from Bank Plain to Prince's
Street. *St Michaels Street,* from St Michael's at Plea Church. *Red*

Well Street is a name first recorded on King's Map of 1766, but there it refers to the street that today is called Queen Street. The 'red well' (*Red Well* 1696 Cleer, 1766 King) from which Red Well Street and also Red Well Plain (*v.* Bank Plain) took their names had perhaps a red frame or curb round its top (K 45). A pump was placed over it in 1629 (Stacy 57).

RIGBY'S COURT
Pit Lane 1746 B, *Pitt Lane* 1766 King, 1789 H, 1830 M&M
Rigby's Court 1845 White, 1885 OS

This is a passage that connects St Giles Street and Bethel Street only a few yards before their junction. The old name referred to a refuse pit in Over Newport (St Giles St.) called *Lothmere* (1289 NoLeet, 1316 K) which was 'filled up & paved over with Stone' in the early eighteenth century (K 20), probably from OE **lort(e)**, ME *lort* 'dirt, mud' and OE **mere** 'pool'; cf. *Lortemere* 1309 Nt (Forsberg 159) and *Lothburgh Lane* 1612, from *Lorteburn(e)strate* 13 (PN C 45). The modern name commemorates Dr Edward *Rigby* (1747-1822), who had his surgery and apothecary's shop here.

RISING SUN LANE (lost), *Rising Sun Lane* 1766 King, 1789 H, 1830 M&M, 1845 White, 1885 OS, used to lead out from the north end of Golden Ball Street to an open place called Scoles Green (*q.v.*). The northernmost part of present-day Rouen Road roughly follows the line of the old Rising Sun Lane. The name was perhaps due to the Golden Ball public house, which had moved from its original premises opposite the Castle Gate (cf. Golden Ball Street) to a corner house at the west end of this street. The huge golden ball of the sign was thought to be a picture of the rising sun (Riddington Young 94). Wicks (62) maintains, however, that the lane took its name from another pub actually called the Rising Sun.

RIVER LANE, *Water Lane* 1845 White, 1885 OS, *River Lane* 1920 6" Map, turns south out of Barrack Street near the site of the Pockthorpe Gates (Bargate). It no longer reaches the river but formerly led to a landingstage or staithe: *ad Kayum Sci Jacobi* 1313 K (*v.* St James's Staithe.

ROSE AVENUE
Market Street 1766 *Beecheno, Market Lane* 1908 *ib*
Holkham Lane 1861 *Beecheno, Rose Avenue* 1920 OS 6" Map

This is a small street which connects Cattle Market Street with Market Avenue.

ROSE LANE
Nether-Conesford or St Faith's Lane c. 1720 K, *Lane of St Vedast or St Faith* 1746 B
Rose Lane 1688 K, 1766 King, 1789 H, 1830 M&M, 1845 White, 1885 OS

This street, which leads from the Old Cattle Market to Prince of Wales Road, is often described as part of Nether Conesford (now Mountergate) in old records according to Hudson (K 2 note 4). Passing by the south side of the (lost) church of St Vedast (or Faith), this was the original St Vedast's (or Faith's) Lane (*v.* Mountergate--St Faith's Lane).   In 1688 the lane was called *Rose Lane* after the *Rose Tavern* (K 5), which stood at the Rose Lane - - King Street junction (*the Rose Corner* c. 1720 K).
Off the south side of Rose Lane is a cul-de-sac called BOULTON STREET, and off the north side there is another, MAIDSTONE ROAD.   They are both late developments.

ROSEMARY LANE
(*ad*) *iter regium de Litleheylisdon* 1279 *NPD,* (*in*) *lytelheylesdon* 1298   *ib, vicus de Litel Heylesdon*(*e*) *1286 to 1291 K,* (*super*) *viam regiam   que vocatur Litilheylesdon'* 1287, 1290 *R, Letleheylesdon* 1298 *ib, Lytleheylesdon* 1298 *ib, Litel Heylesdon* 1298, 1306 *ib, Litelheylesdon* 1306, 1308 *ib, Lytelheylesdone* 1308 *ib, Litteleheylesdon* 1310, 1313 *ib, Litleheylesdon* 1317 *ib,* (the street called) *Litelheylesdon* 1397 NoRec
Heylesdon Lane 1458 K, *Hellysdon Lane* 1567 *ib, Little Hellesdon Lane* 1626 BLR, 1789 H, 1830 M&M, *Little Heilesden Lane* 1746 B,   *Lit. Heilsden Lane* 1766 King
Rosemary Lane c. 1720 K, 1845 White, 1885 OS

Rosemary Lane is a narrow by-way linking St Mary's Plain to St Miles Alley. One John *de Heylesdon* (1285-1289 NoD) is known to have been an inhabitant of the parish of St Michael Coslany, and so are

Richard *de Heylesdon* (1298, 1310, 1313 K, 1305, 1320 NoD) and another John *de Heylesdon* (1337 NoD). Hellesdon, formerly a village, is some two miles west-north-west of the Market Place. The *Rosemary Tavern*, which gave this by-way its modern name, was once *Pilgrim's Hall*, a fifteenth-century building that escaped the great fire that devastated Colegate and Coslany in 1507 (Knights 73).

ROUEN ROAD is a new road leading from the Old Cattle Market into King Street, named from Norwich's twin town in France. It follows the line of several former streets. The most northerly section roughly corresponds to *Rising Sun Lane* (*q.v.*); the section from Stepping Lane to Thorn Lane corresponds to COW LANE/MARKET LANE (*Cow Lane* 1746 B, 1766 King, *Market Lane* 1845 White, 1885 OS); the section from Thorn Lane to Music House Lane corresponds to ST JULIAN'S STREET (1885 OS, 1920 OS 6" Map); the section from Music House Lane to Mariners Lane corresponds to WILLIAM STREET (1885 OS) *alias* BURLEIGH STREET (1920 OS 6" Map).

ST ANDREW'S HILL
St Andrew's three Steps c. 1720 K, *St Andrews Steps* 1761 *NPD, St Andrew's Steps* 1819 Stacy
7 Steps or Black Friers Street 1746 B, *Black Friers Street* 1766 King, *Black Friars Street* 1789 H, 1830 M&M
St Andrew's Hill and steps 1845 White, *St Andrew's Hill* 1885 OS

This is a street which runs from the London Street--Bedford Street junction northwards to St Andrew's Plain. Like St Andrew's Plain and Street it is named after St Andrew's Church. *St Andrew's (three) Steps* was really only a short descent out of London Street (or *Cutler Row* as it was then called) into the east end of Bedford Street (then *Pottergate*). The Steps were removed in 1761 according to Stacy (57). In 1762 a committee was set up to 'open, widen & enlarge the Common Street or King's Highway at a certain place called St Andrews Steps' (*NPD*). The equivalent of present-day St Andrew's Hill is nameless in K: '... also a Lane running down from thence [i.e. the junction of the Three Steps with Pottergate] North past the East end of St Andrew's Church to the Newhall gate' (28). *v.* St Andrew's Hall (Buildings).

ST ANDREW'S PLAIN, *St Andrew's Plain* 1845 White, 1885 OS, is the junction of St George's Street, St Andrew's Street and Prince's Street between St Andrew's Hall and St Andrew's Church.

ST ANDREW'S STREET
(*in*) *Wimeres strete* 13 *D&C, Wimer Street* 1766 King, *Wymer Street* 1789
  H
vicus Sci Andree Apostoli 1283 K
Wimer's or St Andrew's Street 1746 B, *St Andrew's Broad-street* 1819
  Stacy, *St Andrews Broad Street* 1830 M&M, *St Andrew Broad street*
  1845 White, *St Andrew's Street* 1885 OS

   This street runs from Charing Cross to Redwell Street. *Wymerus*
(NF *Wimard*), a Norman follower of William de Warren, is recorded in
DB as steward of Warren's estates in Norfolk (Knights 75).   For the
French name *Wimard/Guimard*, of Germanic origin, *v.* Dauzat 315.
The OE equivalent of this name, *Wigmær*, was frequent in East Anglia
(Seltén II 166 f.).   Wymer was also the name of one of the four
medieval leets of Norwich (*v.* Leets).   St Andrew's Church stands to
the south of the street, between Bridewell Alley and St Andrew's Hill.

ST ANN LANE
a Lane next the Austin Fryers 1391 K, *the Common Lane on the South
  side of the Augustine Fryers* 1421 *ib*, *a Stath ... near the Mansion of the
  Augustine Fryers* 1457 *ib*
St Anthonys Lane (sic) 1696 Cleer
St Anns Lane c. 1720 K, *St Ann's lane* 1845 White, *St Ann Lane* 1920
  OS 6" Map
St Anns Staithe 1766 King, *Saint Annes Staith(e)* 1789 H, 1830 M&M
Staithe Lane 1885 OS

   The Austin Friars had established themselves in Norwich before the
close of the 13th century.   Their friary and conventual church were
bounded on the north by Mountergate and on the south by this lane (*v.*
Austin Friars).   The forms *St Anns Staithe*, etc., from the maps of
1766, 1789 and 1830 are actually printed along the lane.

ST AUGUSTINE'S STREET. *St Austin's Street* c. 1720 K, 1746 B, 1766
King, *St Augustines Street* 1789 H, 1830 M&M, 1885 OS, *St Augustine
street* 1845 White, runs from the site of St Augustine's Gate to Botolph
Street. Kirkpatrick does not give a separate name to Botolph Street but
regards it as part of St Augustine's Street, and so does M&M (1830).

St Augustine's Church stands by the junction of Pit Street and Botolph Street.

ST BENEDICT'S STREET, *v.* Westwick Street.

ST CATHERINE'S PLAIN, *St Catherines Plain* 1830 M&M, *St Catherine's hill, terrace and plain* 1845 White, *St Catherine's Plain* 1885 OS, is simply a widening at the south end of Surrey Street at the entrance to Finkelgate, where the lost St Catherine's Church once stood.

ST CLEMENT'S ALLEY, *St Clement's Church alley* 1845 White, *St Clement's Alley* 1885 OS, runs from Colegate to Fyebridge Street, round St Clement's Church.

ST CRISPIN'S ROAD is a recent street (part of the Inner Link Road) running from a roundabout at the top of Barn Road (just west of the Wensum) across the town to another roundabout at the west end of Barrack Street. There is no church dedicated to St Crispin in Norwich, but the name of the street is apt for Norwich since St Crispin is the patron saint of shoemakers.

ST FAITH'S LANE, *v.* Mountergate.

ST GEORGE'S ALLEY is a walkway north of St George's Church which connects Muspole Street to St George's Street. It is not on the 1885 OS Map but indicated, though nameless, on the 1920 OS 6" Map.

ST GEORGE'S STREET, *v.* Botolph Street.

ST GILES STREET, *v.* Bethel Street.

ST GREGORY'S ALLEY, *St Gregory's Church alley* 1845 White, *St Gregory's Alley* 1885 OS, is an alley leading from St Benedict's Street to Pottergate and Lower Goat Lane along the west side of St Gregory's churchyard. East of the church is ST GREGORY'S BACK ALLEY (1885 OS, 1887 Knights). Both these passages are marked on early maps, but nameless.

ST JOHN MADDERMARKET

Madelmarkette 1229, 1293 *R,* 1296, 1303 K, *Madelmarket(e)* 1232 to
  1295 *R, Madermarket* 1254-75 Val, 1269 (p) *Ass,* 1286 *et freq* to 1300
  R, 13 *NC Reg,* 1374, 1429, 1459 *D&C,* 1528 *NPD, Maddermarket* 1264
  K, *Madirmarket* 1308 *R,* 1385 Pat, 1400 Fine, *Matermarket* Ed3, 1461
  K, *Matremarket* 1349-65 NLCh, *Mathermerkett* 1535 VE
St John's Street 1746 B, 1766 King, 1830 M&M, 1885 OS, *St John's
  Street, Madder Market* 1789 H

In the quotations above *Madel-, Maddermarket* usually occurs in the
combination *St John Maddermarket,* referring to St John the Baptist's
Church in Pottergate. The market was at the northern end of the
churchyard, where there used to be an open space. Today *St John
Maddermarket* refers to the street along the east side of the church and
churchyard; in Georgian and Victorian times this used to be *St John's
Street.*
      Red dye is got from the root of madder, OE **mædere** *(Rubia
tinctorum),* Kirkpatrick's references (58) show that madder was grown
in Norwich (cf. *Le Mader yerd* 1358 K in St Peter Mancroft, *curia
vocata Madiryerd* 1361 K in St Margaret and St Olave). For the
numerous *l*-spellings (*Madel-*), due to dissimilation, *v.* Zachrisson 120.

ST JOHN'S ALLEY, *St John's Alley* 1885 OS, *St John's Maddermarket
Alley* 1887 Knights, starts as a passage through the tower of St John's
Church in Pottergate. It joins St John Maddermarket Street by
Charing Cross. According to Nobbs (59) it is called MADDER-
MARKET ALLEY by most people.

ST JOHN'S STREET, *Orchard Street -- John Street* 1885 OS, *St John
Street* 1920 OS 6" Map, runs north from Mountergate. It used to
connect with Rose Lane at the point opposite Maidstone Road, but
today only the southern portion remains (leading to a car park). On
the 1885 OS Map this southern part is called *Orchard Street,* from a
tavern on the corner of St Faith's Lane (Mountergate).

ST JULIAN'S ALLEY, *St Julian's Alley* 1845 White, 1885 OS, got its
name from the church of St Julian. It leads from Rouen Road to
King Street.

ST LAURENCE'S LANE

Seint Laurences Lane 1357 K, *Seyn Laurence Lane* 1378, 1389 K, *St
    Laurence lane* 1585 *AddCh, St Lawrence Lane* 1552 *CG,* 1626 BLR,
    1830 M&M, 1845 White, *St Laurences Lane* 1746 B, *St Laurence
    Lane* 1766 King, 1789 H, *St Lawrence's Lane* 1885 OS
Sholdhams Lane 1483 K

A lane passing from Pottergate to St Benedict's Street, named from
St Laurence's Church (*via quae se extendit de Pottergate usque
ecclesiam Sci Laurentii* 1288 K). The surname (*de*) *S(c)huldham* is
well evidenced in Norwich: Reyner *de Schuldham* 1288, 1289 NoRec,
1305 *R,* Johannes *Shuldham* 1391 NoLeet. The latter is probably
identical with the John *de Shuldham* who was one of the Bailiffs in
Richard II's time and owned all the houses on the west side of this
street (K 49). Shouldham is a parish in Clackclose Hundred Nf.

ST LAURENCE'S STEPS, *St Lawrence's Church alley* 1845 White, *St
Lawrence's Steps* 1885 OS, refers to some thirty steps which lead down
from St Benedict's Street to Westwick past the east side of the church.
On the west side is a narrower by-way, ST LAURENCE'S LITTLE
STEPS (*St Lawrence's Little Steps* 1885 OS). Both are mentioned in K
(51 f.) but no names given.

ST LAURENCE'S WELL (lost), *common way leading to St Laurence'
Well* 1297 NoRec, *St Laurence Well* c. 1720 K. On the north side of
Westwick Street, across the road from St Laurence's Church, was an
alley-way that led to a well (K 53).

ST MARGARET'S STREET, *Nether Westwick Lane* 1746 B, *Westwick
Lane* 1766 King, 1789 H, 1830 M&M, *St Margaret's Lane* 1885 OS, runs
from St Benedict's Street to Westwick Street past the west end of St
Margaret's Church. It is mentioned but nameless in K (51). The
north end was formerly wider than it is now and was called ST
MARGARET'S PLAIN (1766 King, 1789 H, 1830 M&M, 1845 White,
1885 OS). East of the church is ST MARGARET'S ALLEY (1885
OS).

ST MARTIN AT PALACE PLAIN

Bichil Hy3 K, c. 1300 *D&C, Bycche Hyl* 1391 K, *Bycheshylle* 1391 *ib
St Martin's Plain* c. 1720 K, 1746 B, *St Martins Plain* 1766 King, 1789 H,

1830 M&M, *St Martin at Palace Plain* 1885 OS

This is a place where several streets meet beside St Martin at Palace
Church (*q.v.*).   The oldest name could be interpreted as a compound
of OE **bicce** 'bitch' and **hyll** 'hill'; cf. Beech Hill, Knaresborough (PN
YW V 111), Bishophill, York (PN YE 282), and Bitch Hill, Wakefield
(PN YW II 166).   OE *Biccan hyll,* where the first element is a
personal name (an assibilated form), is a possible alternative; cf.
DEPN s.v. Beechamwell. The name may perhaps more plausibly be
connected with an assibilated form of OE **bic* or **bicca* 'beak', used in
a transferred sense about a beak-like projection; cf. Adam atte *Bick*
1298 PN Sx 192, and DEPN s.n. Purbeck.   For an exhaustive
discussion, *v.* Dietz in *Anglia* 103 (1985) 1-25. According to Green &
Young (11) merchant ships were berthed on the south side of the river
near the site of St Martin's Church and unloaded onto the gravel
terrace known as *Bychel* (*v.* also NfA 35, 1973, 443 ff.).

ST MARTIN'S LANE
(*Le*) *Horlane* 1273,1329 K, 1308 *R,* 1337, 1498 *NPD, Horelane* 1401,
    1498 K, *Whores Lane* 1746 B, *St Martins or Whores Lane* 1766 King
St Martins Lane 1789 H, 1830 M&M, 1845 White, 1885 OS, *St Martin's
    street* 1819 Stacy

This lane used to link Oak Street to Pitt Street, but the Pitt Street
end was lost in the construction of the Inner Link Road. *Hor(e)lane*
may have meant 'the dirty lane', from OE **horu** 'filth'.   This
interpretation agrees with the fact that there used to be tanneries here.
But since, in pre-Conquest Norwich, settlement did not extend north of
this lane (Campbell 4), it is tempting to assign the meaning 'boundary'
to the first part of the name.   OE **hār** 'grey' was frequently used with
the word *stone* and other words for objects denoting boundary marks.
It has been suggested that *hār* actually came to mean 'boundary'.
According to Smith, however, 'there is no certain compound p.n. where
hār could mean only "boundary" (*v.* **hār**^{2}).   But *Hor(e)lane* could be an
elliptical formation, from **Horstonelane* or the like.   Note that
Hor(e)lane was not far from *Merholt,* believed to have meant 'the
boundary wood' (OE *gemǣreholt*).   The 18th-century form of the
word, *Whores Lane*, probably came about through popular etymology.
Cf. *Turpis Vicus* (Opie Street).   St Martin at Oak Church stands to
the south of this street.

ST MARY'S ALLEY, *St Mary's Church alley* 1845 White, *St Mary's Alley* 1885 OS, runs behind St Mary's Church, Coslany, from Duke Street to St Mary's Plain.

ST MARY'S PLAIN
Souter(e)gate 1323, 1355 K
Colgate 1388 K
Broad Street 1746 B
St Mary's Plain -- *Southergate* 1766 King, 1830 M&M, *St Mary's Plain* -- *Soutergate Street* 1789 H, *St Mary's plain* -- *Southgate street* 1845 White, *St Mary's Plain* 1885 OS

OE **sūtere**, ON **sūtari** 'shoemaker' (MLat *sutor*); *v.* also Muspole Street. Muspole Street and St Mary's Plain were probably at one time regarded as a continuation of Colegate (*v.* the 1388 quotation and K 75). At first the name *St Mary's Plain* only applied to that part of the street which is west of St Mary Coslany Church and which used to be an irregular open space.

ST MILES ALLEY, *St Miles Alley* 1885 OS, runs north and east of St Michael's Church, Coslany. The bit along the east side of the churchyard was long considered part of Rosemary Lane (*q.v.*).

ST PETER'S STREET
Uvere rowe 1269 K, *le Huuerrowe* 1285 R, *Le Uuere rowe* 1292 ib, 1299, 1300 K, *le Vuerrowe* 1294 *AddCh*, (*le*) *Uuerrowe* 1303 NoD, 1304, 1306 (2x) R, *Le Uuer rowe* 1312 K, *Uuerowe* 1325 NoD, 1331 R
Over rowe 1269 K, *Overrowe* 1286, 1346 NoRec, (*le*) *Ouererowe* 1291 to 1313 R, *Overowe* 1293, 1316 ib, *Ouererouwe* 1298, 1311 ib, *le Overe rowe* 1299, 1300 K, *Overrowe* 1300 to 1313 R, *Overrouwe* 1306, 1311 ib, *Le Ouer rowe* 1369 K
(*the*) *Upper Market* c. 1720 K, *Upper market* 1845 White, *Upper Market Street* 1789 H, 1830 M&M
St Peter's Street 1885 OS

St Peter's Street runs along the top of the Market Place, which slopes considerably from this street down towards Gentleman's Walk. OE **ofer**[3] 'over, above', and OE **rāw** 'row'. The modern name is from St Peter Mancroft Church. The modern City Hall, completed in 1938, is situated along this street.

ST SAVIOUR'S LANE

the lane leading to Rotten row c. 1720 K
St Saviours Lane 1746 B, 1830 M&M, *S. Saviours Lane* 1766 King, *St Saviour's Lane* 1789 H, 1845 White, 1885 OS

This lane connects Magdalen Street with Blackfriars Street, the old Rotten Row. It passes along the south side of St Saviour's Church. ST SAVIOUR'S ALLEY runs around the church from Magdalen Street to St Saviour's Lane.

ST STEPHEN'S STREET AND PLAIN

Nedham 13 *Phillipps*, 1253 to 1268 *D&C*, 1285 *et freq* to 1314 *R*, 1289 NoLeet, 1299, 1372 *NPD*, 1333 *SR*, *Nedeham* 1470 *D&C*, 1540 to 1616 *NPD*, *Neadeham* 1552 *ib*
Nedham strete 1373 *NPD*, *Nedeham strete* 1561 to 1585 *ib*, *Needham strete* 1616 *ib*, *Nedeham street* 1624 *ib*, *Needham Streete* 1626 BLR, *Nedham Street* c. 1720 K, *Needham Street* c. 1720 *ib*
S. Stephens Street 1696 Cleer, *St Stephen's Street* c. 1720 K, 1845 White, 1885 OS, *Nedham or St Stephens Gate* 1746 B, *Needham or St Stephens Street* 1766 King, *St Stephens Street* 1789 H, 1830 M&M
Niedham Slothe 1358 to 1391 K, *Nedham Sloth(e)* 1401, 1452, 1503 *ib*, *Needham Slough* 1626 BLR, c. 1720 K
St Stephen's Plain 1845 White, 1885 OS

From the site of St Stephen's Gate this street runs north-east by east to the junction of Rampant Horse Street, Red Lion Street and Westlegate (i.e. St Stephen's Plain). *Ned(e)ham* meant 'the needy or poor homestead'; *v.* **nēd** (Angl), **nīed** (WSax) and **hām**. The name occurs several times in East Anglia and also in Cambridgeshire and Derbyshire (*v.* PN C 269 and DEPN s.n. *Needham*). Kirkpatrick (14) explained the name from OE **nēat** 'cattle' and **hām**. Carter (199) tentatively equates Cowholme and Needham, suggesting that *Cowholme* is a Scandinavian adaptation of the OE name. He modifies Kirkpatrick's explanation as regards the second element, which he prefers to derive from OE **hamm** 'water-meadow'. Since OE *hām* and *hamm* are very difficult to distinguish in later forms, OE *hamm* would not seem impossible, the name meaning 'the poor meadow', but derivation from OE *nēat* is incompatible with the linguistic evidence, for no spelling with *t* has been found. The ME *Nied*-spellings (1358 to 1391) would seem to be normal representations of Angl close *ē*. The earliest forms refer to a city area, the parish and subleet of St Stephen. The present name is from the parish church in Rampant Horse Street, which was the original St Stephen's Street.

The *slough* (OE slōh) referred to the wide northern end of the street (St Stephen's Plain), which was a deep, muddy place caused by 'the conflux of the Water of several Kennels before the streets were paved with Stone' (K 14). The spelling *th* for *h* is evidenced especially in East Anglia (cf. OED s.v. *sloth* sb^2).

From the seventeenth century the Plain went by the name *the Tuns corner* (c. 1720 K), which referred to an inn, *the Three Tunnes* 1626 BLR, and before the 1939-45 war it was popularly known as *Bunting's Corner*, from *Bunting's Store*, destroyed in an air raid (Nobbs 64).

ST SWITHIN'S ALLEY
St Swythun's Lane 1326, 1332 K, *St Swithin's Lane* 1789 H
Venella Sci Swythini 1327 K
St Swithin's Church alley and lane 1845 White, *St Swithin's Alley* 1885
   OS

This is a passage which runs from St Benedict's Street to Westwick Street along the west side of St Swithin's Church. In this alley is HAMPSHIRE HOG YARD, presumably the site of the *Hampshire Hog* public house (Wicks 104 ff., Riddington Young 11, 33). To the west is ST SWITHIN'S TERRACE.

SCHOOL HOUSE DITCHES (lost), *The Common Lane called the Scoole house Dyches* 1602 K, from Adam and Eve's Gardens (*q.v.*) down to the river (K 70).

SCHOOL LANE
Kokeye 1286, *Cokeylane* 1535 NoRec, *Little Cockey Lane* 1789 H
Crouche Lane 1501, 1530 K
Hole in (the) Wall Lane 1830 M&M, 1845 White

This lane used to run from Wymer Street(now St Andrew's Street) to Pottergate (now Bedford Street). It was called *Cokeylane* after the Great Cockey. The prefix *Little* (1789) served to distinguish it from Cockey Lane/London Street. South of Pottergate the Great Cockey passed along *Smithy Lane* (afterwards Little London Street) which was sometimes called *Little Cockey Lane* too (*v.* Little London Street).

The name *Crouche Lane* derived from the church and churchyard of St Crouch, along whose east side this alley-way ran; OE crūc³, ME **crouche** 'cross'.   The church ceased to be used after the Reformation and by the middle of the eighteenth century it had been totally demolished and a public house, 'called the sign of the *Hole in the Wall*', stood on its site (Blomefield IV 299).   Today's *School Lane* coincides with the southern portion of the old *Hole in the Wall Lane* and ends in PARSONAGE SQUARE (so called from the former St Andrew's Parsonage).   In the nineteenth century there was an infant model school in Hole in the Wall Lane (White 171).

SHERBOURNE PLACE, *Sherborne Place* 1885 OS, *Sherborne Place* 1920 OS 6" Map, was a street on the north side of the east (now lost) end of Mariners Lane.   It ran parallel to King Street.   It is only partially preserved.

SHIRE HOUSE GAP (lost), *v.* Castle.

SMALLBURGH'S LANE or HOLE (lost)
Smaleberghes Lane 1328 K, 1331 *R, Smalberghe Lane* 1336 K;
   Smaleberwes hole 1346 *ib, Smalberghes hole* 1350 *ib*
River Lane, Water Lane. Antiently Smallburgh's Lane 1746 B

   This lane ran northwards from Charing Cross to the river, between *Craketaileshole* (Long Lane) on the west and *Blexterehole* on the east.   It is said to have taken its name from one Roger de *Smaleberghe* whose name is on record in a document of 1296 (K 56).   He had a messuage on the west side of the lane.   Cf.   also Geoffrey de *Smalebergh* 1286 NoD, John de *Smalberth* 1298 *ib*, Beatricia de *Smalberth* 1300 NoLeet, John de *Smalebergh* 1313 NoD.   *Smalebergh* is Smallburgh, a Nf village near the river Ant which was anciently called *Smalea* (ERN 372).   For the spelling *-berth* for *-bergh*, cf. *slothe* for *slough* (St Stephen's Street and Plain).

SOUTHGATE LANE, (*mes. in*) *Suthgate* 1329 *R, Southgate Lane* 1845 White, 1885 OS.   The 1329 form probably refers to King Street (*q.v.*). The present Southgate Lane snakes its way from Ber Street down to King Street past the remains of St Peter Southgate (*v.* Churches).   The name Southgate Lane did not appear on maps until the middle of the nineteenth century, but there seems to have been a trackway along this lane at an early date.

SOVEREIGN WAY. Like Anne's Walk, this is a walk-way from Magdalen Street to Anglia Square.

STEPPING LANE
Toftes Lane 1316 *R*
Cokerelle Lane 1329 K, *Kukerellane* 1331 *R, Cokereles wente* 1345, 1349,
    1358 K, *Cokerelles Lane* 1376 *ib, Cokerel lane* 1519 *ib, Cokerell Lane*
    1525 to 1554 *NPD*, 1644 *D&C, Tofts or Cockarel Lane* 1746 B,
    Cockeril Lane 1766 King, 1789 H
Stepping Lane c. 1720 K, 1830 M&M, 1845 White, 1885 OS

This lane leads out of Rouen Road into King Street; the King Street end is a mere footpath. Off the north side there is a cul-de-sac called NORMANS BUILDINGS, a fairly recent development (mid-1930s). The name *Toftes Lane* was due to Adam de *Toftes,* one of the Bailiffs in 1275-6 (NoRec I 218 f.) and 1286 (*ib* II 209); *v.* Blomefield IV 102. *Toftes* is the Nf parish of Toftrees (*v.* DEPN). *Cockerell* is evidenced as a Norwich surname: Peter *Cokerel* and Firmin *Cokerel* 1286 NoRec, Walter *Cokerel* 1325 NoD. The first two, with some others, are described as French merchants ('Mercatores Ambianenses et Corbienses'). Reaney, s.n. *Cockerel,* says that this name is often from OF *cocherel, cokerel* 'poultry-dealer'. *Stepping* in Stepping Lane is probably also a personal name; cf. *Steppings & Tungate's garage* (Banger 52). *Stepping(s)* is a variant of *Stebbing(s),* which in turn is a side-form *Stubbing* (from OE *stybbing* 'clearing'); *v.* Reaney s.n. *Stubbing,* and Cottle s.n. *Stebbing(s). Stebbing(s)* is said to occur chiefly in Essex and Norfolk. A noted Stebbing was Philip S., for whom *v.* Evans 287 f. and *passim.* He lies buried in St Peter Mancroft (died 1705, *v.* Blomefield IV 197).

STUART ROAD, a short street on the west side of King Street, south of the ruins of St Peter Southgate Church, is connected with the more southerly Alan Road by a footpath. Cf. James Stuart Gardens.

SURREY GROVE, *Surrey Grove* 1845 White, 1885 OS, is an alley off the east side of Surrey Street.

SURREY STREET
terram de Thedwardescroft 1157 ChNCP, *venellam de Neugate que
antiquitus vocabatur Thedwardescroft* 1292 *AddR, Thedwardescrofte,
modo appell. Newgate* R2 *Binham*
Neugate Hy3 Misc, 1232 ChNCP, 1250 to 1305 NoRec, 1257 *Ass,* 1292
R, 13, 1304, 1320 *D&C,* 13, 1364 *NPD,* 1317, 1338 K, 1317 (p), 1317,
1320 NoD, *New(e)gate* c. 1250 to 1470 *D&C,* 1264, 1278 K, 1307 to
1313 *R,* 1317, 1333 NoD
Newgatesend 1391 K
Magna Neugate 1257 Ass, 1257 (1450) NoRec, 1292 *AddR,* 1300 to 1324
K, 1304 *R,* 1318 *D&C, Magna New(e)gate* 1257 K, 1286 to 1314 *R,* c.
1311 NoRec, *Graunt Neugate* 1292 *AddR, Graunt Newgate* 1303, 1306
K, *Newgate Street* c. 1720 *ib, Great Newgate Street* 1746 B, *Great
Newgate* 1766 King, *Surry Street* 1789 H, 1830 M&M, *Surrey Street*
1845 White, 1885 OS
Parva New(e)gate 1286 K, 1289 to 1313 *R,* 1306 NoD, *Parva Neugate*
1291 K, 1305 *R, Newegate parva* 1290, 1302 K, 1336 (2x) NoD, *St
Katherynes Lane* 1576 K, *St Catherines Lane* 1789 H, 1830 M&M, *St
Catherine's Street (Lane) or Little Newgate* 1746 B, 1766 King, *Surrey
Road* 1845 White, 1885 OS

The present Surrey Street extends from St Stephen's Street to St
Catherine's Plain.   It is bisected by All Saints Green.   Formerly the
two halves were regarded as separate streets: *Great Newgate* from St
Stephen's to All Saints Green, *Little Newgate* from there to St
Catherine's Plain.   The earliest sources emphasize the identity of
Newgate with *Thedwardescroft* (NoRec I 52 ff.).   OE **Þeodweard* is a
personal name found in place-names but otherwise unrecorded; cf.
Thedwestry (*Theod Wardes Treo, Thedwardestr(e)u, Thewardestre* 1086
DB 'Thedward's tree'), a hundred-name in Suffolk, and the field-name
Thiedwarescroft, Tedwardescroft (AD II 195, 217) at Chattisham Sf
(EHN I 96).   For a discussion of the name **Þeodweard, v.* Forssner
231 and ELPN 2.   The name *Newgate* (OE **nīwe**) was no doubt given
to this street because, at one time, it was new in comparison with some
other street or streets; cf. New Mills, Newbridge, etc.   *Newgate* was not
only the name of the street but also of the land on both sides.   From
the time of William Rufus this land had been under the jurisdiction of
the Prior of Norwich, but in 1291 it reverted to the Crown (*v.* K 16 note
8, Blomefield III 68, NoRec I 20).   The street was later named after
Surrey House (*v.* Buildings).   St Catherine's (or Winwaloy's) Church

stood where St Catherine's Plain now is (at the entrance of Finkelgate).

SUSSEX STREET, *Sussex Street* 1830 M&M, 1845 White, 1885 OS, links Oak Street to St Augustine's Street.

SWAN LANE
Rackeyslane 1315 (2x) *R, Rakeytheslane* 1316 *ib, Rakheytheslane* 1317
   ib, Racheytheslane 1329 *ib, Rakheythe Lane* 1331 *ib,* 1376 K,
   Racheislane 1332 *R, Rakkey Lane* 1450 K, *Rackey Lane* 1626 BLR,
   Racky Lane 1746 B, 1766 King
Swan Lane 1830 *D&C,* M&M, 1845 White, 1885 OS

Swan Lane runs from Bedford Street to London Street. The early name was from one Robert de *Rakheythe,* who had a messuage here t. Ed1, later the property of Eda de *Racheyth* (K 47). Rackheath is a Nf parish. 'The Swan Tavern stood on the right-hand side of Swan Lane from Bedford Street' (Wicks 78).

SYNAGOGUE STREET (lost), *Synagogue Street* 1885 OS, 1920 OS 6" Map. From the mid-1800s to 1942, Mountergate was connected with St Ann Lane by Synagogue Street. The synagogue, at the Mountergate end, was built in 1848. (The medieval synagogue had been near Orford Place; *v.* Jewry.) The whole street was destroyed in an air-raid in 1942.

TEN BELL LANE
(*Le*) *Hollegate* 1288, 1293 K, 1298 to 1331 *R, Holgate* 1314, 1359, 1379
   K, 1379 *NPD, Holleweye* 1372 K
St Swithins Lane 1746 B, 1766 King, 1789 H
Ten Bell Lane 1830 M&M, 1885 OS, *Ten-bells lane* 1845 White

This lane runs from Pottergate to St Benedict's Street and joins the latter at a point opposite St Swithin's Church. Rainwater, flowing down from the present Cow Hill, probably washed the lane hollow in the old days. Cf. Mariners Lane (formerly *Hollegate*). OE **hol¹**, ON **hol**, OE **hol²**, ON **holr**. *The Ten Bells* refers to a pub in St Benedict's Street, on the corner of Ten Bell Lane, which dates back to the mid-eighteenth century (Wicks 103). Riddington Young (33) suggests that the name alludes to the fact that at one time the bells of ten churches

could be plainly heard from this spot.   A place called *le Heselyerd* 1299
NoD was situated near *le Hollegate* in St Swithin's.

TENTELANE (lost), *Tentelane* 1383, 1392 K, seems to have extended
from St Giles Church to what is now Chapel Field Gardens (*v.* K 21), 'a
lane where there were tenting frames' (for stretching cloth to dry in
shape); ME *tente*, MLat *tenta* 'tenting frame' (Latham).   There is
documentary evidence that there used to be tenter-yards in the vicinity
of St Giles's (K 21). ModE *tenter* is another word for 'wooden frame
on which cloth is stretched', AN **tentur*, MLat *tentura* (*v.* Latham,
ODEE).

THEATRE STREET
Chappelfield Lane 1567 K, *Chapel Field Lane* 1766 King, 1789 H, 1830
   M&M
Theatre Street 1845 White, 1885 OS

   A separate name for this street, which runs from Church Street
(opposite St Stephen's Church) to Chapel Field North, occurs late;
earlier it was no doubt regarded as part of the *Horse Market* (now
Rampant Horse Street).   It used to pass along the grounds of the
College of St Mary in the Fields, hence the name *Chappelfield Lane.*
   The first theatre was built in 1757, the second was erected in 1826
and destroyed by fire in 1934.   The present theatre, built in 1935,
occupies the same site as its two predecessors on the south side of the
street immediately to the west of the Assembly House.

THORN LANE
Sandgate Hy3 K, 13 *Phillipps*, c. 1260, 1284, 1322 *AddCh*, 1540 *NPD*,
    1286 *et freq* to 1323 *R*, 1766 King, 1789 H, *Sondgat'* 1288 *NPD*,
    Sangate 1290 *R*, *Sandegate* 1391, 1530 K, *Sandgate Lane* 1626 BLR,
    1638 K,   1746 B
Thorn(e) Lane 1696 Cleer, 1845 White, 1885 OS, *St Michael of Thorn*
    Lane c. 1720 K, *Sandgate or St Michael at Thorn Lane* 1830 M&M
St Michael's hill 1819 Stacy

   This lane runs down-hill off Ber Street and ends in Rouen Road; it
originally led to King Street.   The old name probably referred to the
character of the road surface (OE **sand**); cf. *Ston(e)gate* (now Lower
and Upper Goat Lane) and, perhaps, *Horlane* (now St Martin's Lane).

The present name is from St Michael at Thorn Church (destroyed in the 1939-45 war).

On the south side of Thorn Lane is GARDEN STREET, which used to connect with Horns Lane (*v.* the 1920 OS 6" Map) but is now closed at the south end. PARADISE PLACE is a modern development on the north side of Thorn Lane.

THREE KING LANE

Bachouse Lane 1330 K, *le Bakhouse Lane* 1386 *ib*
Seint Margaret's Lane 1357 to 1720 K, *St Margarets Lane* 1746 B, 1766
    King, 1789 H, *St Margaretts Lane* 1830 M&M
Three King Lane 1885 OS

Runs northwards from Pottergate into St Benedict's Street opposite St Margaret's churchyard. OE **bæchūs** 'bake house' occurs in place-names but is not found on independent record; *v.* Löfvenberg in *ESts* 43 (1962) 38. A bakery has been excavated here. The modern name derives from a tavern that stood at the junction of this lane and St Benedict's Street. Its sign represented the Three Kings or Magi who brought offerings to the infant Jesus (Wicks 102).

TIMBER HILL

Durnedale 1325 *NPD*, 1335, 1397, 1413 *R*, *Vicus de Burnedale* 1329,
    1335 K, *Dunsdale* 1766 King
Holde Swyn market hille 1299 K, *Oldswynemarket hil* 1312 *R*,
    Oldeswynemarkethill 1330 NoD, *Oldswyne markethill* 1333 *ib*, *Olde
    Swyn Market hille* 1337 K, *Oldswynmarkethil(l)* 1437, 1449, 1454
    NPD
Tymbermarket hill 1507 K, *Tymber Hill* 1523, 1548 *ib*, *Tymbyr Hyll* 1544
    ib, *Timberhill* 1631 *NPD*, *Timber Hill* 1696 Cleer, 1766 King, 1789 H

Durnedale has been explained as OE (Angl) **derne**, (Wsax) **dierne** 'hidden, secret' plus OE **dæl** or ON **dalr**, ODan **dal** 'valley', i.e. 'the secret, hidden or overgrown dale' (Campbell 25). However, *Durne-* is not the spelling to be expected in East Anglia for the element suggested, so the origin remains obscure.

The swinemarket was early replaced by a timbermarket (*v.* All Saints Green). This timbermarket was situated at the upper end of Ber Street (*v.* Cleer and H). The name *Timber Hill* is a reduced form of *Tymbermarket hill.* The old name *Durnedale* would seem to have

denoted the stretch of road which today goes by the name of Timber
Hill (from St John's Church to Orford Hill).

TOMBLAND
Tomeland c. 1250 NfD, (*le*) *Tomlond* 1276 *et freq* to 1543 *NPD*, 1285 *et
   freq* to 1349 *D&C,* 1287 to 1295 *R,* (*le*) *Tomelond* 1271, 1306 *R,* 1276
   to 1407 *NPD,* 1280 *et freq* to 1351 *D&C,* 1306, 1307 Ch, *le Thomelond*
   13 to 1343 *D&C,* 1285 to 1312 *R, le Thomlond* 1285, 1343 *D&C,*
   Tomelonde 1303 ChNCP, *Tomland*(*e*) 1303 to 1540 *NPD,* 1324, 1329
   D&C, Le Toomlond 1387 K, *Thoomlond* 15 *Norvic*
Tumlond(*e*) 14 *Binh,* R2 NoRec, 1422 *NPD, Tumelond* 1480 K, 15
   Norvic, Twmlond 1471 Past, *Tumland* 1529, 1533 *NPD*
Tombelond 1400 K, *Tombland* 1626 BLR, 1678 *Buxton,* 1746 B, 1845
   White, 1885 OS, *Toombland* 1696 Cleer, *Tomb Land* 1766 King, 1789
   H, 1830 M&M

This place at the western entrance of the Cathedral Close was the
civic centre of Anglo-Saxon Norwich. OE *tōm* 'free from' is a *hapax
legomenon* (*Christ* line 1211); ME *tōm* 'empty', ModE (dial.) *toom,* is
considered to be of Scandinavian origin (Björkman 256). The OE
equivalent of *tōm* was *īdel,* and *Tombland* is parallelled by *Ydellond*
1435 Exeter (PN D 23). For the spelling *Tombland* with its intrusive *b,
v.* Jordan § 212. The situation of Tombland would seem to favour
popular association with *tomb.*

TOMBLAND ALLEY, *Tombland Alley* 1885 OS, runs from Augustine
Steward's Tombland house (built in 1549; *v.* Solomons 7) to Prince's
Street.

VINEGAR LANE
Sevecote Rowe 1289 to 1527 K, 1334 NoD, *Seuecote rowe* 1291 *ib*
Sevencote Rowe c. 1720 K, *Seven Cote Rowe* c. 1720 *ib, 7 Cote Row* 1766
   King
Cole Row 1746 B, *Coal Row* 1789 H, *Seven Coal Row* 1830 M&M
Cote Row (*now Vinegar Lane*) 1887 Knights

Seuecote rowe was the old name of the Tombland end of St Faith's
Lane, along the east side of St Cuthbert's churchyard (lost). An
alternative name was *St Cuthberts Lane* (1486 K). The interpretation
'seven-cottage row' (OE **cot**), suggested by Kirkpatrick (64), is

probably correct. The name may have been transferred to a street in Heigham: *in suburbe in Sevecote rowe* 1297 *R*, *in the suburb of Norwich at Sevecoterowe* 1324 NoD, *in the suburb of Norwich outside Westwyke Gates at Sevencoterowe* 1324 *ib*. It is unlikely that the two streets should have been given the same name independently (cf. K 64 note 4). Cf. Onecote St (*Anecote* 1199 DEPN). ON **sef** 'sedge, reed', surviving dialectally as *seave* (EDD), is formally possible as the first element; but, in the first place, *seave* is not a Norfolk word and, secondly, houses thatched with reed were probably too common in Norwich to attract any attention.

Vinegar Lane is the name of that part of St Faith's Lane that runs along the west side of the Cathedral Close. According to Nobbs (75), it owes its name to the Vinegar Works (erected in 1762 by J. Poole) in Recorder Road: *Vinegar Yard and Office* 1766 King, *Vinegar Yard* 1830 M&M, *Distillery and Vinegar Works* 1885 OS.

WAGGON AND HORSES LANE
Hundegate 1320, 1367 K
Prynce Inne Lane 1497 K, *Prinse In Lane* 1509 *ib*
the Lane by the Elme 1583 K, (*the*) *Elm Lane* c. 1720 *ib*, 1766 King, *Elm Hill Lane* 1789 H
Wag(g)on and Horses Lane 1830 M&M, 1845 White, 1885 OS

This lane runs from the north end of Tombland westwards to Elm Hill. The Prince's Inn was situated in the neighbouring alley-way today called Plumbers Arms Alley (*v*. Buildings). The change from *Elm Hill Lane* to *Waggon and Horses Lane* (from a pub at the Tombland end of the lane) would seem natural from the confusing similarity between the two names *Elm Hill Lane* and *Elm Hill Street* (the former name of the nearby street today called *Elm Hill*).

WATER LANE[1]
communis venella 1324 K, *a common lane* 1392 *ib*
St Margarets Stathe 1746 B
Water Lane 1766 King, 1789 H, 1830 M&M, 1885 OS

This is a footway that runs from Colegate (opposite St George's Church) to the river. The Norvic shoe factory is built around it, so there is no public right of way (Nobbs 75). St Margaret Newbridge stood east of the lane. On Blomefield's Map (1746 B), *St Margarets*

Stathe is actually printed along the lane (*v.* St Margaret's Staithe).

At the south end Water Lane connects with St George's Street by means of a footpath. This was the original Water Lane (*Water Lane* c. 1720 K). It is called LITTLE WATER LANE on the 1885 OS Map.

WATER LANE[2] (lost)

Commune Adaquare 1351 K, *Commune Aquare* 1368, 1386 *ib*, *placeam*
   aquaticam 1503 *ib*
Le Wateryng in Coslany 1514 K, *Water Lane* 1766 King, 1845 White

This lane ran from Oak Street to the river and led to the Calk Mills according to Kirkpatrick (K 73). MLat *aquare* 'watering-place' (LathamD).

WEAVERS' LANE

Cobler Rowe, now the Lynnen Weavers' Lane 1626 BLR, *Weavers' Lane*
   c. 1720 K, 1845 White, 1885 OS, *Cobblers Row or Weavers Lane* 1746
   B

The country linen weavers used this street for their stalls on Saturdays (K 38). *v.* Market Place, Cobblers' Row.

WELLHOUSE YARD (lost)

Communis via qua itur ad fontem de Sellaria 1287, 1305 K, *Communis*
   Venella ducens a foro regio usque ad fontem communem 1324 K
Welleyerd 1285, 1293, 1305 *R, the Welhousyerd* 1331 K
Kokeys, or Kokeys Lane 1344, 1351 K

A passage that ran from the east side of the Market Place (now Gentleman's Walk) to the ancient Saddlegate Well, just north of the present White Lion Street. It crossed the Great Cockey. A document testifies to the existence of saddlers' workshops here in 1318: *Rengea selariorum* (K 28). For *Sellaria, v.* White Lion Street. OE **wella, welle** (Angl), OE **geard**.

WELLINGTON LANE, *Wellington street* 1845 White, *Wellington Lane* 1885 OS, runs along a line just within the old City Wall from the site of St Giles' Gate to the site of St Benedict's Gate, thus being a section of the old *Via sub Muros* (Campbell Map 6). The *Wellington* tavern (built in 1647) stood just off Upper St Giles Street close by the old wall

(Wicks 123, Riddington Young 23). The portion of the lane which is north of Pottergate used to be considered a separate street, *Duck Lane* 1845 White, 1885 OS, 1920 OS 6" Map, presumably named from another pub. Between Wellington Lane and the remains of St Benedict's Church there is a housing development called WELLINGTON GREEN.

WENSUM STREET

Vicus Cocorum Hy3 K, *(in) vico cocorum* 1277 to 1318 *NPD*, 1317 *R*

in (vico de) Cueria 1283 NoRec, 1286 *et freq* to 1317 *R*, 1295, 1327, 1500 *NPD, Cueria de Phibriggate* 1307 *R, Cueria de Fybriggate* 1313 *ib*

(le) Cookrow(e) 1288 NoLeet, 1317 *et freq* to 1428 *D&C, (le) Cokrowe* 1314 K, 1367 Pat, *Kokrowe* 1315 *NPD, Kocrowe* 1315 *ib, (le) Cokerowe* 1325, 1329 K 1541 *D&C, le Cook rowe* 1351, 1358, 1368 K, *le Cookerowe* 1403 *ib*, 1426, 1428 *D&C, Cooke Rowe from Tombland to Fybrigg* 1626 BLR, *Cook Row* 1746 B, 1766 King

Coquinaria 1292 *R, Vicus de Coquinaria* 1302 K, *vicus Coquinarie* 1325 *ib*

le Cuerrowe 1345 *OFB*

Cook Street 1789 H

Fye Bridge Street 1830 M&M

Wensum Street 1845 White, 1885 OS

This street was sometimes looked upon as a part of Fye Bridge Street (*q.v.*). MLat *coeus (coquus)* 'cook' (LathamD). MLat *cueria*, which normally signified 'the ofice of cook', meant 'cooks' quarter' in Norwich (*v.* Latham and LathamD). The same seems to apply to *coquinaria*. Cf. also OF *curie* 'kitchen' and the street-name *Petty Cury* in Cambridge (PN C 47 f.).

WESTLEGATE

Nedham 1285 K

Wastelgate 1340, 1343, 1380 *D&C*, 1381, 1386, 1485 K, *Wassell Gate* 1626 BLR, *Wastlegate or All Saints* 1766 King, *Wastlegate Street* 1789 H,   1830 M&M, 1845 White, *Westlegate Street* 1885 OS

This street, which runs from St Stephen's Plain to All Saints Green, must at one time have been regarded as a prolongation of Needham Street, now St Stephen's Street. Cf. *Wastelgate* (1313) in South Creake

Nf. For the etymology of *Westelgate, v.* Wastel Market (Market Place).

WESTWICK STREET, ST BENEDICT'S STREET
Westwik Hy2 K, 1186-1210 Holme, 1287 *R*, *Westwic* 1153-68 Holme, c.
 1200, c. 1250 *D&C*, *Westwyk* 1175-86 Holme, 1285 (2x), 1287 (2x) *R*,
 1310 to 1340 *NPD*, *Westwyc* 1223 K, 13 NfD, *Westwich'* 1254-75 Val,
 Westwike 1334 NoD
Neder Westwic 1257, 1258 K, *Netherwestwic* 1267 *AddCh*, *Netherwestwyk*
 1298 *R*, *Nether(e) Westwyk* 1315 *R*, 1385, 1462 K, *Nether Westwik*
 1342 *ib*, *Nether Westwick* 1766 King, *Nether Westwyk Strete* 1626
 BLR, *Nether Westwick Street-St Laurence's Street* 1746 B; *Inferior*
 Westwyk 1284, 1304 *NPD*, 1286, 1305 K, 1289, 1315 *R*, *Inferior*
 Westwik 1289 *R; Lower Westwick Street* 1789 H, 1845 White, 1885
 OS, *Lower Westwick-street or St Swithin's street* 1819 Stacy; *Heigham*
 Street 1820 M&M
Letestere rowe 1308 K, *Littestere rowe* 1333 *ib*, *Litsteresrowe* 1355 *ib*,
 Listere rowe 1362 *ib*, *Lyster rowe* 1378, 1392, 1401 *ib*, *Littestere or Dyers*
 1746 B, *Litsters Row* 1766 King
Uuere Westwik 1262, 1289 K, *Uverewestwic* c. 1263 BM, *Vuerwestwic*
 1267 *AddCh*, *Overe Westwik* 1289 *R*, *Ouerwestwyk* 1313, 1316 *ib*, *Ouer*
 Westewyk 1337 K, *Ouer Westwik* 1343 *ib*, *Over Westwick Strete* 1626
 BLR; *Superior Westwik* 1285 to 1289 *R*, *Superior Westwyk* 1287 to
 1307 *ib*, *Superior Westwick* 1303 *ib; Upper Westwick Street* 1789 H,
 1845 White; *S. Benedicts Street* 1696 Cleer, *Over or upper Westwick*
 or St Bennet's Street 1746 B, *Upper Westwick or St Bennits Street* 1766
 King, *Upper Westwick-street or St Benedict's street* 1819 Stacy, *St*
 Benedicts Street 1830 M&M, *St Benedict's Street* 1885 OS

Westwick was the name of one of the nuclear settlements out of
which the city of Norwich developed; *v.* **west, wīc**. The earliest forms
refer to the city quarter or leet of Westwick or Wymer (*v.* Leets).
Westwick Street, from Charing Cross to the site of Heigham (or Hell)
Gate, was formerly *Neder Westwic*, etc.; St Benedict's Street, from the
site of St Benedict's (or Westwick) Gate to Charing Cross, was *Uuere*
Westwik, etc. The latter was re-named after the parish it belonged to.
The eastern, converging ends of the two streets were also known as
Upper and *Lower St Laurence's Streets* from the church between them.
Letestere rowe was the north side of the eastern part of the present
Westwick Street; *v.* K 52, Campbell Map 6. ME *litester(e)* 'dyer'
(Fransson 105).

WHITE LION STREET

Sadelgate 1246 to 1378 K, 1248 NoRec, 1248 *NPD*, c. 1250, 1343 (p)
D&C, 1285 to 1306 *R*, 1332, 1333 (p) NoD, 1363 AD, *Sadilgate* 1310
K, 1313 (2x) *R*, 1315 to 1339 NoD, *Saddilgate* 1322 (p) *ib, street of
Sadlery* 1295 NoD, *Sadelere rowe* 1313 K, *vicus vocatus Sadelgate als'
dicitus Sparyer Rowe* 1395, 1418 *ib*
Sel(l) aria 1285 to 1310 *R*, 1303 NoD, 1317 *D&C, Sel(l) eria* 1293, 1305
R, 1301 to 1304 NoD, 1307 K, *Selerya* 1293 *R*
Le Lorimers Rowe 1322 K
Bridelsmethis rowe 1364 K
Le Sporiere Rowe 1320 K, *Sporiere Row* 1373 *ib, Sporyer Rowe* 1395,
1418 *ib,* 1461 Past, *le Sporyerrowe* 1420 *NAR, Sporierrowe* 1438
Beecheno, *Sporier rowe* 1452 K, *Sporerys rowe* 1476 *ib, Sporyrowe* 1489
ib, Sporowe 1499 *ib, Sporerrowe* 1508 AD, 1535 NoRec, 1537
MinAcct, *Spurry Rowe* 1626 BLR
the Lyon Lane 1626 BLR, *White Lyon Lane* 1696 Cleer, 1746 B, *White
Lion Lane* c. 1720 K, 1789 H, 1830 M&M, *White Lyon Lane or
Sadlers Row* 1766 King, *White Lion Street* 1819 Stacy, 1845 White,
1885 OS

Runs from Hay Hill to Orford Hill. The making and selling of
saddles, bits, bridles, spurs, etc., was concentrated to this street in the
Middle Ages. MLat *sellarius* 'saddler', *sellaria* 'saddlers' quarter'; OF
loremier, lorenier 'bit-maker, spurrier' (from *lorain* 'harness-strap'); ME
sporiere, a derivative of OE **spora** 'spur'. *v.* Fransson 147. The *White
Lion* Inn stood 'about the midst of the North side of [the lane]' (K
28).

WILLIAM BOOTH STREET, *v.* Church Street.

WILLIS STREET, *Willis Street* 1885 OS, 1920 6" Map, off the east side
of Peacock Street, is now a cul-de-sac but used to reach Cowgate.

WILLOW LANE, (*the*) *Willow Lane* 1696 Cleer, c. 1720 K, 1746 B,
1766 King, 1830 M&M, 1845 White, 1885 OS, connects Cow Hill with
St Giles Street and joins St Giles Street at the point opposite Rigby's
Court. It took its name 'from Willow Trees which grew on the S. of it,
upon the Wast ground next the Churchyard [of St Giles], where now [c.
1720] Houses are built' (K 50). In 1542 'the Stewyng [i.e. 'checking'] of
ye Willoughes stondyng upon ye common grounde in ye parish of St

Gyle' was committed to the Mayor (K 50).   In OED *stew* 'check, restrain' is evidenced from c. 1205 to c. 1400.

WORLD'S END LANE (lost)

Worlds End 1696 Cleer, *World's end Lane* c. 1720 K, *Worlds End Lane*
   1746 B, 1766 King, 1789 H, *World's end lane* 1845 White, *Worldsend*
   Lane 1885 OS

The piece of roadway north of St Martin at Palace used to extend further east and this easterly continuation went by the above name. It passed the north side of the great messuage called *Rome Hall* (*v.* Buildings) and led to the *High Schools of Norwich (v.* Buildings). The *World's End* public house is indicated on the 1885 OS Map but was no longer in existence in 1925 (Wicks).

WOUNDED HEART LANE (lost)

Cosyns Lane 1315 to 1405 K
Herlewynes Lane 1392 K, *Herlewyns Lane* 1746 B, 1766 King
(*the*) *Wounded Heart Lane* c. 1720 K, 1789 H, 1830 M&M, *Wounded*
   Hart Lane 1845 White, 1885 OS

This was a short lane that ran due west from what is now St Peter's Street (the west side of the Market Place), about mid-way between Bethel Street and St Giles Street.   John *Cosyn*, who was one of the Bailiffs in 1307 (*v.* NoD II 1), had a messuage here, and so had the linen-draper John *Herlewyne* (1310 *et freq* to 1319 NoD); *v.* K 30.
   The *Wounded Heart* was an inn on the south side of the lane, next the Market Place (K 30).   On its sign was painted a heart pierced with five swords, an emblematic representation of the Sorrows of Our Lady (*v.* Knights 49).   On a later sign the heart was corrupted to a hart wounded by an arrow (*v.* Riddington Young 29); cf. the 1845 and 1885 quotations.

YORK ALLEY

le Castledyck lane 1569 *Beecheno, le Casteldike lane* 1571 *ib, le*
   Castildicke land 1577 *ib*
York Alley 1908 *Beecheno*

Today this little street connects White Lion Street with the modern thoroughfare called Castle Meadow. It was described in 10 Eliz as a 'common way leading from the Parish of St Peter Mancroft to *le Sherehows*' (*Beecheno* 81). Formerly the *York Tavern* (1845 White) and the *York Hotel* were situated here.

INDEX

Early spellings and names no longer current or lost have been printed in italics.

Old Shirehouse 24
Oldswinemarket 82
Oldswynemarket hil 147
Old Swynemarket
  Street 83
Omannebrugge (Bk) 15
Omanseterow 77
Omnium Sanctorum
  de Fibrygge 34
Onecote (St) 149
One Post Alley 122
One post passage 122
Opie Street 122
Orchard Street 136
Orford Hill 122
Orford Place 123
Orford Street 124
Oserie 116
Outer Court 33
Ouere Cunesford 114
Ouer Westwik 152
Overeneweport 88
Over(e) rowe 139
Over Stongate 108
Over Wastelgate 93

Palace Gate 32
Palace Street 124
Palace Yard 124
Paradise Place 147
Parchemyners Rowe 124
Parmentergate 119
Parmenter Row 77
Parmenterestrete 52
Parsonage Square 142
Parva Newgate 144
Parva Stongate 108
Peacock Street 125
Peleteria 77
Pelliparia 77
Pelloures Medwe 23
Pellour Lane 125
Petty Cury
  (Cambridge) 151
Pigg Lane 126
Pig Lane 24
Pilgrim's Hall 133
Piscaria 73
Pistrinum 27
Pit(t) Lane 131
Pitt Street 126
placeam aquaticam 150
Pluclingiswente 127
Plumbers Arms
  Alley 127

Pockthorpe 20
Pockthorpe Gate 19
Pockthorp Street 87
pons Sci Martini 15
Popingay Inn 63
porta de Swynemarket 16
Porta S. Egidii 20
Post Office Street 104
Pottergate 127
Poultrymarket 78
pratum Castri 23
Prince of Wales
  Road 128
Prince's Inn 63
Princes Inn lane 127
Princes Inn Yard 127
Prince's Street 128
Prioratus sce
  Trinitatis 25
Preachers Street 94
preechyng yard 31
Prynce Inne Lane 149
Pudding Lane 128
Puddingmarket 78
Pull's Ferry 33
Pump Street 95
Pyeslane 124

Quakers Lane 129
Quakers Street 129
Quay Side 10
Queen Street 129
Qwetemarket 80
Qwittowermarket 81

Racky Lane 145
Rakheytheslane 145
Rampant Horse
  Back Street 123
Rampant Horse
  Street 129
Ramping (Rampant)
  Horse Lane 123
Ratones Lane
  (London) 130
Ratton Row 130
Recorder Road 130
Red Cow 100
Red Knappe Closse 88
Red Lion Lane 130
Red Lion Street 130
Redwell Plain 85
Red Well Street 130
Red Well Street 129
Refectory 33

MAPS

Fig. 1. Map of the City of Norwich showing the medieval leets with subleets as indicated in the Leet Roll of 1288 (from NoLeet) and the positions of eleven staithes.

Conesford
1. North Conesford
2. South Conesford
3. Berstreet
Mancroft
4. St Stephen
5. St Peter Mancroft
Wymer or Westwick
6. St Giles

7. St Gregory
8. St Andrew
9. St George
Ultra Aquam
10. St Michael
11. St Clement
C. Fee of the Castle
N. Norman's Hospital
G. Great Hospital

For a recent reconstruction of the Norwich subleets, *v.* map in Kelly 17.

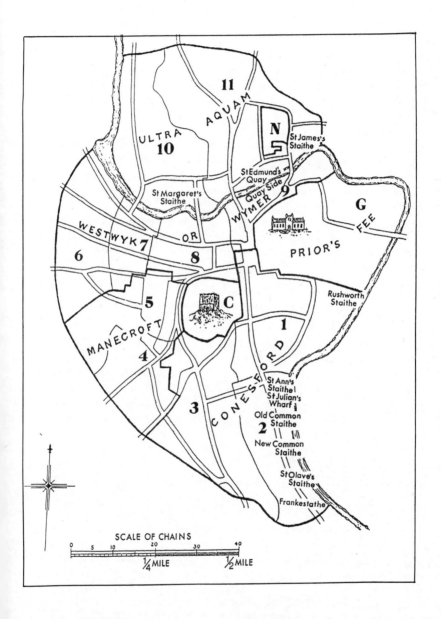

ULTRA
10

AQUAM
11

N
St James's
Staithe

St Edmund's
Quay

St Margaret's
Staithe

Quay Side

WYMER 9

OR

G
FEE

WESTWYK 7

8

PRIOR'S

6

C

Rushworth
Staithe

5

1

MANECROFT

4

3

CONESFORD

St Ann's
Staithe
St Julian's
Wharf

Old Common
Staithe

2

New Common
Staithe

St Olave's
Staithe

Frankestathe

SCALE OF CHAINS

0   5   10   20   30   40

¼ MILE   ½ MILE

Fig. 2. The Cathedral Close, based on reconstructions of the medieval close (OR 1972 and Campbell 1975) with a couple of modern names added. The map is for the reader's orientation and does not intend to show the area at one particular time in the Middle Ages.

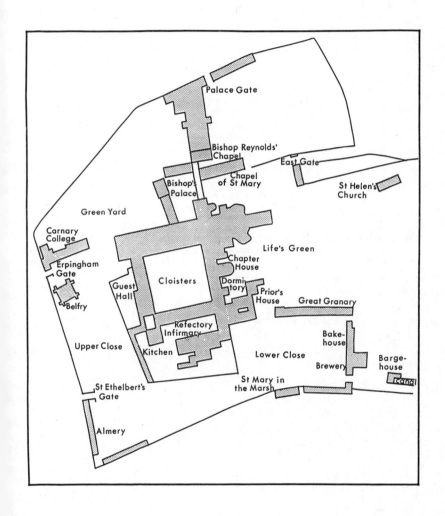

Palace Gate

Bishop Reynolds' Chapel

East Gate

Bishop's Palace

Chapel of St Mary

St Helen's Church

Green Yard

Carnary College

Life's Green

Erpingham Gate

Chapter House

Belfry

Guest Hall

Cloisters

Dormitory

Prior's House

Great Granary

Refectory

Bake-house

Upper Close

Infirmary

Lower Close

Kitchen

Brewery

Barge-house

Canal

St Ethelbert's Gate

St Mary in the Marsh

Almery

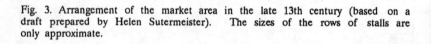

Fig. 3. Arrangement of the market area in the late 13th century (based on a draft prepared by Helen Sutermeister). The sizes of the rows of stalls are only approximate.

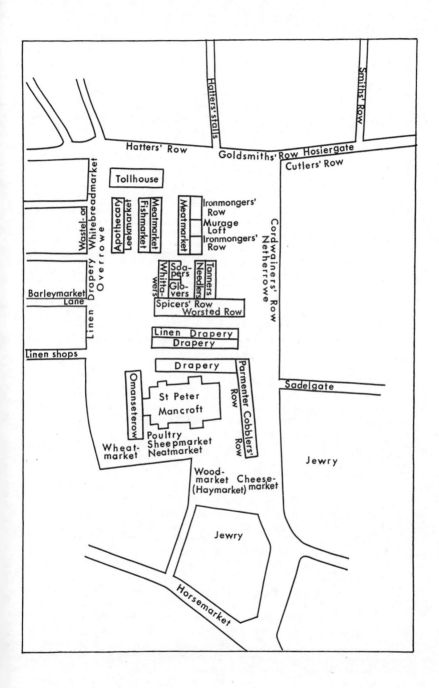

Fig. 4. Arrangement of the market area in the late 14th and 15th centuries (based on a draft prepared by Helen Sutermeister). The sizes of the rows of stalls are only approximate.

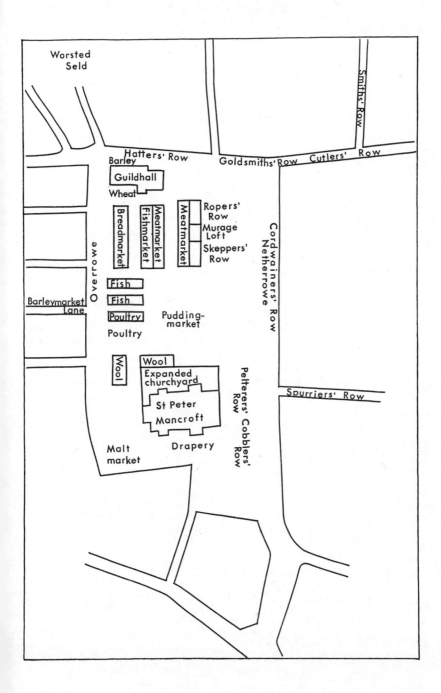

Fig. 5.   The City of Norwich.   For the readers' orientation a selection of the modern street-names have been printed on a plan of Norwich about 1348 as reconstructed by Barbara Green, Keeper of Archaeology, Castle Museum, Norwich (in Green & Young).   A couple of names which are no longer current have been added.   A = Austin Friars, C = Carmelites or White Friars, D = Dominicans or Black Friars, F = Fransiscans or Grey Friars, G = Great Hospital, N = Norman's Hospital, 1 = St Miles Bridge, 2 = Blackfriars Bridge, 3 = Fye Bridge, 4 = Whitefriars Bridge, 5 = Bishop Bridge, 6 = Cow Tower.

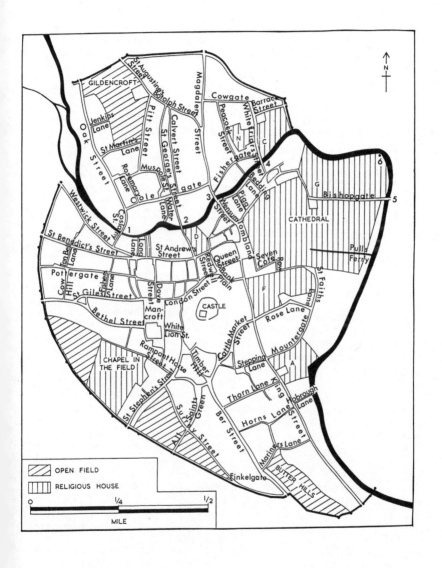

GILDENCROFT

Oak Street

Jenkins Lane

St Martin's Lane

Rosemary Lane

Muspole Street

Cole gate

Water Lane

Cosiany St

Long Lane

St Augustine's Street

Botolph Street

Pitt Street

St George's Street

Calvert Street

Magdalen Street

Cowgate

Peacock Street

Fisher gate

Barrack Street

White Friars Street

Bedding Lane

Pigg Lane

Wensum Street

C

N

4

9

6

G Bishopgate 5

CATHEDRAL

Pulls Ferry

1

2

3

D

St Benedict's Street

Ten Bell Lane

Pottergate

Cow Hill

St Giles Street

Fishers Lane

St Andrew's Street

Dove Street

London Street

Bedding Street

Queen Street

Redwell Street

Bank Plain

Seven Cole Rose

St Faiths Lane

Man- croft

Bethel Street

White Lion St.

CASTLE

F

Rose Lane

Mountergate

Rampant Horse Street

Timber Hill

Castle Market Street

Stepping Lane

A

CHAPEL IN THE FIELD

St Stephen's Street

Surrey Street

All Saints Green

Ber Street

Thorn Lane

Horns Lane

King Street

Hobrough Lane

Mariners Lane

Finkelgate

BUTTER HILLS

OPEN FIELD

RELIGIOUS HOUSE

0   1/4   1/2
MILE